Special CORRESPONDENT

INVESTIGATING IN THE SOVIET UNION

Vitali Vitaliev

HUTCHINSON
London Sydney Auckland Johannesburg

© Vitali Vitaliev 1990

The right of Vitali Vitaliev to be identified as Author of this work has been asserted by Vitali Vitaliev in accordance with the Copyright, Designs and Patent Act, 1988

This edition first published in 1990 by Hutchinson

Century Hutchinson Ltd
20 Vauxhall Bridge Road, London, SW1V 2SA

Century Hutchinson Australia
20 Alfred Street, Milsons Point,
Sydney NSW 2061, Australia

Century Hutchinson New Zealand Limited
PO Box 40–086, Glenfield, Auckland 10, New Zealand

Century Hutchinson South Africa (Pty) Ltd
PO Box 337, Bergvlei, 2012 South Africa

British Library Cataloguing in Publication Data
Vitaliev, Vitali
    Special correspondent: investigating in the Soviet Union
    1. Soviet Union. Organised crimes
    I. Title
    364.1'06'047

Photoset by Speedset Ltd, Ellesmere Port
Printed and bound in Great Britain by
McKays of Chatham Ltd, Chatham, Kent

Contents

The dead have been awakened – shall I sleep?
The World is at war with tyrants – shall I crouch?
The harvest's ripe – and shall I pause to reap?
I slumber not; the thorn is in my Couch;
Each day a trumpet soundeth in my ear,
Its echo in my heart –

Lord Byron *Journal in Cephalonia*

If I ran out of ink, I would open my vein
  and start writing with blood.

Vissarion Belinsky, Russian literary
critic and philosopher of the first half
of the Nineteenth Century

From the Author

This book is the product of glasnost' and perestroika. There is no exaggeration here: just a few years ago the whole project would have been absolutely hopeless.

I have tried my best to write an honest book to enable a Western reader to look into the processes which are under way in our country, from the inside, and to understand what it means to be an investigative journalist here in the Eighties. I do not think that there is a correct concept of Soviet journalism before or after perestroika in the West: the books on this subject have been written either by emigrants or by Western correspondents in Moscow. These books, though often well done, are inevitably incomplete. In the case of emigrants they are likely to be prejudiced. In the case of Western correspondents they are more or less superficial in their approach.

The stories comprising my book are taken from our real everyday life and have for the most part been published in the Soviet Union during the last eight years. They are strictly documentary, though some of the names have been changed so as not to embarrass my living 'heroes' for a second time. The publication of their names in the Soviet press was enough of a punishment. It is still considered a great disgrace here if your name is mentioned in a newspaper or magazine in a negative sense. While investigating into moonshiners in Central Russia, I remember being approached by a female home-brewer who knelt before me and implored: 'I am ready to go to prison rather than have my name published.'

But all the characters are nevertheless real.

The very concept of investigative journalism is quite new for the Soviet Union. During the so-called stagnation years which coincided with the second half of Brezhnev's rule (1972–82) no serious investigation by a journalist was possible. Due to the considerable social inertia, this concept is still not well developed. All the people involved in real investigative journalism could be counted on the fingers of one hand. But I am sure there will be more of us in the near future.

It is difficult for a Soviet journalist now to keep abreast of the ceaseless changes in our society. This gives the profession an additional challenge. I am proud to say that many of these revolutionary reforms, as you will see from the book, have been prepared and nurtured by the journalists.

A revolution is indeed under way in our country. It is fascinating to be taking part in it, to watch this huge land awakening from many years of slumber. Not only to watch, but to be part of an alarm-clock helping the country to wake up. There are still lots of problems, but no revolution makes everyone happy quickly. Perestroika is facing strong opposition from the bureaucracy. This makes the role of a journalist even more challenging.

Before I start my narrative I am bound to name the people without whom this book would have been impossible. First of all these is Martin Walker – a prominent British journalist and my good friend. He gave the idea of the book his ardent support. The outlines of my future work have been shaped and heatedly discussed with him during our numerous Russian-style kitchen sessions when Martin was the Moscow correspondent for the *Guardian*. It was he who introduced me in London to Clarissa Rushdie of A. P. Watt Ltd, who became my literary agent and has contributed tremendously to the project. I am also thankful to my *Krokodil* colleagues who in agreeing to grant me an unplanned long leave to write this book, took some of my daily journalistic routine on their shoulders. I am grateful to the journalists and editors of the *Guardian* and of *Punch*, who helped me to believe in my ability to write a book in English while I was in London.

I am very much obliged to the two charming British women who happened to become the first readers and critics of this book's script: Ruth Jones from St Andrew's University who helped me with typing, and my editor Kate Mosse, whose high professional skills and wonderful human qualities were very essential for me as a newly-born 'English' writer.

Most of all I want to thank my family, especially my wife Natasha, who voluntarily took on the burden of becoming my secretary, cook, public relations officer and so on for the time of writing. Her help in sorting out thousands of letters and in compiling the bibliographic index (see Notes) has been indispensable. And, of course, she went on being my wife, which was probably the most difficult part of her duties. My son Mitya, who is eight, gave me a lot of inspiration. And my mother Rimma, being the author's 'author', supplied some invaluable advice.

At the peril of sounding obsequious, but from the very depth of my heart, I want to thank our President, Mikhail Sergeyevich Gorbachev, whose courageous policy of unprecedented reforms has made this book a reality.

Vitali Vitaliev,
Moscow, May 1989

1

'Clean Skies over the City of Kharkov'

I give all this background information because I do not think one can assess a writer's motives without knowing something of his early development. His subject matter will be determined by the age he lives in ... but before he ever begins to write he will have acquired an emotional attitude from which he will never completely escape ... if he escapes from his early influences altogether, he will have killed his impulse to write.

George Orwell[1]

I was born in 1954, in the Ukrainian city of Kharkov. It belonged to the Ukraine only geographically. Bordering upon Russia, it was traditionally inhabited by Russian-speaking residents. Kharkov was a large industrial centre – probably the third largest in the country, after Moscow and Leningrad. At the time, its population was close to a million.

My mother was a chemical engineer, my father a physicist. A couple of months after my birth he got a job at a research institute in Zagorsk, a town near Moscow, where we all moved. Zagorsk is the centre of the Russian Orthodox Church, and my first childhood impressions were linked with the chiming of church bells and the black-robed priests and holy-water springs in which Zagorsk abounded. I remember vaguely the time-worn icons and brand-new portraits of Stalin put out on display in the windows of log cabins.

Because my parents were at work all day, they had to hire a child-minder to look after me. She was an old woman (babushka) and resembled the Baba Yaga – a long-nosed witch in Russian folk tales who lives in a hut standing on chicken's legs.

Once, coming home from work, my parents saw the Baba Yaga with me in a bundle in her arms. She was standing near the church asking for alms to feed 'the poor little orphan' that was me. My parents didn't think of me as an orphan, and the begging Baba Yaga was sacked the same day. When leaving for good, she boasted of having christened me secretly, though no

1

one knew if she really meant it. Probably she did, since God (or someone else up there) was to save me from real trouble many times in my future life (fingers crossed). Then I got another child-minder – a woman who was so keen on photography that she often forgot to feed me, being preoccupied solely with developing films and printing photos.

There was also a theological academy in Zagorsk, and the town swarmed with young, newly ordained priests, but my mother said that all 'good' citizens were forbidden to have contact with them at the peril of losing their jobs. No wonder – it was still the Stalin era, though Stalin himself was dead.

My father was working on his thesis, but a few years later – in 1957 – we had to leave Zagorsk owing to the illness of his mother and return to Kharkov. So my parents had temporarily to separate: my father had to stay most of the time with his ailing mother, who didn't get on well with mine. I was staying with my mother's parents, and coming to see my father only at weekends. My mother went to see her husband more often, and I remember tying her hand to my bedpost with a rope to stop her going. Crying, she used to untie the rope and leave, to come back next day after work.

Granny Niura and Grandpa Misha were both old Bolsheviks. Apart from the Baba Yaga and the woman photographer, they were my first and main educators. We lived in a quiet and fairly privileged part of Kharkov, with lots of greenery and comparatively clean air. Our apartment block was called 'The House of Old Bolsheviks', though in fact there were not so many authentic Bolsheviks living in it. The neighbouring apartment blocks were The House of Actors, The House of Writers and The House of Artists, though again, for the most part just rank-and-file people lived there.

Both Grandpa Misha and Granny Niura joined the Communist (Bolshevik) Party in 1919, two years after the October Revolution. During the Civil War of 1918–20, Grandpa was in the Red Army, fighting the White Guards. He was badly wounded at the front, fell ill with typhoid in the trenches and nearly died. He was saved by my Granny, who was a nurse with the Red Army – that's how they met. After recovering, Grandpa went on a reconnaissance mission to 'White' Poland, posing as a businessman. I remember very well his tattered old travelling bag, which he kept in the attic. In this leather briefcase he used to carry the underground Bolshevik literature, to be distributed in Poland. Several times he was nearly captured by gendarmes, but always managed to escape. Grandpa's travelling bag was my favourite toy. Its leather interior smelt of adventures and history. It even had a false bottom.

It's interesting that right up to his death in 1968, Grandpa's mission to Poland was supposed to be hushed up so as 'not to spoil the friendly relations between the two countries', though of course at the time of the Civil War the two countries were far from being friendly.

After the Civil War, Grandpa worked as a professor of political economy. When Stalin's purges started, he expected to be arrested any minute. My mother remembers how in 1937, he – a robust and strong-willed man – would faint when there was a knock at the door in the evening . . .

My father's parents were old Bolsheviks too, and his father, whom I hardly remember (he died when I was two), was once even the secretary of the city's executive committee (a magistrate). In the late Thirties, he too escaped arrest, but was removed from his post and had to work as a photographer. He was lucky not to be shot, as happened to most old Bolsheviks at that time.

One sunny afternoon, when I was six, Grandpa Misha picked me up from the kindergarten a couple of hours earlier than usual. 'Let's go and greet Comrade Khrushchev,' he said, and explained that Nikita Sergeyevich was passing through Kharkov on his way to Moscow from the summer residence on the Black Sea coast. We went into the main street, called Sumskaya, and joined hundreds of other onlookers. Soon a cavalcade of open cars passed us at high speed. In one of the cars, a stout, elderly man sporting a green pork-pie hat was sitting in state. It was Khrushchev. The crowd started cheering and crying 'hooray', but the man didn't even look at us or remove his hat to acknowledge our presence. The cavalcade sped towards the railway station, and the crowd started to break up. We went home too, both feeling disappointed.

The failure of Khrushchev's agricultural policies became apparent in the early Sixties. I remember the endless queues for butter and white bread, winding like serpents all along Culture Street, where we lived. The head of the serpent was usually inside the Tempo food shop. I was often taken to the queue by adults, since bread and butter were rationed per capita. People were making ersatz butter from sour cream. I remember biting into a piece of newly acquired butter just there in the street, to the general sympathy of the queue: 'Look, this boy likes butter so much he eats it on its own!'

Despite all the shortages, people were very enthusiastic. The country had just been freed from the yoke of Stalinist terror and was starting to breathe more freely.

3

On our old KVN TV set, I liked to watch funny animated cartoons praising maize as the tsarina of agriculture. Maize-growing was one of Khrushchev's obsessions.

During the Cuban missile crisis of 1962, we were sitting in my father's flat listening to our old-fashioned black radio. The faces of the adults were very grave. 'Is there going to be a war?' I asked, hoping secretly for an affirmative answer (wars seemed so exciting for a boy of eight). 'We don't know yet,' my parents answered.

Soap and matches were disappearing from the shops at the speed of light. It was at that time that I first heard over the radio the song 'The Skies Are Clean over the City of Kharkov'. The song was performed in the Ukrainian language, and the melody was awkward, but catching. Even now, when I have the blues, I'm in the habit of humming to myself its plain refrain 'The skies are clean . . .' It was funny that clean skies were the last thing that Kharkov could boast of. With lots of factories and smoking chimneys, the sky over the city was grey and the air polluted. But songs, as you know, do not generally correspond to reality. And needn't do . . .

At school, I did well in all the subjects, but after some time I lost interest in physics and mathematics and was attracted to literature, languages and geography. I was lucky to have an excellent Russian language teacher; her name was Svetlana Mikhailovna Karolinskaya. She was young and beautiful, and I was in love with her in a funny childish way. Svetlana Mikhailovna was an intelligent, kind-hearted woman who knew her subject from A to Z and found ways to introduce it to her pupils in an unbiased, unusual manner, in contradiction to the boring curriculum. This slim, diminutive woman taught us to speak our own language properly, and to think and express our opinions correctly. It was thanks to her that I came to admire Yevtushenko's poems, and really learnt to appreciate Pushkin, Lermontov and Tolstoy. My first youthful poems were inspired by, and dedicated to, her, and it was she who urged me to send my first short stories to *Pionerskaya Pravda* – the Moscow children's newspaper. She also knew English well, and her favourite adage was 'No pains, no gains!'

From the age of eight, I started learning English with a private teacher and enjoyed it immensely. My English teacher was an old mustachioed man who had been educated in a pre-Revolutionary grammar school. He was fluent in several languages and was a real pedagogue: he played games with us – four little boys – and encouraged our learning by presenting military badges and postcards for good answers. When after several years he died, I got another teacher – not as good as he was. But by that time the foundations of English had been firmly laid.

At fourteen, I wrote my first article to be published in the city's evening newspaper *Vechernii Kharkov*. The article was prompted by the fact that someone in our school administration decided to write a Letter to the Future, to our progeny. We compiled this long and pompous letter, glorifying Brezhnev and our happy life, put it into a specially designed capsule and buried it in the wall of our school assembly hall. The niche was covered with a marble plate which bore the inscription 'Open in fifty years'. It was similar to burying the ashes of a statesman in the Kremlin wall, with the only difference that the Kremlin wall niche is not supposed to be opened at all.

My article was called 'A Letter to the Future' . . .

Soon afterwards local newspapers started publishing my poems. They were mainly romantic stuff: trains, stations at night and daydreams:

Railway stations at night . . .
You are dear to all wanderers,
You attract them with your lights,
You are the sentries of my separation from the loved one.

Anyone can enter here
To find the smell of the road, sacks and suitcases,
But when in the morning he lifts himself from the wooden bench –
He will feel warm and hopeful.

No matter how dark the night,
No matter how much soot there is around you –
Just look: the express train of dawn is already piercing the darkness,
Carrying the sun on its tail like a signal lamp . . .

Of course in Russian the poem rhymed . . .

The poetic string was touched in me solely because of my mother. Being an avid reader of poetry, she would take me to the local philharmonic society for literary recitals. People said that my poems, apart from being youthful and romantic, were rather professional. I was praised at the sessions of the literary studio which I started to attend. In 1970, aged sixteen, I was even sent as a guest to the plenum of the Ukrainian Writers' Union. It was there that I first met my namesake Vitali Korotich – then a young poet – who now heads the famous *Ogonyok* magazine.

The long-awaited medal for valour found Grandpa Misha already in his grave. It was his only decoration in life, or in death, to be more exact. His death was a sudden one and left a deep imprint on my childish soul. One week before Christmas in 1967 he went to the market and bought a big Christmas tree for me. He had to carry it on his back all the way home. That very evening he suddenly felt unwell and was taken to the special Old Bolshevik's hospital. I decorated the fir-tree with paper flags, fragile glass toys and walnuts wrapped in foil and tied it tightly to the radiator lest it should fall down. As soon as I opened my eyes next morning I saw the tree lying flat on the floor. Fragments of broken toys were scattered all over the room. I instantly had the heavy premonition of a disaster. Within an hour there came a call from the hospital with the news of Grandpa Misha's sudden death during the night. Up to now I cannot understand how the Christmas tree could have possibly collapsed: it was tied to the radiator with very strong ropes. And what's more, it is completely beyond my comprehension why I wasn't awoken by all the noise of falling tree and breaking toys when as a rule my sleep was very sensitive. I didn't hear a thing, lying there in the same small room! I think that each life must have some inexplicable mysteries of its own. This is one of the biggest enigmas in mine . . .

Grandpa died rather disappointed in what was going on. After Khrushchev's thaw, the country was approaching another cult – this time Brezhnev's. At the end of the Sixties, Stalinism was being revived, little by little. In the history manual for the Tenth form of secondary school*, thirty-five years of Stalinist terror were dealt with in a single line that mentioned 'some mistakes'. Some mistakes indeed, which cost us millions of lives! In the edition of this same manual, printed several years earlier – in 1965 – the description of Stalin's 'mistakes' took the whole page . . . so the trend towards stagnation was evident and Grandpa Misha couldn't but notice it. As an old Communist he regretted it very much, but what on earth could he do? The only thing he could actually achieve was to convey to me his firm belief in the eventual triumph of Communist ideas. I did believe in them firmly and was a good Komsomol (Communist Youth Organisation) member.

There was no question for me about where to go to study after school. I had chosen the foreign languages department of Kharkov University – a prestigious faculty with the dim perspective of a job abroad. People said that you were supposed to have considerable influence to be accepted there. I didn't have any. What I did have was a pretty good command of English, and I passed the entrance exams with flying colours, scoring 20 points out of 20 possible. I couldn't afford a failure, since otherwise I would have been drafted into the Army.

It was very exciting for me to study at the university. The teachers there

*Soviet schoolchildren start their secondary education in the First form at the age of seven, and finish it in the Tenth, aged sixteen/seventeen.

were excellent. Among them there was a man – Leonid Nikolayevich Prudnikov – who was fluent in eighteen languages. And he had never been abroad. Leonid Nikolayevich lived the life of a recluse and never married. With his unparalleled scholarship, he could speak professionally on any subject – from secrets of Thai cuisine to the design of a spacecraft. He died suddenly three years ago, aged fifty-two, without ever getting a glimpse of the outside world – the typical fate of a Russian intellectual of his generation.

I took to translating Henry Longfellow's poems, which in the long run became the subject of my diploma paper. Being an active member of the Komsomol organisation, I worked hard in the collective farms where all the students were sent each September to help the farmers to harvest the crops. In the summers, I joined the students' construction teams working in Siberia, Central Asia or the Far East.

I studied at the interpreters' department, where only boys were accepted. Our faculty also had a teacher training department, where mainly girls studied. This separation of the sexes contributed perhaps to my keen interest in girls at that time, and partly accounts for my early marriage at the age of nineteen.

All went well until the fifth year – my last at the university. At this time only one word was on the undergraduates' lips: *raspredelenie* (assignment). By law, all graduates must be provided with a job, where they must work for at least three years, and after that they are free to stay or leave. This is what was meant by *raspredelenie*.

With East–West relations going from bad to worse, interpreters were not in great demand in Kharkov. Our predecessors had to be satisfied with positions as English teachers in village schools. But we didn't want to follow their example. And the administration this year was sympathetic. 'Go and find yourselves a job,' the Dean announced to the undergraduates. 'If they agree to have you, we won't mind.'

So we went to look for jobs in different parts of the country. Most of my fellow students were lucky to find appointments with the Black Sea shipping company in Odessa. They were going to work as barmen, waiters, stewards etc on cruise ships carrying foreign tourists. This definitely meant trips abroad, and they were happy. The others were selected by the military. I myself didn't like the prospect of serving, in any sense of the word, so on a friend's advice, I went to the Baltic town of Kaliningrad (formerly Königsberg) and quickly found a place as an interpreter for an organisation with the intricate name of Zaprybprom-razvedka. Its aim was to explore the sea, locate shoals of fish and convey the information to the fishing fleet. I was supposed to become a real sea

7

wolf – to cross the rough seas and visit foreign ports. They gave me an official invitation, and I came back to Kharkov full of glowing prospects.

But I was too quick to rejoice. The atmosphere at the faculty was getting very tense. The students who were not lucky enough to find a good job were feeling envious. They started reporting their luckier comrades to the administration, accusing them of drunkenness, promiscuity and every mortal sin. The same was true for the teacher training department. Many of the girls were hurriedly marrying the would-be interpreters with good 'assignments'. The others faced the gloomy prospect of going to a village, which seemed unfair to them.

Naturally, my wife became an object of envy. Being straightforward and talkative, she couldn't refrain from sharing her radiant hopes for our future life with her friends. This, of course, couldn't fail to drive them crazy with envy and in the long run it ruined both of us. 'Anybody can sympathise with the sufferings of a friend', Oscar Wilde once said, 'but it requires a very fine nature to sympathise with a friend's success.' My wife's friends were far from being fine-natured girls.

I will never forget that terrible day in June 1976. The assignment had taken place already and I was officially 'assigned' to Kaliningrad. The only thing left was to collect my references, approved by the district Party Committee, from the Dean's office and send them to my future place of work. In four days' time I had to take my final exam in scientific Communism, then to defend my diploma paper – and that's all . . .

The Dean looked away when I asked for my references. 'Go down to the university Party committee,' he said sternly. 'Someone there wants to talk to you. And ask your wife to come to my office.'

Puzzled, I went to the Party committee, the most obscure room in the university; I'd never been there before.

A short, podgy man in a rumpled black suit (his name was Romanov) introduced himself as the deputy secretary of the university Party committee.

'What are your plans for the future?' he asked drily.

'I'm planning to go to Kaliningrad, to work there,' I answered unsuspectingly.

'Are you? We have different information.' Saying this, he produced several sheets of crumpled paper from his breast pocket. 'Just listen to what your wife's friends write.'

In a dull voice, devoid of any emotion, he started reading. At first I could understand nothing. It was something about my wife's allegedly anti-Soviet views, about her fascination with Western clothes and the Western way of life . . . In the end, there was a conclusion that the real aim of our work in Kaliningrad was to defect to the West. 'As true friends, we can't stay indifferent . . .' and that sort of crap. At the bottom of the paper, there were four signatures and the date. I couldn't believe my ears: the denunciation had been written a week before, and only yesterday these very girls who signed it had come to our house and asked me to help them prepare for their foreign literature exam. I gave them books, we joked a lot. Are there any limits to human hypocrisy?

I was in shock, and it took me several minutes to regain my senses.

'Well, what would you say to that?' asked Romanov with a nasty smile.

'What would I say . . . what would I say? . . . It's the meanest thing I ever heard . . . Just filth . . . filth and shit . . .'

'Behave yourself, Comrade Vitaliev. You are at the Party committee, this is not the place for using dirty language . . .'

'How can you, an adult, reasonable person, take all this seriously? Or maybe we are back in 1937? Don't you understand there is just envy behind this? Envy and nothing else! It's just a pack of lies. A pack of foul, dirty lies!'

'No, it is not. It's a document. Look: there are signatures here and the date. We couldn't just dismiss it, could we? There's no smoke without fire, you know. You understand that until we find out the truth, we can't send you to Kaliningrad, having a wife like that,'

'But I only have four days to go.'

'Never mind. Write a short note to the effect that you ask to postpone the final decision as to your assignment, for personal reasons.'

And here I made a mistake. I wanted only one thing: to end this nightmare as soon as possible. Besides, I completely lacked any experience of that kind. And I wrote the note.

Romanov beamed.

'OK, that does it. You may go now, and don't tell anyone about our talk. And don't beat up your wife on an impulse . . .'

I rushed to find my wife.

She came out of the Dean's office, all in tears. At the same time as I was 'talking' with Romanov, she was being interrogated in the Dean's office. They told her: 'You have just two options – either you confess your anti-Soviet behaviour, or we call an emergency Komsomol meeting and you will be thrown out of the Komsomol and the university, together with your husband.' Dirty blackmail. The poor girl was so terrified that they had managed to trick her into a kind of written confession in which she called her behaviour 'unworthy of a Soviet student'.

'Did you really make these pro-Western remarks?' I asked her.

'No. But I was so frightened.'

Of course I told my father everything. He was a Party leader at his research institute. He was furious. 'I will go and talk to them properly!' he shouted. Here I should say that my father was far from being what we call a feeble intellectual. He came from a worker's background, starting as a turner aged fifteen. During the Second World War when his family was evacuated from Kharkov to Ufa in the Urals. Being still a teenager he worked at the ammunition factory and had a number of adult apprentices whom he taught. He recalled that during sixteen hour shifts his fingers used to freeze on to his machine-tool.

My father preserved his worker's skills up to his very last days, though for many years he had been a scientist. Like Jack-of-all-trades he was constantly fixing and repairing something. All the furniture in our flat was designed and made by him. He also assembled a tape recorder and, shortly before his death, a colour TV set. His kitchen workshop was full of home-made tools and machines. It was his favourite place in the whole world where he liked to rest from formulas and equations which haunted him at his office. Besides he was a very good sportsman, an athlete and a gymnast with high rating. So, as you see, he was the one who could really talk to Romanov *properly*. So my father did go to him the next day.

He came back looking grim and pale. 'He said she had confessed everything. Why on earth did you write the confession? – Though I understand how you must have felt. Bastards. What have they done to you?'

That day he had a severe heart-attack.

What could we do? Nothing. I wrote a letter to one of the Politburo members who worked with my grandfather before the war, but I never got a reply.

In a couple of days, having mobilised all my willpower, I passed my exam in scientific Communism. Then I took my diploma on Longfellow's poetry and got the highest mark for that. It went so well that the university newspaper ran an article on it. But I was jobless, and got what they call 'free assignment' – that is, I had to look for a job again. They never returned my references, and without them I couldn't go to Kaliningrad on my own.

At that time I started having terrible pains in my stomach. The doctors said I had a gastric ulcer and put me into hospital for a month. So I managed to earn the professional journalist's disease without yet being a journalist. Wasn't it symbolic?

It was there in the hospital bed that I realised that my wife's friends were not particularly to blame. They were just envious – it was understandable. The real culprits were the cowardly bureaucrats of

Brezhnev's time. Their logic was simple: even if there was one chance in a million that what the girls had written was true, it would be safer for them to believe the lies and not to let us go to Kaliningrad. They didn't want to run any risks, being preoccupied with only one thought: how not to lose their positions. If for that they had to ruin a couple of lives, well, who cares? . . .

It was my first encounter with reality. For the first time in my life I came up against a wall – the wall of injustice, the wall of conservatism, the wall of Stalinism if you wish. And though it may sound high-flown, there at the hospital I promised to devote myself my whole life to demolishing this wall, or at least to making a hole in it . . .

When I came out of hospital, my wife divorced me. I don't blame her: she had to sort out her life somehow. I was jobless, sick and stigmatised, and thus a poor provider, especially for the materialistic-minded girl she proved to be. Shortly after our divorce she married a well-off foreign student.

Everyone sympathised. My university teachers telephoned and moaned: 'Oh, what have they done to you, our best student?' But where were they at the time of trouble, I thought. Not one of them ventured to put in a word for me. And the reason was the same – fear, animal Stalinist fear, deeply rooted in their souls. 'It's good your Grandpa didn't live to see that,' my mother kept telling me. 'He wouldn't have survived it.'

But *I* had to survive. At this time, some of my Jewish friends started emigrating to the West, but for me this was out of the question. I had to stay here and prove to everyone (myself included) that I could not be easily beaten. And I didn't want to leave my country. I wanted to improve it.

In a couple of months I found a job as a translator at a small research institute of micro-biology. It was a curious institution. With only about forty people on the staff, it possessed huge grounds and a large assembly hall where Stalin once spoke. Probably from just that time, the assembly hall was closed for good and the meetings of the staff were conducted in the corridor.

I had the whole room to myself and practically nothing to do for 90 roubles a month – the minimum salary. By way of comparison, an average bus-driver was getting 280–300 roubles a month. I'm sure the institute director just took pity on me, as they didn't actually need a translator. She also wanted me to give her granddaughter private lessons in English, which I did with pleasure. I conducted English courses for the institute staff members too, just to keep everyone busy.

There were only two young men on the staff – the director's driver and me. My main duty was to switch off the tea-kettle when it started boiling in my room. My other assignment was to provide a coffin when someone on the institute staff died. It happened fairly often, since most of the personnel were elderly people. I became a constant customer at the city's funeral bureau – everyone there knew me by name.

My room was located in the former refuge for people bitten by dogs, which was on the institute grounds. The building was 200 years old and was swarming with rats. The first thing I did in the morning when I entered my 'office' was to clear my desk of rats' droppings. After that I used to go to sleep peacefully on the pile of dictionaries. When someone approached up the creaky, wooden stairs, I sat up, took a pen in my hand and went on sleeping with my eyes open. In the next room, a young woman researcher sat all day long with an obscure scientific bulletin open in front of her at one and the same page, number 44. I suspected she was day-dreaming or sleeping too.

As a matter of fact, in the many years of its existence the institute had created only one brand of medicine. People said it was fairly good, but being in short supply, it couldn't be got at drugstores for love or money.

Out of boredom, I had several short romances with the young laboratory assistants (one-day stands). But the living being to whom I was most attached was a miserable ram named Borya, who was kept at the vivarium. He had his blood taken for serum and was slowly dying. I used to feed him with grass and took him to graze just under my window. He learnt to recognise me and bleated gratefully whenever he saw me.

This rueful bleating of his was driving me up the wall. Was this all that I deserved after so many years of studies? My fellow students were coming back from abroad and were enthusiastically sharing their impressions with me, which only added to my depression. I started writing poems again. Strange, but these were funny poems. People laughed when reading them, but while writing them I was on the point of tears.

> I'd like to become a cow,
> To drive away the seconds with my tail,
> To gape sternly at people
> And to moo, to moo, to moo.
>
> I'd like to become a bird,
> To look down at the world under me,
> And then, floating in the clouds,
> To eat up a dragonfly.
>
> I'd like to become an elk,
> To play on the grass in the forest,

And to come home with horns
On my poor head.

Well, to dream is not harmful at all,
If you have something to dream about.
Human life is sometimes miserable:
Just a bed and four stone walls.

When I read this poem at a session of the literary studio, a high-ranking Komsomol official, who happened to be there, was infuriated and condemned me in his speech for 'pessimism' and 'decadence'. To some extent he was probably right, but what could I derive optimism from? Anyway, I have been banned from attending the studio since . . .

God knows what would have happened to me after several years of funeral-arranging and grass-feeding if it were not for the sympathetic institute director. Seeing that I was on the verge of a nervous breakdown, she decided to send me to Moscow for half-year extension courses to study patentology. The institute had no more need for a patentologist than it did for a translator, so on the director's part it was just a gesture of good will. But for me it was a bonanza, a chance to start a new life.

So in November, 1977, I went to Moscow, knowing in my heart of hearts that I would never return to live in Kharkov – the city with the clean skies over it.

2

Moscow Does Not Believe in Tears

'Moscow does not believe in tears' is a Russian proverb. Some years ago, there was a good feature film directed by V. Menshov, under the same title. It tells the story of three girls from the provinces who come to Moscow in search of happiness. Having experienced many hardships and disappointments, they eventually settle down in the capital. And the one who is the least lucky at the beginning proves to be the most successful in the end.

The film is indeed rather sentimental, but its sentimentality, to my mind, is its main merit. Our life is full of sentiments – there is no hiding the fact.

Fascination – that was the prevailing sentiment during my first months in Moscow. I frequented museums and theatres, I took up an evening course in Italian (English and French I knew pretty well by that time); occasionally I managed to buy a week-old copy of *The Times* or the *International Herald Tribune* at the Intourist Hotel, acquiring my first notion of the Western press, practically unknown in Kharkov. So it was a real breakthrough. As to the patentology courses, they were not much of a burden.

For the first couple of months I rented a room in a small flat in Cheryomushki, one of Moscow's newly built areas. The room teemed with cockroaches and there was no bed-linen. As to the cockroaches, I got used to them quickly, and even felt lonely when there were fewer of them than usual. But the bed-linen was a problem. I couldn't afford to buy it and was at a loss as to what to do. Once I went to the theatre to see a new production of *Othello*. I had two tickets, and gave one to an elderly woman begging for a spare at the theatre doors. When we entered the auditorium, we saw an open stage with Othello's huge bed, covered with black linen.

'Othello was lucky to have a bed with such good linen, even if it is black,' I confided to my companion. 'Black is better, since it doesn't need washing too often. As for me, I don't have any linen at all.'

'You know,' the woman answered, 'I'm so grateful for the ticket that I'd love to help you. I'll lend you some linen – white though, not black.'

We met the next day, and she indeed brought me some white sheets, a pillow and a blanket. And so the linen problem was solved, thanks to Shakespeare.

The man I was sharing the flat with was an alcoholic. From time to time he used to down my shampoo and aftershave lotion standing in the bathroom. But apart from that he was quite a nice fellow.

One fine night I found myself out in the street. The woman who owned the room, but lived elsewhere, appeared suddenly at 2 am, saying that her mentally deranged brother had just escaped from the lunatic asylum and would be here any moment. 'Get out fast if you want to stay alive,' she urged. I followed her advice, forgetting to demand the return of my rent, which I paid in advance. This was probably the reason for my sudden eviction, since I was told afterwards by the local militiaman that she had played these tricks on her tenants before.

I stayed at a hotel for a fortnight and then found another room in a General's widow's flat. I was leading a well-deserved normal life, and only the thought of having to go back to Kharkov prevented me from being totally happy.

Then I met Natasha, who soon became my wife. She was a Muscovite, and insisted that we stay in Moscow. But her parents were opposed to our marriage. The point was that by Soviet law, you were not allowed to live permanently in any particular city or town without being registered by the militia, who put a stamp in your passport. Moscow registration is the most coveted, since it gives you the right to live in the capital and take advantage of the better food supplies and a richer cultural life. As the husband of a Muscovite, I automatically acquired the right to Moscow registration, but since Natasha was living with her parents, she couldn't register me without their consent. A vicious circle. So we reached a compromise: we promised not to live in her parents' flat and to rent a room instead, but in exchange we asked my in-laws to agree to my temporary registration – just for one year – in Moscow, to which they reluctantly consented.

'You'll have a hard time finding a job, pal,' said a ruddy militia captain, putting the stamp in my passport. 'Do you know that in Moscow we mainly give temporary registration to convicts who've just come out of prison? It's bad luck about your in-laws.'

How right he was! Though the difficulty in finding a job did not only originate from temporary registration: for a long time my job-hunting never reached the stage of anyone wanting to look at my passport. In the long run, this very problem of *propiska* (registration) stood me in good stead for my future journalistic career by providing a subject for one of my investigations. But then – in 1978 – I couldn't foresee this, of course. The main problem proved to be different.

Each morning I got up at eight, and roamed the city in search of a job. Naturally, I wanted to work as an interpreter, but no one seemed interested in the extent of my knowledge. The first question that greeted me everywhere was: 'Who are you from?' An interpreter's job was supposed to be prestigious, and they didn't want to take 'just anyone from the street' as they put it. You were supposed to have powerful connections to get a job like that, and the only connection I had in Moscow was my wife, who was a student. It seemed as if all the officials I applied to were in a kind of secret conspiracy not to give me a post. For the first time in my life the word 'mafia' occured to me . . .

Nowadays all these instances of pull and nepotism are being publicly condemned as characteristic of the stagnation period. For me, these are not mere words: I felt the stagnation on my own skin.

In desperation, I tried to find a job with the Church, which was rather unusual for a Komsomol member. 'The Church is separated from the State,' I was thinking. 'The State doesn't want to give me an interpreter's job – so probably the Church would.'

At the publishing office of the Russian Orthodox Church, I was given a short questionnaire to fill in. It had a space for religion. After some hesitation, I honestly wrote 'none'. The young priest to whom I submitted the completed form was rather taken aback. 'So, you're an atheist,' he said. 'We don't employ atheists.' References to my childhood in Zagorsk didn't help.

At the office of the Baptist Order, where I was addressed as 'brother', there was no one at the international section. It was explained to me that all its staff members were on missions abroad. The only man who remained was repairing his Zhiguli car in the courtyard. He explained that to work with them I must be a member of their order. I expressed a readiness to join any kind of order, provided I got a job. The man didn't like my eagerness. 'It takes a long time,' he said. 'You'll have to undergo a test period of several years.' Suddenly he smiled. 'It's a good job we have here, travelling abroad all the time, so it's worth trying.' But several years of waiting – no, it didn't suit me at all. Besides, I could imagine how my parents would have reacted if they found out that I had become a Baptist.

And I went to the international relations department of the Soviet Muslim board. It was located in a small wooden hut near Dinamo metro station. The hut was guarded by ferocious dogs, and there were a number of black Volga sedans parked in the courtyard. Inside, a middle-aged, narrow-eyed Uzbek sat under the huge wall-hanging with some Arabic signs on it. He was desperately trying to reach Tashkent by phone, and he couldn't get through, which made him angry. 'What do you want?' he snapped at me. 'I want a job,' I answered meekly. 'Are you a Muslim?' 'I don't think so.' 'All right, just leave your address with my secretary and go. I'm very busy.' It was hopeless, and I went to the Synagogue.

An old orthodox Jew in a yarmulka was washing his hands in the lobby. It was not a praying day, and he led me inside, where I saw a rabbi sporting an ordinary working-class cap instead of a yarmulka. He was sitting under the Yiddish and Russian slogan 'Our father in Heavens, bless the government of the USSR', and speaking over the telephone: 'How are you, eh? How is your health, eh? What does he want?' he asked in a low voice, pointing at me. 'A job,' my yarmulkaed escort answered. 'Send him to the Council for Religious Affairs!' the rabbi screamed suddenly, not acknowledging my presence at all. I was being sent packing again.

Following the rabbi's advice, I did go to the Council for Religious Affairs. This organisation is attached to the Council of Ministers of the USSR and is designed to supervise the religious institutions on behalf of the State. A polite man with steel-grey eyes examined me thoroughly. 'So if I've got you right, you're an interpreter, aren't you?' 'Yes, I am.' 'You've got no job, and you decided to go to the Council for Religious Affairs to ask for one, didn't you?' 'Yes, I did,' I answered nonchalantly. 'The idea of such a thing!' he shouted all of a sudden. 'Are you crazy or what? We don't know ourselves how we got our jobs here! And we don't take anyone from the street!'

This was the end of my short association with the Church. It took me just the one day to visit all the above-mentioned establishments. My friends laughed their pants off when I recounted my ordeal to them. But it didn't sound funny to me: only extreme desperation could prompt such a hopeless attempt.

'Why don't you try to bribe some bigshot to give you a job?' my Moscow friends kept asking me. But this was totally against my principles, and even a bribe couldn't make up for my damned temporary registration anyway.

My troubles ended only a few years later in 1980, when we finally got a room of our own. It was in a big flat where two other families lived, but at least it was ours, and I was able to get properly registered there. I then found a permanent job at a medical institute, where I was supposed to do written translations working at home, and simultaneously I found a part-time job with the Ministry of Culture of the USSR. This second employment for me was much more important than the first one. It was 1978, and the policy of détente was still in full swing. Lots of people from the West were coming to Moscow and a good many of them came via the Ministry of Culture: artists, museum curators, musicians etc. My job was to act as an interpreter for these people and to accompany them on their tours throughout the country.

My first 'delegate' was an American woman – an impresario and pianist. Her name was Mary. We toured Central Asia, the Caucasus and central Russia together. Here on the road, I brushed up on my spoken English, formerly known to me mainly from text-books. Once Mary came to my hotel room in Baku to discuss the details of our programme. 'You can undress here,' I offered hospitably. She blushed and took a step back. The fact is that in Russian, *Rasdet'sya* sometimes means just to take off one's coat, which was what I had meant of course. But she took the words in their English sense. I remembered this first lesson in colloquial English for the rest of my life.

Mary was quite an attractive woman. Once in Alma-Ata, the director of the local philharmonic society, having previously pumped a lot of cognac into us, tried to assault her sexually in his Volga car. At that moment I was nearby, admiring the evening lights of the city. Suddenly I heard her screams. I reached the car just in time to stop the drunken director. Next day he called me to his office: 'Tell the guys at the Ministry not to send that woman here again,' he said. 'She's a lousy pianist.' I can only imagine what impressions this trip left on the poor woman: a wild interpreter inviting her to undress and a rapist of a philharmonic director.

I also worked with a number of Australian museum workers negotiating exhibition exchanges with the Hermitage Museum. One of them, the director of the National Gallery Victoria, was such a heavy smoker that he even smoked in his sleep. I witnessed this strange phenomenon when we took an overnight train from Moscow to Leningrad. All night through he slept and chain-smoked, automatically putting out one cigarette stub and lighting another, without waking up. In the morning he said that he had dreamt that our train was stopped in the snow-covered steppe and attacked by a pack of wolves. 'And you were probably trying to drive them away with the smoke of your cigarettes,' I remarked. . . .

The negotiations were as a rule very tense: the Australians couldn't offer any adequate exchange for the treasures of the Hermitage. But they were very nice and quick-witted, and always managed to achieve their goal by means of diplomacy. I enjoyed interpreting at negotiations but they said I was especially good at banquets, which at that time were an integral part of any official visit.

At one official banquet in honour of the Guyanese Minister of Culture, held in Moscow, the USSR Deputy Minister of Culture, Ivanov, asked what parts of the Soviet Union our guest would like to see. While the Minister was ruminating, the Guyanese ambassador, also present at the banquet, intervened: 'Just don't send him to Gorky, where you have exiled your Academician Sakharov.' I diligently interpreted his remark, and at that very second was tugged by the sleeve. It was a woman adviser from the Ministry sitting beside me. 'Change the subject quickly,' she hissed. 'Ask whether they have read *The Lower Depths* by Gorky.' And without waiting for me to react, she interrupted in her broken English. Our guests were either easily diverted or just polite, and didn't press the subject any further. Afterwards, the woman approached me and said: 'Vitali, you've committed a major political mistake. You shouldn't have translated that sentence about Sakharov.'

'But as an interpreter I must convey all remarks adequately.'

'A Soviet interpreter is more than just an interpreter,' she declared gravely, and retired to the cloakroom.

'More? Or less?' I kept wondering.

Several times, I was solemnly allowed to act as a translator for the Minister of Culture of the USSR himself. This was the all-powerful candidate Politburo member P. N. Demichev, who as it now turns out did a lot of harm to our culture. It was an unforgettable experience to interpret the words of the Librarian of Congress of the USA at his meeting with Demichev. The Minister of Culture asked our American guest what his impressions of our country were. 'I think,' the Librarian of Congress replied, 'that your country is dominated by fear, that there is no respect for free thought and fresh ideas.' My habit was always to interpret in the first person. So, looking into the eyes of the candidate Politburo member, I found myself saying in Russian: '*I* think that the country is dominated by fear. . . .' And the ceiling of Demichev's huge office didn't fall upon me for such a sacrilege. Neither was I arrested or even sacked from my job . . . but the sensation was precarious. Yet I must say that Demichev was much more polished and quick-witted than most of his subordinates, who could only drone on for hours about how many clubs we have and how privileged Soviet children are.

I already knew who had the real privileges. It was the high-ranking bureaucrats. I will never forget how, working with the Guyanese Minister of Culture, we were accommodated at the government dacha called 'Durmen', near Tashkent (Uzbekistan). The cottage with its thirty or more rooms was surrounded by a huge garden with a swimming pool. There were only four of us staying in the whole house, and at least thirty people to wait upon us. In the dining room, there stood two (!) Blüthner grand pianos and the waiters, when you asked them what was for

19

breakfast, replied: 'Everything.' They did have everything indeed, and the cost was very low – about ten times less than in ordinary restaurants . . . Once in the evening I decided to have a swim in the swimming pool. As soon as I emerged from the water, a blonde, plump Russian girl materialised from the bushes. In one hand she was holding a towel, in the other there was a small tray with a bottle of ice-cold beer on it, though I hadn't asked for any . . . And when we were playing billiards with the guests in the dacha's special rest-room, an old Uzbek woman followed our every move with an ashtray to pick up the ash from our cigarettes. This small patch of Communist (or capitalist?) paradise was separated from the rest of the world by a high stone wall with barbed wire on top of it, and was guarded day and night by the militia. Beyond the wall lay the ordinary difficult life, with no meat, no butter and long queues for milk at the shops. We saw one such queue on the way to Tashkent airport at 6 am; it was at least a kilometre long. No wonder: one of the most corrupt of Brezhnev's henchmen, Rashidov, was ruling in Uzbekistan at that time . . .

The foreigners couldn't help noticing the difference, but being reticent they seldom mentioned it. As for me, after four days at 'Durmen', I felt so shocked and disgusted, that I was about to quit my job with the Ministry . . . Where was the social justice my grandfather had fought for? There was no sign of it. I was sure that such perversions couldn't last very long and that the time would come when we would be able to speak about them in the open. But I couldn't imagine that this time would come so soon – less than ten years later.

The other moral difficulty of the job was that being together with my 'delegates' for many days, I grew quite attached to most of them. But as soon as I bade farewell to them at Sheremetievo airport and the turnstile at passport control clicked, it was as if a bullet-proof glass wall emerged between us. I knew only too well that this wall was impossible to penetrate and that I would never see my friends again. They were ready to invite me to their countries (some even jokingly proposed to kidnap me). But who on earth would have allowed me to go?

My job with the Ministry of Culture finished in 1979, when the Soviet troops were sent to Afghanistan and cultural relations with the West practically came to a halt. In 1989 a Soviet TV presenter called the Afghanistan war a crime of Brezhnev and his crew. Back in 1979, we all understood that it was a crime, but could only say that to our closest friends and in a whisper. The country was again – as under Stalin – paralysed by terror. People were arrested just for cracking jokes about the leadership and the poor economic state of our huge land. Solzhenitsyn was stripped of his citizenship and thrown out. Academician Sakharov, whom the press is now calling the conscience of the nation, was labelled by the mass media as an enemy and traitor.

In the summer of 1980, Muscovites were suddenly granted three weeks off from Communism. During the Olympic games, boycotted by many Western countries because of Afghanistan, Moscow shops were bursting with foodstuffs and high-quality goods brought from all over the country and from abroad. It was the greatest show of Brezhnev's régime. Queues disappeared and the shop assistants, as if by a miracle, grew polite and helpful overnight. Oranges, different types of cheeses and sausages, Finnish butter, New Zealand mutton were on sale everywhere. I remember being struck dumb when the saleswoman, who only yesterday was screaming at the top of her lungs her traditional 'You are many and I am one!' asked me: 'What can I do for you?' and smiled . . .

The militiamen were swarming all over the city, sporting white uniforms, and also being nice and helpful. The streets were clean and deserted. Schoolchildren, prostitutes, homosexuals and people with criminal records were temporarily evacuated from Moscow, for the duration of the Olympics. The city was also closed to any Soviet visitors lacking Moscow registration. Ice-cold Pepsi was sold from the street stalls, and special American-made trucks commuted between them with loads of ice. All these were aimed at impressing foreign guests. There were not too many of them, as a matter of fact, but some of the hotels stood empty just in case . . . Wild rumours were circulated in the city: about Negroes who covertly injected fatal drugs into Soviet citizens' behinds in the underground crowd, about foreigners who treated Soviet children with poisoned sweets, and so on. These rumours were spread from the top to reduce any possible contact with the visitors from abroad.

The grandiose show was marred by only one fly in the ointment: on 25 July, Vladimir Vysotsky, the famous actor, poet and singer, died suddenly, aged forty-two. He was the idol of the Soviet intelligentsia. During the Olympics, he was made to appear on stage several times a day as a part of the cultural programme. He was suffering from heart disease and his heart couldn't stand the pressure. The queue to pay a last tribute to him was at least fifteen kilometres long. Coming there with my pregnant wife, I couldn't get inside the smallish Taganka theatre where the poet lay in state. The place was swarming with plain-clothes militia and it was a scorching hot day. Death didn't want to play its part in the show . . .

But the biggest shock came with the closure of the Olympics. The three-week paradise ended. One fine day the shop assistants became rude again, delicacies disappeared from the counters and militiamen resumed wearing their grey-blue uniforms. The trucks no longer brought ice to the Pepsi stalls, and the famous American drink was sold tepid and tasted of sugar. As for the queues, they were longer than ever before: the whole country rushed to the re-opened capital, attracted by the rumour of unseen abundance. But there was nothing left. This sudden transition from fairy tale back to gloomy reality was done with unparalleled cynicism towards the people, especially Muscovites. The authorities didn't even try to conceal the meanest act of throwing dust into the eyes of the whole world. As for the Muscovites, we had enough dust in our streets again. The Olympic show didn't impress us in the least, causing feelings of shame and bitterness.

I was not very upset by the end of my interpreter's job. I didn't want my well-being to depend upon the quickly changing international situation any longer. I was also annoyed by the elements of servility and showing-off that were part of an interpreter's job during stagnation time. I wanted to do something useful for my country, to help it climb out of the swamp. The only way for me to do it at that time was through honest writing. I felt that I would succeed in it.

After some hesitation I decided to try my hand at satire. It was impossible to write seriously about serious problems – no one would have published that. But satirists were always allowed a bit more leeway than 'serious' writers: satire as a genre was supposed to be critical.

I started by taking some of my old comic verses to *Literaturnaya Gazeta*: I had to establish my name before trying to touch upon real problems. In *Literaturnaya Gazeta* there was the famous page 16 – 'The Twelve Chairs Club', compiled by the department of satire and humour and edited by Victor Veselovsky. 'The Twelve Chairs Club' was well known all over the country. Everyone started reading the paper right at page 16. They managed to publish very courageous jokes, but the main merit of the page was the so-called second meaning. Using euphemisms and Aesopian language, the authors of the page ventured to criticise the most burning problems with a good deal of humour. Page 16 had its constant fictional personage – a nincompoop writer 'Yevgeny Sazonov', who was used to mock the bureaucrats from the Writers' Union. One of his favourite expressions was: 'If something is prohibited, but desired very much, then it is allowed.' . . . So it was to page 16 that I brought my poems.

They were published very quickly, within a fortnight[1] – incredible speed for 'someone from the street'. Why did it happen so? Because honest and hard-working people who recognised no connections were on the staff of page 16 of *Lit. Gazeta*. The other departments also managed to publish occasional unorthodox, courageous articles and the newspaper was widely read. '*Literaturka*' – that is what the intelligentsia fondly called it.

After my first publications in *Literaturka*, I experienced a certain setback. One of my comic poems was a parody, mimicking the style of an obscure poet;[2] it was published all right, but who could know that this poet had recently died? It became known only after publication. The poet's widow stirred up a big row, accusing me of making fun of a dead man. She demanded either a printed apology in *Literaturka* or . . . the publication of her late husband's verses. The editors chose the second option, and one of his poorly-written poems did appear in the newspaper. I was advised to take a break from publication 'until the fuss subsided', and I suffered greatly because of it: I had just got a taste for being published in the best newspaper in the country.

But remembering only too well the proverb 'Moscow does not believe in tears', I didn't give up writing. By that time, my son Mitya had been born, and with just one room for the three of us, I had to work in . . . the cupboard. Literally in the cupboard, but a big one! The room's previous tenant was a radio pirate who had used the cupboard for illegal broadcasts and kept his home-made radio transmitter there. I just made a bigger hole in the door to let me breathe, installed an electric lamp there and arranged a small table with a stool. In this improvised 'office' I could type the whole night through without risking waking up the baby.

I was freed from my voluntary cupboard exile several months later by a telephone call. Viktor Veselovsky, the editor of page 16, was calling: 'Come to the office quickly,' he said.

'We need feuilletons,'* he blurted as soon as I appeared on the threshold of his tiny cubicle of an office, in Tsvetnoi Boulevard.

'But I've never written feuilletons.'

'You will. I like the style of your short stories and poems. You've got a good feel for words. I know you'll succeed.'

'But what shall I write about?'

'Anything. Just go to any town you wish, and write a feuilleton from there. You are free to choose the subject.'

He switched on the small fan on his desk, indicating that the audience was over. I felt as if I was being swept out of the office by the fan's rotating blades.

I was indeed taken aback. It is one thing to write short and cryptically venomous stories or poems, but to produce a big concrete article on God

*Feuilleton is a French word, which originally meant a serialised story. In Russia it denotes a special genre of journalism – a satirical article, mostly based on concrete facts, denouncing a negative phenomenon.

knows what, and to make it funny – that was definitely a horse of a different colour. After some shilly-shallying, I decided to take the challenge and to ride this differently coloured horse to Archangel, a town in the north of the country, where I had never been before. 'Why not just write about the experience of an ordinary traveller?' I thought, and carefully hiding my brand-new correspondent's card, took the train to Archangel. This simple trick of changed (or rather hidden) identity was to become one of my favourite methods in future investigations.

Like any Soviet town, Archangel was suffering from a shortage of hotels. Of course, for a correspondent of a Moscow newspaper, there was no problem getting accommodation, but I was determined not to show my card under any circumstances, and managed to get a room at a newly-built hotel only after putting (on the advice of the doorman) a three-rouble note into my passport. The note was readily accepted by the passport-checking hotel clerk, and I got a room facing the river.

It was the start of my week-long struggle to overcome the rigours of hotel life: the rudeness of the personnel, cockroaches, the inexplicable obstinacy of the doormen who refused to let my guests into the hotel until greased with a rouble. Once, having returned to my room late in the evening, I found an elderly floor-lady* sleeping in my bed. When I woke her up, she got very angry: 'I thought you were not coming tonight, and decided to take a nap here. Why the hell did you return so late?'

I called the story 'Reports from a Hotel Bedside Table'[3] and invented a personage – a poet named Arkady Malokrovny – whose letters to his wife I allegedly found in the drawer of the bedside table in my room. He was trying to write poems (they also became part of the story) but the hotel personnel made it impossible for him to work.

I also wanted to mention the severe food shortages in the Archangel shops: there was practically nothing on sale there but spaghetti (the contribution of an Italian ship which had just visited the local port). Milk was sold only on prescription to the sick. But the editors in *Literaturka* told me later that it wouldn't do: at that time food shortages were still taboo for the press.

The story occupied half of page 16 and was rather a success. As one of the readers put it in his letter, it helped to expose the stupidity of our provincial life.

Immediately after that, I volunteered to write a feuilleton on the extreme difficulties of getting tickets to the best Moscow theatres. The problem was that up to 90 per cent of the tickets for each show were

*Floor lady – in Russian hotels – a vigilant guardian of the inmates' régime and morals whose main task is to keep outsiders away.

reserved for the privileged and well-connected. For an ordinary person 'from the street', it was next to impossible to see a good play. The story[4] was written all in verse, but at the last moment when it was about to appear, the duty editor (the one who is responsible for the whole issue) insisted on removing all mention of Moscow from the story. The reason behind this was that V. Grishin – a Politburo member, and the first secretary of the Moscow city Party committee – would tolerate no criticism of the 'exemplary communist city' (as Moscow was labelled at that time) in the central press. And so my page sixteen editor hastily had to change the verses in which Moscow theatres were touched upon, to make the story sound neutral. To save the feuilleton, he managed to do this, though some of the new rhymes were rather far-fetched and approximate, and the whole message became very vague. Of course, Grishin-gave no specific orders not to mention Moscow, but the editors were well aware of his likes and dislikes.

The other stumbling block of the story was one of the invented personages – the fictitious bigshot named Leonid Andreevich. My poor editor was hauled on to the carpet by the deputy editor-in-chief, and warned that he would be sacked if another 'Leonid' ever appeared on page 16. The reason was that Brezhnev's full name was Leonid Ilyich, and not even the slightest echo of this name was allowed to appear on the 'humorous' page. It was stupid, it was absurd, but it was reality. If you read the feuilleton (or rather what is left of it) in *Literaturka* now, you'll see that instead of Leonid Andreevich, my personage, who is by the way mentioned in the story only once, is called 'Alexander Andreevich' . . .

All this was very upsetting for me as a tyro journalist, just a beginner. I thought that in my editor's shoes I wouldn't have complied with it, since to agree to such humiliating corrections certainly meant playing into the hands of stagnation forces. But it was easy for me to judge. To act was much more difficult . . .

At least, I consoled myself, they had managed to preserve *something*. Details, I mollified myself again, in the long run were not that important. To show how the system worked and to expose the phenomenon – these were the main things, I told myself soothingly . . . I felt with horror that a little demon of a self-censor (still a baby, but a naughty one) was being born inside my brain. 'If it is useless to criticise Moscow, since they won't publish it anyway, why should I write about anything at all?' Such treacherous thoughts were brewing in my mind. No matter how hard I tried to drive them away, they were still there.

By the end of 1981, I had published one more big story in *Literaturka*. Subconsciously I had chosen a more 'neutral' subject – poetry for children. The story was entitled 'Engineer Tyutikov's Presents'[5]. Again there was a fictional hero, engineer Tyutikov, who tried to educate his little son by reading him children's poetry books. But the poems were such gibberish that he succeeded only in provoking his son's tears and a family scandal. The feuilleton was also a cross between fiction and documentary prose, which was very unusual for the Soviet press on the whole. One of the country's leading literary critics, S. Chuprinin, said at a session of the *Literaturka* editorial board that I had created a new satirical genre. Besides, the story proved to be not that innocent: some literary bosses liked to while away their time writing awful verses for children. I mentioned a couple of them in the feuilleton and quoted some of their hopeless rhymes, bringing vociferous telephone calls to the editor.

On the eve of the new year, I was awarded the Golden Calf literary prize – the most coveted award for a Soviet satirist. It was given to me for the three above-mentioned stories after only half a year of being a journalist. I couldn't believe my eyes and ears, but it was true.

The importance of the award for me could not be stressed enough. I was in desperate need of moral support to strengthen the belief in my own abilities which had been shattered by years of injustice and bad luck, and there could be no better support than the Golden Calf, which immediately led me from obscurity to the first ranks of Soviet satirists. I came to realise that journalism really could become my profession. In just three years, I had gone all the way from the miserable grass-loving ram in Kharkov to marriage, a son, and the prestigious 'Golden Calf' in Moscow. The clatter of my typewriter from the cupboard was growing more and more optimistic.

The proverb proved to be right: Moscow does not believe in tears, but it does believe in effort.

3

Just a Magazine Cutting

Shortly after winning the Golden Calf, I was offered the position of literary consultant to page 16 of '*Literaturka*'. My job was to answer the readers' letters and to review the innumerable stories, poems and jokes sent to the editorial office.

I published some more feuilletons in the same fiction/non-fiction manner. In February 1982, a selection of Henry Longfellow's poems, translated by me, appeared in *Lit. Gazeta*[1]. This was largely due to the well-known Soviet journalist and translator Oleg Bitov, who was the editor of the foreign culture page of *Literaturka* at that time. He greatly liked my translations and preferred them to those by the more venerable translators. Later Bitov became famous (or rather infamous) all over the world for his sudden defection to Britain and his even more unexpected return to the USSR a year later. I was very proud of this publication, which happened to be the last my father saw. He died suddenly of a heart-attack on the last day of February, aged fifty-six. The ambulance, called by my mother when he collapsed, arrived in forty minutes, just in time to confirm his death. I still think that if they had arrived thirty minutes earlier he could have been saved. The ambulance station, by the way, was only 200 metres from my parents' Kharkov house.

That very spring I wrote a story about the excruciatingly bad conditions under which emergency medical services worked in the city of Gorky. The story was set, but never saw daylight: it was removed from the paper at the very last moment, with no plausible explanation. I suspect that the reason was that Sakharov lived in Gorky at that time. Probably the censors didn't want to highlight the fact, since Sakharov himself was an elderly and sick man and might need an ambulance any time. This could have created a negative reaction in the West.

Some other journals started commissioning articles from me. *Literaturnaya Rossiya* – the organ of the Writers' Union of the Russian Federation – asked me to write an essay on any Moscow schoolteacher who was a doctor of science. I telephoned the city's education department and found out there were about a dozen teachers with PhDs working in Moscow schools, whose names they dictated to me. All of them but one sounded obviously Jewish. When I showed the list to *Literaturnaya Rossiya* they told me point-blank to write about the only gentile one. They were not actually rampantly anti-semitic, it was simply that a lot of Jews were emigrating from the country then, and the editors just didn't want to play with fire, that is to provoke displeasure from those at the top. There was a precedent – a misprint in Brezhnev's last name in one of the provincial newspapers. It called him 'Brezhner', which in Russia sounds like a Jewish surname – and the editor was sent packing.

I wrote the essay on the chosen man, who really was a good teacher.[2] After publication there was a big row: it appeared that this safely gentile teacher had resigned from the Communist Party several years before on his own volition – a unique case for this country. The angry official from the district Party committee telephoned *Literaturnaya Rossiya* shouting: 'Whom do you publicise? A dissident?!' Certainly the blame fell upon me: I should have made enquiries and found that out, they said. They simply needed a scapegoat. I suspected from the very beginning that there must be something fishy about this black sheep of a man who was the only non-Jewish person on the list. For a scholar it's a lowly position to teach in a school, which is probably why all but one of them were Jewish and hence denied better jobs. The editors wanted to play it safe, and as a result they found themselves in a mess. But I didn't sympathise with them. That was the end of my association with *Literaturnaya Rossiya*.*

It never rains, but it pours. In the spring of 1982, I suffered another set-back at *Literaturka*. I wrote a big feuilleton, 'H$_2$O for a Wide Readership',[3] making fun of stupid introductions to books both by classic and modern authors. (It's a tradition to publish an introduction at the beginning of every book.) In the story, I criticised the summary (mind, the summary, not the book itself) of a pamphlet by a certain Kabanov, *How to Feed a Pig*. The introduction stated that the book was designed for a wide readership (a pun was involved here: 'kaban' in Russian means a 'boar'). How could I know that Comrade Kabanov was none other than the head of the cattle-breeding section of the Agricultural Department of the Central Committee of the CPSU?! After the story was published, he personally visited the editor-in-chief of *Literaturka* and demanded an apology. This time, unlike the case of the poet's widow, the apology was granted and printed in the next issue of the paper. By the unwritten laws of stagnation epoch journalism, a printed apology was a disgrace for a

It's interesting to note that now – in 1989/90 – it has become one of the strongholds of anti-Semitism in the Soviet press.

newspaper. So I was ordered not to cross the threshold of *Literaturka* for at least a year.

This of course was the end of my literary consultancy too . . . Was it just? Certainly not! First, the paper had its own research bureau which was supposed to know everything: they should have checked who Kabanov was, and crossed his name out if they wanted. Secondly, even if someone was a top-ranking official, why couldn't you criticise just an introduction to his book? But trying to find justice was still hopeless. 'The pointsman is always to blame for a train crash,' a Russian saying goes. All these mishaps were good for me in a way! They helped me to acquire a certain stamina which proved indispensable for my future – much more serious – investigations.

Of course there were some high spots too. In 1982, a group of young Moscow satirists united around the newspaper *Gudok* (The Hooter), the organ of the Ministry of Railways. *Gudok* was at the height of its fame in the Twenties, when a bunch of prominent writers – Bulgakov and Ilf and Petrov among them – were on the staff. These people compiled the satirical page 4, which was applauded throughout the country. In the post-war years, the paper had gone from bad to worse, and turned into an ordinary blue-collar daily. In 1982, Alexander Kabakov, the editor of the feuilletons department, decided to revive the old traditions. He started publishing monthly issues of page 4 under the title 'The Ilf and Petrov Club', which quickly established itself as the country's best satirical page, outstripping even page 16 of *Literaturka*. I became one of the main contributors, writing a feuilleton for each issue. Analytical and even philosophical stories were welcomed there, together with the so-called non-concrete feuilletons in which you could ruminate and philosophise on certain general problems. There I also edited the column 'Punch from a Classic' in which readers' letters were commented upon by suitable quotations from classic works. This column was very popular with the readers. But one couldn't possibly maintain a decent living from the *Gudok* publications: the royalties were very low, and besides, the 'Ilf and Petrov Club' appeared only once a month.

And so I went to *Krokodil* magazine. Why didn't I do that earlier? Because *Krokodil*, as the oldest and largest satirical magazine in the country (its circulation in 1982 was close to 6,000,000 as compared to the 3,000,000 of *Literaturka* and 500,000 of *Gudok*), had the reputation of being tame, biddable and rather conservative. This reputation dated back to the Stalinist epoch, when the magazine was violently attacking innocent persons stigmatised as 'enemies of the people', 'cosmopolitans without kith or kin' (meaning Jews) or 'wrong-doers', and was a powerful instrument in the hands of Stalin's henchmen. Published by the newspaper *Pravda*, it seldom ventured to touch upon crucial problems, though by its very nature it was supposed to be critical. In fact, the magazine carried lots of high-level cartoons, but its literary section left much to be desired. People mostly did not read it but just flicked through, stopping to giggle occasionally at a cartoon or an anecdote. But even so, the magazine was influential, widely circulated, and – not unimportant – it paid good royalties.

'What would you like me to write about?' I asked the editor of one of *Krokodil*'s departments, who was leafing idly through the papers piled high on his desk.

'Write about drunkenness,' he mumbled without looking up.

Trying to remain quiet, I promised to give it some thought, but inside I was boiling with anger: drunkenness. The idea of such a thing! For so many years, journalists, writers, artists and poets had been ridiculing this ancient Russian vice, making fun of it, drawing innumerable cartoons of red-nosed alcoholics sitting inside vodka bottles, but drinking only kept growing. To write about it had become a banality in itself, a worn-out cliché. Jokes about drunkards sounded almost as tasteless as mother-in-law anecdotes. 'They just want to get rid of me,' I decided, and left dead sure that I would never return.

But at home in the cupboard, I did give some thought to the editor's suggestion. Suddenly it didn't seem so absurd to me. Yes, drunkenness was growing. It was our national affliction. It ruined lives, families and careers. But why was it so? Had any journalist ever attempted to look seriously into the social roots of the problem? Maybe most people drank not just as a tradition, but because of their sheer inability to find an outlet or a place to go after work, because of their disbelief in official propaganda. Superficial articles of condemnation together with crude red-nosed cartoons only aggravated the situation. But what if I found a basically new approach, an unusual angle? For years we had been writing about the evils of drink, but this didn't seem to frighten away a single alcoholic. What if I made a 180-degree turn – praised drinking (ironically, of course), applauded the effect of drink on public life and economy, dished out eulogies to hard drinkers and alcoholics? Wouldn't the final effect be much more powerful than that of a direct and therefore all the more crude criticism?

That evening a new personage, a new hero (or rather anti-hero), was born. I christened him Ya. Khmelnoi (I. Blotto) and immediately found a job for him – '*Our Fellow Drinker*' magazine. He was destined to become my boozy alter-ego – but first I had to register my new-born hero, that is, to have his birth approved by *Krokodil*.

The department editor liked the idea. He only advised me to cross out the word 'Our' from the name of the invented '*Our Fellow Drinker*' magazine, so as not to imply that *we all* were fellow drinkers. So far, so good.

The deputy editor-in-chief was strongly opposed to Comrade Blotto. 'Are you trying to make fun of our colleagues, journalists?' he said.

The argument was solved by the editor-in-chief, Evgeny Panteleyevich Dubrovin: 'Good idea, and a good hero,' he concluded, and so the fate of the new-born journalist I. Blotto was determined. Thus my fate was determined too, but I didn't know it at the time.

So I went on my first mission, posing as a '*Fellow Drinker*' magazine correspondent. For that I chose the city of Kirov, formerly Vyatka, notorious for its traditions of heavy drinking.

The city was indeed drinking itself into oblivion. There was nothing in the food shops, despite the ration cards on which the locals lived. There had been some feeble attempts to combat drinking in Kirov, but they were not effective and the local spirits factories which I visited kept supplying the city's shops with thousands of decalitres of cheap, strong wines popularly nicknamed as *bormotukha* (literally 'the stuff that makes you mumble').

My first story under the name Ya. Khmelnoi was entitled 'Notes of an Inebriated Journalist'.[4] It sang the praises of the Kirov authorities for their valiant struggle against sobriety and mildly criticised some of the city's anti-alcoholic campaigners.

The result was beyond all expectation. The readers wholeheartedly joined in the game. *Krokodil* was showered with ironic letters addressed to the 'esteemed Ya. Khmelnoi', inviting him to visit other places to pay tribute to local drinkers. And the Kirov authorities reacted very quickly, promising in their official reply to put an end to unlimited drinking. This was my first major success in pursuit of the vow made several years before in my hospital bed: to try and make my country better.

So Comrade Blotto had to go on yet another mission – this time to Perm, a city in the Urals, to glorify local taxi-drivers who were bootlegging spirits by night at twice the daytime prices. The Perm story was called 'Alcoholic Ambulance',[5] and was followed by Riga, Ternopol, Kharkov – Comrade Blotto was in great demand. He and I made a tour of villages in the Ryazan region to publicise the achievements of home-brewers ('Manuscript in a Bottle').[6] Gradually some of the details of Blotto's daily routine became known to the readers. Being a journalist, he had a desk with a 'working liqueur glass' on it; he took part in editorial meetings, only in the '*Fellow Drinker*' they were called 'alcotorial meetings'; he was fond of going on missions, since it enabled him not to have to account for every copeck to his ever-nagging wife, and to spend freely his drinking money, allotted by the magazine. As a real journalist he got letters from his readers, one of whom invented a measuring unit of drunkenness – one bout. The formula for one bout was as follows:

$$\frac{\text{gramme} \times \% \text{ of alcohol}}{\text{person per second}} = 1 \text{ bout}$$

All these small ficticious details became part of the stories.

Here I would like to break the chronological order of my narrative for a short while and to dwell upon the letters phenomenon in the USSR. Whenever I come back from a mission, I find a big pile of letters waiting for me on my office desk. To read them is my favourite occupation; often unable to do this during office hours, I take them home and try to answer each one, though it is time-consuming: I receive up to 5,000 letters annually.

While on a short attachment to the *Guardian* in Britain, I saw that its correspondents were also receiving letters, but in much smaller numbers. It probably happens partly because our country is much larger than Britain and the 1989 circulation of *Krokodil* (5,300,000) is quite a lot bigger than the *Guardian*'s (400,000). But the main reason, to my mind, is that in Russia, with its huge distances, letters have always been special. For many people, they are often the only means of communication with their relatives, friends and loved ones. That's why letters in our country are generally much more informal, much more personal, than in Britain.

I treasure my readers' letters very much. They help to overcome inevitable fits of pessimism and fear. They prove that your work is necessary for your people and for your country. I have old and trusted correspondents in many parts of the Soviet Union, in its most distant nooks.

As soon as a letter arrives at the editorial office (unless it is addressed to someone in person), it ceases to be just a scribbled piece of paper – it becomes a document and is taken under control. A special filing card is provided for each, and a number assigned. On the cards, the girls from our letters department sum up the contents in a few sentences. Then the letter is forwarded to one of the other departments, depending on the subject. A copy of the card goes to the special card index, soon to be joined by an official reply from the organisation to which it was forwarded, or a resolution. When readers enquire by phone or by post what happened to their letters, the card index is consulted and they get a quick reply.

Writing letters to newspapers, magazines, radio and TV studios is quite popular in my country, especially under perestroika. In recent years they have become much more frank and sincere. My readers tend to expose their souls, to share their joys and grievances with me in their letters. Very often, they inform me of some unlawful procedure of which they have become victims. They criticise their bosses, express their opinions of how to change the country. They say why they like or dislike this or that story of mine.

Each letter can easily launch me into a long mission somewhere to Siberia, Central Asia or the Far East. Of course, it's impossible to visit every correspondent of mine, so when urgent measures must be taken, and someone is in trouble, I forward the letter to local militia or Party headquarters, asking them to look into the case and to inform me and the reader of the results of the check-up. More often than not, it helps: a letter forwarded from *Krokodil* is not usually ignored even by the most bureaucratic of bureaucrats.

Letters are part and parcel of my journalistic life. Not all of them are pleasant or complimentary. It's only natural. 'The funniest desire is the desire to be liked by everybody,' Goethe once said. Dealing with such contentious subjects as corruption, organised crime, fascism and the like, I receive lots of letters with curses and threats. But they don't distress me: if someone is irritated by your story, it's the surest indicator that it worked, that your words hit home . . . Hostile letters though are well outnumbered by letter-confessions, letter-autobiographies, letter-whodunnits and so on. After 'The Plague of Love'(see chapter 4) I got a lot of letters from lonely young women, telling me their sad life stories. One of them wrote that as soon as she finished the letter, she would turn the gas on and die. 'You are the last one in all the world to whom I want to speak,' she acknowledged. Unfortunately there was no return address on this letter, and I couldn't check whether she was serious or not. But I was flattered, of course.

I also get many letters from jail. After 'Amur Wars' (chapter 6), prisoners seeking justice started addressing me regularly. There were some truly remarkable letters amongst these. One man, imprisoned for fifteen years in a correction labour camp in the Far East, recounted how he and some of his prison mates were selected by the corrupted members of the camp's administration for thefts and robberies. They were given arms and at night were driven outside the camp in a lorry. After robbing a shop or a flat under the supervision of their guards, they were taken back. All the loot went to the administration. I checked up on the letter and it proved to be true. The corrupted camp supervisors – all military officers – were tried and punished.

The letter I got in 1988 from a group of convicts alleged that they had been unjustly condemned. Such letters are not unusual. But this one was special because it was written in blood. Though this time the prisoners' allegations proved to be false.

Another prisoner wrote that he knew where the Sailor's money and his militia file (see chapter 6) were hidden. I went to see him in the labour camp only to make sure that he had been bluffing and was only trying to commute his long sentence by any possible means.

Some time ago, we had big problems with unsigned, anonymous letters. What was to be done with them? Chuck them into the waste bin? And what if they contained important facts and the authors were just not brave enough to put their signatures, for fear of possible prosecution by those whom they criticised? It was a dilemma. But practice showed that as a rule anonymous letters were lying and slandering innocent people. So in 1988, at last, we made a big decision in *Krokodil* – not to consider unsigned letters at all. We even arranged a demonstrative public burning of some of the *anonimkas*, as we call anonymous letters, and informed our readers about this auto-da-fé in the magazine. This made our lives much easier.

But there remained another problem: letters signed in someone else's name. As a rule, these letters are just libel, but to find this out a journalist sometimes has to travel thousands of miles.

Several years ago, I received a series of letters from a man calling himself Ivanov, a sleeping car attendant, living in Kirov. In them he described his awful working conditions and his corrupt colleagues and bosses. I decided to go to Kirov to find out whether these vivid condemnations of his were true to life. On arrival, I went straight to the railway office where Ivanov allegedly worked and where I had the following dialogue with one of the officials:

'Can I speak to Comrade Ivanov?'

'No, you can't.'

'Why not?'

'Because he doesn't work with us any longer.'

'Have you sacked him, or what?'

'Yes, we have dismissed him.' ('So you've sacked him for being critical,' I thought with fiendish pleasure.)

'For what reason have you dismissed him, if I may ask?'

'For the reason of his death. He died more than a year ago . . .'

'? ? ?'

I was struck dumb, since Ivanov's last letter had been posted, according to the stamp, just a week before. So I was corresponding with someone from the other world!

But there was no mysticism about this story. Being a slanderer and a coward too, in an attempt to blacken his colleagues my Kirov pen-friend was signing his libellous letters in the name of his late comrade who had perished in an accident.

Thus my connections with the other world were finished, though only temporarily, I suspect . . .

For me, readers' letters are very much like human beings. They may be kind or angry, clever or stupid, sad or funny, warm or cold, friendly or hostile. An affectionate reader's letter has always been my best award.

After each publication, I look forward impatiently to the readers' reactions. It is the best indicator of whether the piece has been successful or not, whether it has struck a responsive chord among the public or has died a death. I am proud to say that such stories of mine as 'Just a Magazine Cutting' (see below), 'The Plague of Love' and 'Führers from Fontanka' (chapter 8) have set *Krokodil* records in the number of letters received, with the latter an all-time absolute champion, getting more than 3,000 replies which are still coming in.

The letters received from my British readers after my five stories were published in the *Guardian* in October–November 1988 are among my most treasured ones. The fact that these articles (and the one in *Punch*) were enjoyed by the British was encouraging, since I had written them in English, which was quite a challenge.

Letters are sensitive barometers for any kind of journalism. That is why I thought it essential to reproduce some of them in this book. At first I wanted to do this in a separate chapter, but later I changed my mind, thinking that it was no good to separate the letters from the stories that triggered them. So I decided to install 'Letter-Boxes' throughout the book. You will find them in the end of most of the chapters. I invite you to look into them and to hear the authentic voices of my country folk. The first 'Letter-Box' is just round the corner – or rather next door: at the end of chapter 4.

Apart from letters and visitors to the office, an important way of communicating with my readers is meeting them publicly. These meetings are conducted in the form of dialogues. When on missions to different parts of the country, I never miss an opportunity to address my readers. Such meetings occur at cinemas or theatres, at research institutes or factories during lunch breaks. I speak about my work, recite my poems and short stories, and the readers readily share their problems with me. There is a tradition of asking questions in a written form and passing them over to the stage, rostrum or table where I stand facing the audience. I collect these scraps of paper with questions and treasure them no less than the letters, since they are also the voice of my readers, the voice of my waking country. Here are some of them:

'When will the top-ranking bureaucrats who do not use ordinary shops and who live in luxury become the object of satire? In other words, when will everyone enjoy equal benefits and experience equal shortages?'

'What's your attitude to women feuilletonists?'

'Do you think our country is democratic?'

'Is it true that mafiosi will soon be buying the positions of first secretaries of district, city, and other Party Committees?'

'Is the mild sentence given to Churbanov, Brezhnev's son-in-law, also a mafia trick?'

'What are the Politburo and Gorbachev going to do about all the outrages you write about?'

'From 1945 to 1953 there was a steady reduction of prices every year. Since then prices have just climbed and climbed. Why is this so?'

'What is the fate of Korotich, the editor-in-chief of *Ogonyok*? Has he really been assassinated or sent to UNESCO?' (These were just widespread rumours. Korotich is safe and sound and keeps his post.)

'Aren't you going to write a documentary novel "Leningrad Wars" as opposed to "Amur Wars". We Leningraders need your help desperately.'

'Why don't you write much about the Memory Society? What do you think of it? Your opinion is important for us since we respect you very much.'

'Have you heard of the Memory Society's nationalistic demonstrations in Leningrad? Do you know that these chauvinistic gatherings were not only guarded by the militia but were approved of by the regional Party Committee?'

'What are the roots of all the negative social phenomena you write about? Is the system to blame?'

'Are you aware of the existence of a taxi mafia at railway stations? It is impossible to hire a cab there . . .'

'Have you got any information as to the negative moments in the work of our ideologists?'

'What's your attitude to the so-called 'special militia units' employed to disperse peaceful demonstrations, as happened in Moscow and Minsk?'

'Your work must be pointed at the sore points of our society. The national question is one of them. Will you expand on this painful subject?'

'Do you get many letters with threats from neo-fascists? How do you react to them?'

There is nothing more encouraging for me as a journalist than to hear people expressing themselves freely after such a long silence. As to the above questions, I shall try my best to answer most of them in this book.

And now, back to my narrative.

Apart from I. Blotto, I began to appear in *Krokodil* under my own name as well. Literary games were not very welcome on its pages, so I practically had to forget my *Literaturka* fiction-documentary tricks. I tried to raise more crucial subjects instead.

In a letter from Turkmenia (Central Asia), a reader informed us that the hospital for war veterans in the town of Marie was located in a former stable. I immediately flew to Marie, which is in the extreme south of the country. It was 42° in the shade there. The air-conditioning in the hotel didn't work. Nor did the shower.

The hospital was indeed in the former stables, but it was OK: the patients were clean, well fed and well looked after. But what I came across in Marie was much worse than just a stable hospital. I investigated how hard it was for a war invalid to prove that he was really a war invalid, how many bureaucratic obstacles were in his way. Although war invalids have lots of privileges in my country – low rent, better food supplies etc – all these benefits are available only if one is *officially* recognised. The procedure of 'recognition' is humiliating and time-consuming, and is based on the crazy old instructions issued in 1956. These instructions, for instance, require the applicant to submit certificates from the hospital at the front to the effect that he really was wounded in action. What if he was lightly wounded and wasn't hospitalised? Now, after forty-odd years, even a light combat wound can turn one into an invalid. The instructions don't care: bring the certificate, that's all. (They don't take into account that pretty soon there will remain no more Second World War veterans, to say nothing of war invalids, at all!) The instructions also specify that a limbless invalid's stump must be carefully measured and if it is one or two centimetres longer than the 'required length', he won't be recognised as an invalid!

I wrote a piece on this incredible bureaucratic procedure calling for the recognition of every (no matter how lightly) wounded Second World War veteran as an invalid. The article was called 'Just a Magazine Cutting'[7] because sympathetic publications in the press were all that most war veterans could count upon. 'We must issue new, more humane instructions', I wrote. 'We need them now, immediately. With every passing day, the necessity will diminish.'

This essay became *Krokodil*'s champion in the number of readers' letters – about 2,000. They were mainly from war veterans who would also telephone me, or would find me in the street when I was walking with my son, just to thank me for it. We were planning to publish the collection of readers' letters, but the censors didn't let it happen. They thought that there was no need further to embarrass people on the eve of the 'glorious fortieth anniversary of our victory'. Four or five years ago it was still useless to argue with them. Now the situation has changed and the censors keep (or try to keep) to their constitutional duties: to guard State secrets, and not to allow pornography, racism and war propaganda in the press. Nowadays, I'm sure such a collection would be published, but thankfully there would be no need: the humiliating instructions were changed shortly after publication of my article, for which I was given my first *Krokodil* annual award. I shared it with Comrade Blotto for 'Alcoholic Ambulance'.

During the pre-perestroika years (1982–5), I wrote dozens of articles, essays and feuilletons for *Krokodil*, where I became a staff special correspondent. I also contributed to *Lit. Gazeta*, which in a year or so forgave me my 'blunder', and also to *Gudok, Trud, Sovetskaya Rossiya, Nedelya* and other publications. I was constantly on the move between the Far East and Central Asia, the Baltic Republics and Siberia, spending more time elsewhere than in Moscow.

When out of Moscow, you always had to be on the alert: you came to criticise, so you should be beyond criticism yourself. From time to time, I was openly provoked. In a town in central Russia where I was exposing some petty corruption, two naked girls were pushed into my hotel room during the night. They were very drunk. Someone from the dark corridor was ready to photograph me in their company. Luckily, he didn't have a flash. I quickly switched off the light and pushed the girls back into the corridor, slamming the door behind them at the peril of being inhospitable. Looking out of the window I could see them, now fully dressed, in the company of the corridor photographer, stopping a militia car and driving away. One of my colleagues who had found himself in a similar situation could think of nothing else but to jump out of the window. Luckily he was staying on the ground floor . . .

Such blatant provocations were pretty rare. Much more often, there were attempts to force a present or even a bribe upon me. The bribe could be a hidden one: you come back to your hotel room exhausted as hell, and find your fridge bursting with exquisite foodstuffs and drinks – caviare and cognac. You rush to a floor-lady shouting: 'Who's brought all these bloody things?' 'No idea,' she shrugs . . . The only thing that remains is to throw all the stuff into the corridor and settle for a cup of wishy-washy tea with a suspicious-smelling sandwich at a hotel buffet . . .

Here I am not trying to parade my honesty. Circumspect behaviour was simply a must, since the subjects I touched upon were very sensitive. Potential stories could be easily ruined by the smallest ill-considered step jeopardising the author's credibility. You can judge for yourselves.

The zoo in the city of Karaganda (Kazakhstan) was a place of increasing danger. Not for visitors but for animals. They were so badly treated and undernourished that some of them preferred to escape from their cages, as happened in 1982 with the zoo's ancient elephant, when the whole city was mobilised to catch him. Next morning, the poor elephant was spotted on the tennis courts of the local park. The first people to locate him were unsuspecting pensioners from the physical fitness group who came to the courts for their morning exercises. People say that on that fine morning the pensioners broke several sprinting records . . .

Eventually the elephant was caught and put back into his tiny cage. The peacock – the pride of the zoo – was less lucky: a persistent visitor tore away all the feathers from his beautiful tail. Unlike the elephant, the peacock couldn't escape, having had his wings clipped, and he had to go on living tail-less in the cage.

The zoo had also suffered from a big fire caused by the sheer negligence of the staff, and many animals had been burnt alive. To crown it all, the director once decided to feed to the tigers three rare Asian piglets which had fallen ill and were dying because of maltreatment. This was done in daytime, in full view of the visitors, mainly children. My story was called 'The Love of Three Little Pigs'.[8] It was not easy to investigate, since at first all the members of the zoo staff denied their atrocious feeding methods. But in the end they confessed.

As Comrade Blotto's godfather, I went on exposing drunkenness and ran a number of stories on this painful subject. In Petrozavodsk (Karelia) I discovered a tragic case of a timber-mill worker, an inveterate drinker, who once appeared at the mill drunk, and with a hunting rifle shot dead his forewoman right there in the workshop. This woman had been the only person brave enough to keep challenging him for his drinking, the rest of his co-workers preferring to turn a blind eye when he became drunk and violent, as if they didn't see him. So I called the story, which despite its tragic plot remained within the frame of a feuilleton, 'The Invisible Man'.[9]

'Pensioner on the Banisters'[10] described the life of a genius of a crook from Belorussia who first fiddled a diploma as a vet, then brilliantly simulated brain-damage and spent many years living comfortably on five (!) wangled pensions at a time, having no legal right to any of them. The intricate web of crookery he had spun was just incredible: he was drawing his five different pensions in five different towns, and brilliantly forging forms, stamps and certificates. Actually, he twisted the whole State bureaucracy around his little finger. Eventually he was arrested and sentenced to fifteen years in prison. I went there to meet him and was surprised by his plain, if not sheepish, look and behaviour. But then I realised that it was this very same simpleton's mask that had helped him to mislead officials for so many years.

In 'Father Vasilii's Revelation',[11] I used my beloved device of a fictional hero – a newly-ordained priest called Father Vasilii. He found himself in his first parish, where seemingly devoted parishioners systematically embezzled church funds, incited by a Moscow crook posing as a restoration worker. The main hero was fictitious but the parish (in Krasnodar region), the church and the crook were real. After the publication of the story recounted by Father Vasilii in exalted high church language, criminal procedures were started against the supposed restorer, who went into hiding but eventually was caught. The feuilleton, designed to be atheistic, proved in effect rather pro-clerical, since it helped to restore the famous church in Taman frequented in the olden days by Lermontov himself, and to punish the hypocrites wearing the disguise of true believers. The invented Father Vasilii, the priest, was quite a positive hero – a very unusual thing for the pre-perestroika press, which was in the habit of portraying clerical people as nothing but crooks and liars.

The letter from the students of the veterinary department of the Blagoveshchensk agricultural institute was hard to believe at first. It was a cry for help. On receiving it I flew to the Far East (the flight from Moscow to Blagoveshchensk takes nine hours). The veterinary students' hostel was run by a sadistic warden (a student himself) who turned it into a kind of military prison – there was even a 'curfew' which started at 7 pm, when the doors of the hostel were locked and no one could enter it for love or money. The main punishment for 'bad behaviour' was the confiscation of the culprit's bed: the offenders (those who were late for compulsory morning exercises, say) had to sleep on the bare floor for at least a month. The warden was also fleecing money from the 'inmates', and he and his henchmen habitually beat them up and broke into their rooms at night. All this was tacitly approved by the rector and the Dean's office. After 'The Sufferings of a Young Vet'[12] was published, the rector, the Dean and the warden, of course, were removed from their posts.

The stagnation years provided an excellent climate for different kinds of crooks some of whom proved very ingenious and quick-witted. They flourished under the loose or non-existent control of the authorities. The directors of the agricultural institute in Tula were ordered to open a new department in a small provincial town of Odoev. Finding this too much trouble they *invented* one instead – with fictitious dead-soul students and a complete bureaucratic structure. This existed happily on paper alone for a long time, and brought the crooks lots of money which they readily shared with their superiors in Moscow. The whole scheme was plotted in the best traditions of Gogol's *Dead Souls*. 'The Department That Never Was'[13] – that's what I named the feuilleton.

Knowing only too well how difficult it was for real war invalids to get their well-deserved privileges, I was genuinely surprised at how easily these were awarded to a crook from Sochi who forged himself a glorious war record and a chestful of medals. He implored some high-ranking war officers to testify in writing to his non-existent combat feats. To get rid of the nuisance some colonels and generals co-operated, thus providing the crook with a fictitious war biography and the quite real privileges stemming from it. The story of the crook who was eventually tried and stripped of all his gains was described in the feuilleton 'Ivan on the Neck' (there is a Russian expression 'to sit on someone's neck', meaning to live as a parasite).[14]

Bribery and bribe-taking were among the most 'popular' crimes in Brezhnev's era; sometimes they went to amusing extremes. In exchange for 'good treatment' a deputy minister of power engineering from Moscow demanded from the director of a subordinate plant in Penza . . . a tractor, a personal tractor to cultivate his out-of-town plot of land. And he got it! The director was eager to have a 'third hand' – that is an influential person patronising him from Moscow – so 'The Third Hand'[15] was the title of the story.

The resourceful café manager in the little working-class town of Shchekino (Tula region) was blackmailing the members of the rock group performing in the café. He demanded part of their salaries for the sheer permission to play there. The musicians knuckled under for some time, but soon they rebelled and denounced the man to the militia. This was the coda of the 'Symphony for a Café with Orchestra'.[16]

I do not want to give the impression that I was always looking for negative moments in life, though a *Krokodil* journalist is supposed to find faults. Travelling round the country, I met hundreds of wonderful people who had managed to preserve their identities despite the shortages and pervasive hypocrisy. To praise them was beyond my duty, but I always admired their ability to keep intact their hopes for a better life. It was their belief that gave me optimism, that kept me moving all through the huge land, my native country, and it was thanks to them that my urge to investigate kept growing.

When Brezhnev died in 1982, I was in Perm investigating bootlegging taxi-drivers. On the day of the funeral, I came on business to the city's militia headquarters. There I was politely invited to the 'red room' (a kind of social club) where local militia chiefs were already watching the funeral, broadcast live from Red Square. There were majors, colonels and even a couple of generals in the room. In the middle of the broadcast, the door opened and a civilian appeared on the threshold. 'Comrades,' he announced gravely, 'there is a recommendation from the district Party committee to watch the ceremony standing.' Everyone in the 'red room' sprang up and stood still until the end of the funeral, when the ornate coffin with the 'great leader's' body was literally dropped into the grave. At one moment I heard a whisper. A colonel was saying to a major: 'Why don't we telephone Lieutenant-Colonel Ivanov? He has a cold and is staying at home, knowing nothing about the district Party committee's recommendation. So he is likely to be sitting or even lying in bed.' 'Outrageous!' his interlocutor answered, and they both smiled.

So the people understood all right the absurdity of what was going on, but were still too embittered to speak up.

It was the press, which often, despite severe censorship, did try to tell the truth. We journalists couldn't generalise yet, but by giving seemingly trifling and disconnected pictures of life we created realistic impressions that made people think, and so paved the way for the impending reforms.

The readers doted on the best publications, they made cuttings and stored them in special files. It was very moving for me to see such a file at the house of one of my readers in Riga in 1986. He was a retired colonel and a journalist, and he kept the clippings of all my *Krokodil* articles.

Just a magazine cutting . . . it was the best reward for me at that time.

4

The Plague of Love

A whiff of fresh air blew over the country with Yuri Andropov succeeding Brezhnev at the post of the CPSU General Secretary. He started by reorganising the militia and combating corruption, but being an aged and ailing person, he had little time at his disposal. Within a year or so he died of kidney failure. Konstantin Chernenko – an old comrade of Brezhnev – came in his stead, and the changes which had just started were abruptly ended.

People keep asking now how it was possible that a petty functionary by nature and a mediocrity of a man was appointed to the highest post in the country. A difficult question. The appointment of the highest apparatchiks was always covered by a veil of obscurity. But most probably the rusty machinery of the administrative command system initiated by Stalin was to blame. Chernenko also was very ill. To have a dying man as the General Secretary probably suited some of the top-ranking bureaucrats who had felt jeopardised by Andropov's reforms.

Chernenko could hardly speak because of asphyxia. He seldom made public addresses – they were read aloud for him by someone else. The country too was once again suffering from asphyxia. Corruption, hypocrisy and nepotism flourished anew. But it was evident that Chernenko couldn't last long. He died early in 1985, hardly to anyone's surprise – the country had grown used to the quick death of its leaders, three in a row. A popular anecdote at that time was the story of a man trying to get to the Hall of Columns where Chernenko was lying in state, to pay his last tribute. He was stopped by a guard: 'Your pass, comrade!' 'I haven't got a pass,' the man retorted, 'but I've got a season ticket.'

In the early spring of 1985, the country received a new leader, Mikhail Gorbachev, a comparatively young man of fifty-four. I still think that we should bless our lucky stars for such a turn of events. The nation would not have survived another Brezhnev or Chernenko. Now, for the first time since Lenin, we had an intellectual and a lawyer as our leader. From his very first days in office Gorbachev proved a polished speaker, a quick thinker and a very charismatic personality. We were all charmed by him, being unused to a leader who could speak his own words without looking at the text, who could express himself clearly, and smile openly. Women especially were fascinated by him and sung his praises in the shops, the streets and the underground.

Gorbachev's reforming urge became apparent in his initial public speeches, where the words perestroika, glasnost' and democracy were sounded for the first time. And everyone realised he meant it.

But the legacy he inherited from his predecessors was a heavy burden. It had been piling up for so many years that it couldn't just be dismissed. Besides, Gorbachev had to overcome considerable resistance on the part of the Brezhnev-style bureaucrats. That is why the process of the reforms went rather painfully and slowly at first, but in the course of time it started to gain momentum.

We journalists rejoiced at the changes. Suddenly we were able to write the truth – not the whole of it for the time being, but still . . . Completely new domains were opening up for us, new topics could be raised.

At this time, on a mission to Karelia, I discovered a stunning story in its capital, Petrozavodsk. The city's main hospital had just celebrated its second centenary. It was founded by Gavriil Derzhavin – an outstanding Russian poet and mentor of Pushkin, to whom he presented one of his books with the dedication 'To the winning pupil, from the losing teacher'. Derzhavin was also a prominent statesman of his time. At the end of the eighteenth century he was appointed the governor of Olonetskaya *guberniya* (an administrative unit in pre-revolutionary Russia), comprising the whole of present-day Karelia. The hospital in question was designed and opened by him. He donated money to it and personally supervised its construction. So it was only natural that to commemorate its 200th anniversary, local enthusiasts decided to erect a memorial tablet saying that the hospital was founded in 1784 by the great Russian poet Gavriil Romanovich Derzhavin. The plaque with this inscription was made by local craftsmen and was about to be put up in the hospital building. All that remained was to have it approved by the Petrozavodsk city Party committee – such was the procedure.

It was here that the problems started. The first secretary of the city Party committee demanded that Derzhavin's name be removed from the plaque. He said that Derzhavin was the Tsar's henchman, a landowner and oppressor of the common people, and so he didn't deserve such an honour. No matter how hard the local intellectuals tried to prove that in spite of being a landowner Derzhavin was a democrat and a great man who had done a lot for Russia, arguing that Pushkin, Lermontov and

Tolstoy were also landowners and noblemen (Tolstoy was even a count), the Party boss was like a stone wall. The memorial board was remade and the inscription changed. Now it read simply that the hospital had been founded in 1784. I decided to write a story and called it 'Memorial Boredom'.[1] 'It won't make it,' my colleagues said. 'There's no precedent for the press showing up a bureaucrat of that level as an orthodox blockhead.' But I was so outraged by the facts that I wouldn't listen to them and delivered the story to *Krokodil*. It came out very quickly, and not a single word was changed. After the publication the memorial tablet was replaced for the third time and the name of Derzhavin was finally reinstated on it. So I'm proud of having been able to kill two birds with one stone – to pay tribute to a classic writer, and to create a precedent for mocking the stupidity of a high-level Party official.

'Memorial Boredom' didn't go unnoticed abroad. The Russian services of several Western radio stations (the German Wave among them) ran broadcasts on it, concluding that the article was the sign of coming glasnost'. There were no repercussions for me after the broadcasts – another sign of changing times.

Suddenly it was possible to deal with serious social phenomena, not simply go on exposing the peccadilloes of petty crooks. I remembered the subject I had harboured in my mind for many years. This was prostitution. Not the infamous prostitution in the West, but our native prostitution.

On the surface it looked like a crazy idea: all our dictionaries and encyclopedias kept saying that prostitution was characteristic of the decaying West, that in Western countries it was caused by the social inequality created by capitalism, and that in the Soviet Union it didn't exist because our socialist society lacked the social roots of prostitution. But everyone knew it was not so.

Prostitution was especially rife in Moscow and Leningrad, and my first intention was to write about prostitutes from these cities. But this was rejected point-blank by my *Krokodil* bosses, who were not yet sure whether such a subject would be allowed at all. 'If you're so eager to write about this,' they suggested, 'start from somewhere in the provinces, so as not to shock the readers too much. Certainly you can go on such a mission, but mind, we can't guarantee that the story will be published.' I could understand their position: their long journalistic experience proved that it was always risky to be the first.

Late in 1986 I decided to go to the famous Black Sea spa-towns of Sochi and Tuapse, both of which were frequented by foreigners. What I came across there far exceeded my expectations.

'We can't go on living like this,' said the second secretary of the Sochi

Party committee where I went to get a stamp put on my travelling credentials.* 'The town is being swamped by prostitutes from all over the country. I have two daughters, and I'm seriously worried for their future.'

His words were confirmed by the local militia chief: 'The foreigners come to us asking to be protected from the prostitutes. But what can we do?'

The militia were practically helpless, in fact. Since prostitution was not officially recognised as existing in our country, logically there was no law against it. To introduce such a law would mean its recognition, and this was unacceptable to the stagnation era officials who preferred turning a blind eye and a deaf ear to all major social vices, in keeping with *their* notion of socialism. To say nothing of the legal situation, the very word 'prostitute' had been taboo for many years. In statements by the militia, the ladies of the night were cautiously referred to as 'women of easy behaviour' and even 'women with low social activity'!

What's in a name? That which we call a rose
By any other word would smell as sweet . . .

These are my favourite lines from Shakespeare. Indeed, a rose smells like a rose, and a skunk smells like a skunk. No matter what we called the prostitutes, they did exist.

My first urge was to interview some of these ladies of the night, and I was granted the opportunity by the local militia, who on the whole were very cooperative. They were holding a woman in a preliminary detention cell, on charges of hooliganism and having no identification papers. They had found her under the sofa in a foreigner's hotel suite, where she had hidden when the militia were called in by a floor-lady troubled by the sounds of a row coming from the room. Nineteen thousand roubles and several hundred dollars were found in her handbag. Hearing this story, I immediately nicknamed the girl 'Laura from under the sofa'. Laura was her 'working' name; her real one was Lena. Prostitutes tend to work under sweet-sounding foreign names – Laura, Isabella, Marianna – thinking their Russian ones too plain to attract a Westerner.

She comes into the room stealthily, with short tense steps. On entering, she modestly holds closed the flaps of her grey prison gown, which is too big for her but still cannot hide the outline of a very slim figure. She is nineteen, and rather good-looking with her round face, tiny nose and narrowish brown eyes.

*Travelling credentials (*komandirovochnoie udostoverenie*) are forms issued to correspondents sent on an official mission, and are supposed to be stamped and signed in every town or village they visit.

She lowers herself onto a metallic prison chair screwed tightly to the floor and asks for a cigarette. I offer her my pack of Astra – a cheap and strong unfiltered brand popular among journalists.

'Yuk!' She wrinkles her nose. 'I don't smoke that stuff.' She pushes the pack back firmly with her tiny palm. 'Have you got a Marlboro?'

'No, I haven't, sorry. Tell me something about yourself. What are you by profession?'

She smiles. 'I used to be a salesgirl. After vocational school, I stood for three years behind a counter for one hundred bloody roubles a month.'

'Now you must be earning much more . . .'

'Right you are. They don't pay good money for nothing, these blokes, so I have to work hard.'

'What do you call yourself now?'

'Putana. That's a girl who goes with foreigners . . .'

To sleep with a foreigner is very profitable for a prostitute. She usually cannot buy anything for the dollars, pounds or any other hard currency he gives her in ordinary Soviet shops, but she can always sell foreign money to black-marketeers, or to the pimps who swarm around the whores like moths around a street lamp. One dollar fetches four or five roubles, one pound, eight to ten.*

'What do you spend that sort of money on?'

'Living and dressing properly. I can't walk the streets naked, can I? A good dress on the black market costs 800 roubles, shoes 300. In the shops of course it would be much cheaper, but there's nothing worth looking at.'

Putana's 'work' requires some special knowledge. She must be well acquainted with hard-currency exchange rates, have a keen eye for finding a relatively wealthy client among the hordes of foreign tourists, and be able to falter out in the main European languages a few useful phrases of the order of 'I like you', 'Will you buy me a drink?', 'What will you give me if I behave like a good girl?' There is also hard competition for a wealthy foreigner, sometimes ending in fights. Putanas tend to age very quickly. By thirty as a rule they are 'retired'.

Putana's work is full of surprises. A Sochi whore nicknamed Rogatka (the Catapult) was thrown out of a foreigner's suite stark naked. Despite the fact that her birthday suit was her favourite dress, she felt uneasy sporting it in the brightly lit hotel corridor. Even though she had had three large whiskies in the foreigner's suite, she didn't lose her way and broke

*Nowadays the unofficial rate is three to four times higher.

into one of the unlocked rooms. There she tried to filch a dress but was caught red-handed and ended up in jail. The most awful thing about Rogatka was that she taught her trade to her five-year-old daughter – the youngest (I hope) prostitute in Sochi.

Yet another Sochi Putana, Liudmila (working name Laura . . . another Laura – poor Petrarca), was murdered in her work place, ie in bed. Alas! there was no Petrarca around to write a sonnet 'On the Death of Putana Laura'. She had to be satisfied with the militia report.

'Have you got a house or a flat to live in?' I ask Laura/Lena.
She smiles playfully. 'Yes, an Intourist hotel.'

True enough, Sochi's Intourist hotels – especially in summer – are riddled with prostitutes, who come from all over the country. It's a mystery how they penetrate the hotels, negotiating the Cerberus-like doormen. Some of the whores manage to book a room, but for the most part they don't bother and just visit their well-to-do 'friends'.

In Tuapse, someone pointed out a 'retired' whore from the port. Straight as a ship's mast, dressed in bright red (a professional habit), she resembled a walking dummy from a second-hand clothes shop. The passers-by were smiling and pointing, but her Frankenstein face, with its imprint of vice, remained indifferent.

Tuapse is more of a port than a seaside town, and the profits of local Putanas are lower than of those in Sochi. For six to ten dollars 'the trade union members', as local prostitutes cynically call themselves, are ready to oblige a foreign sailor or even a bunch of them in a row. Tuapse is always full of Greek, Norwegian and Philippine sailors, so there is a lot of work for the young street-walkers, many of whom by the way, are Komsomol members.

The 'working conditions' are much worse in Tuapse. Local Putanas take the sailors from a restaurant to an improvised brothel. One of them is popularly known as 'the California Hotel'. Despite the name, it's just two tiny windowless cells – a wooden extension to the garage of the 'owner', himself a former sailor. He charges each couple ten roubles and provides the guests with ancient time- (and not only time-) worn striped mattresses which are spread on the floor. No beds, no anything. But in the adjoining garage stands the 'owner's' brand-new Zaporozhets car.

'Where do you come from?'
'From the Volga region. I lived in the country.'

'Would you like to have a family?'
'If I got married, then it would only be to a foreigner.'

To marry a foreigner is a cherished dream of any Putana. Some of them do succeed, but having got the marriage certificates, they often prefer to stay in the Soviet Union. Such a certificate gives them a legal right to possess hard currency and to buy goods in the special 'Beriozka' shops for foreigners – that's all they ever want.

Two prostitutes from Leningrad were detained in Sochi for hard currency dealings. One of them, named Svetlana, was married to a Western business man and bore his name. The husband came to see his faithful wife twice a year and replenished her already high currency resources. In the absence of the loved one Svetlana entertained his compatriots – and not only them.

In Moscow, I've heard of wealthy Putanas who buy Western husbands for themselves for thirty or forty thousand dollars. Some hard-up foreigners are ready to cooperate, certain that no one at home will ever know of their Russian marriage.

'Could you imagine wanting to have a child?'
'And what of it? I'll have one all right. Not too expensive and no more problems with parasitism, as they call it.'

By Soviet law, every healthy person must work. Not some activity of his or her own, but official employment by the State or by a cooperative. Mothers with small children are exempt from this rule. This explains why so many prostitutes are ready to become mothers.

In a Tuapse restaurant, I saw how local prostitutes Masha Electronik, Olga the Fish, French Horse, Dirty Heel and about twenty more were courting foreign seamen. They embraced the seafarers with their snake-like hands during the dance, they pecked at their beards with brightly lipsticked mouths. Every now and then one of the newly formed couples disappeared for a while (to the nearby 'California Hotel' perhaps?), then returned red-eyed and happy. I knew that most of these playful whores had unfed little kids waiting for them at home. 'Prostitutes' children are easy to distinguish from other pupils in the class,' a teacher from a Tuapse school confided. 'They always have sad and hungry eyes. I would have executed such mothers,' she added fervently. Thank God she didn't know about Rogatka's daughter.

'Have you ever been honestly in love?'

'Honestly?' Laura smiles sullenly. 'That means free of charge, doesn't it?'

A Moscow putana arrested for currency peddling told the Sochi militia that the money was presented to her for 'love'. But she couldn't recall the difficult foreign name of her sweetheart.

Love – the most human of feelings – for putanas is just a dirty joke or a stack of foreign banknotes with a portrait of an alien president.

'The Plague of Love' – that's what the Russian poet Sasha Chiorny called prostitution. And that's what I decided to entitle my story.[2]

'What do you think honour is?'
'Something military . . .'

Here are some extracts from militia documents to illustrate the last point.

From a prostitute's written statement to the militia: 'We came to Dahomys hotel to meet foreigners and to determine which country has the best men . . .'

From the detention sheet: 'She was detained for pestering foreign tourists near Dahomys hotel. She demanded to be taken to a hard currency bar, and when they refused hurled four-letter words at them . . .'

From the statement of fifteen-year-old Christina: 'I went into the foreigner's room, just to see how he lives . . .' (Christina came to Sochi with her mother, who encouraged her to sell herself to foreigners.)

From the record of the interrogation:

Question: 'Why did you steal 50 dollars from a sleeping foreigner?'
Answer: 'I didn't steal. Simply, I'm paid 60 roubles a night as a rule. I converted this sum into dollars, and seeing I had been underpaid, just took away the difference . . .'

From a court testimony: 'Sveta suggested we could have fun with her foreigner together, and when he fell asleep, take his wallet and run . . .'

From the statement: 'I asked the foreigner what he would give me for love. "An umbrella," he said. "Too little," I objected, "I want two umbrellas" . . .'

Honour for two umbrellas – a fair deal, isn't it?

'How much were you paid by your last client?' I asked 'Laura from under the sofa'.

'Five hundred Bundesmarks, a carton of cigarettes, twenty-five roubles and small things like Western-made crackers and canned sausages . . .'

'If you manage to catch a foreigner, will you stay here or emigrate?'

She pauses, thinking the question over. 'Probably I'll emigrate.'

'And do you know that many girls who've gone to live abroad with their husbands feel nostalgic and are eager to return, being unable to adjust to foreign life, feeling miserable?'

'Double Dutch! Only the ones who marry lousy students or manual labourers are miserable. I'm not interested in proletarians if you ask me, no sir!'

Strange words for the daughter of a 'lousy' peasant! And for a Komsomol member too . . .

It's interesting that both a six-dollar whore from Tuapse and a schoolgirl who had robbed her sleeping client belonged to Komsomol, the 'front rank of Soviet youth' as its Statute says.

Our Putanas are already getting famous in the West. In several countries, sex tours of Russia are gaining in popularity. They even publish special catalogues with prices for our women. I have seen one of them with my own eyes.

Random memories: I was sitting in a Tuapse restaurant watching local prostitutes at work. A drunk Greek sailor, swinging and stumbling with every step as if he was treading a rolling deck, dropped anchor at my table. 'Have you got a spare glass, sir?' he asked in broken English. 'Sit down for a while,' I said. The inebriated Hellene slumped onto the chair. 'Do you like being here?' I asked. 'Yeeeah,' he drawled, 'very much. The girls are especially likeable – so pretty and so cheap!'

At the end of my essay 'The Plague of Love', I suggested that a law against prostitution and a special 'morals militia' should be introduced. These were officially accepted after some time. Now we have 'morals militias' in several big cities, and a rule by which prostitution is punished by a fine of 100 to 300 roubles.

But the law proved abortive. Firstly, it's next to impossible to prove the fact of somebody selling her body unless the partner himself testifies to it, which is highly improbable. Also, the fine of even 300 roubles is nothing for a hard-working Putana who can earn several times more in just one night. But the main reason for its failure is different. It stems from the sheer inability of any law to eliminate a social vice. And prostitution, in contrast to the accepted dogma, is always socially connected – both in the West and in the East. Its growth in our country in the Brezhnev years came from shattered ideals, from the beliefs broken by lies and hypocrisy, from chronic food and goods shortages. Now I'm sure that the only way to combat prostitution is to build a healthy society. I was mistaken when I called for the introduction of the law.

As Professor Gilinsky aptly put it in the *Sociological Studies Journal* at the end of 1988: 'Prostitution will exist as long as commodity-money relations exist. Neither appeals nor bans will be able to eliminate it. Thousands of years of human history testify to this. Our blind belief in the power of bans and repression can be explained only by mere neglect of history, science and reason. A street-walker is no more despicable than a prostituted writer, scientist, journalist, politician. Prostitution will diminish only by overcoming the stimuli for money-grabbing and easy gain; in the process of developing the feelings of pride, dignity and self-importance in people's souls, any form of mercenary behaviour or haggling will begin to be viewed with contempt and repugnance'.[3]

The effect of 'The Plague of Love' was like a bomb exploding. More than a thousand letters were received by *Krokodil* over a couple of weeks. They could be roughly divided into three categories: angry (from the readers who just didn't want to know what was going on and preferred the peace of ignorance), furious (from readers calling for the instant execution or at least isolation of all prostitutes) and moderate (from those who regarded prostitution as normal and called for the legalisation of brothels). There were also a number of letters from prostitutes themselves. (See the Letter-Box.)

But the main thing was that the gates of a formerly forbidden subject were suddenly flung open. Many journalists, as if by order, started writing about prostitution. Most of these articles, though critical on the surface, had rather an advertising effect. Some unsophisticated reporters were subconsciously savouring the luxurious lives the prostitutes led, their gorgeous clothes and high earnings. The subject was quickly overdone and stopped attracting public interest. It was quite natural for the press, which was learning to be free, but it was harmful for the problem itself, which continued to grow. Young girls who read such shallow articles were attracted by the prostitutes' seemingly easy-going existence.

Moscow's youth newspaper, *Moskovski Komsomolyets*, ran an article on famous Moscow prostitutes – Blokha (the Flea), Yaponka (the Japanese girl) and some others – who were described as sporting mink coats, driving Mercedes cars and staying at the very best hotel suites for months on end.[4] Blokha's earnings were said to amount to $100,000 for a few years' work. These prostitutes were the talk of all the city. Inspired by their examples, lots of teenage girls went on the streets in an attempt to pick up a wealthy foreigner. No one seemed to be afraid of AIDS, which was still far from being a menace to Soviet society. A group of girls even applied to the authorities through *Literaturnaya Gazeta* asking for permission to open a prostitutes' co-operative. Their letter was never published, but I saw it in the *Literaturka* office.

A public opinion poll revealed that more and more educated women were involved in the prostitution business too. Out of 532 prostitutes from Georgia who participated in the poll, three out of four had secondary and higher education. There were even several doctors of science among them.[5]

Newspapers received letters from schoolgirls asking how to become a part-time prostitute. In yet another poll, a group of senior Moscow schoolchildren named prostitution among the twenty most prestigious professions. It shared ninth to eleventh place with the posts of salesman and shop-manager, overtaking such professions as diplomat, teacher, taxi-driver, car-mechanic and butcher.[6]

The advertising of prostitution in the press should have been stopped. I published an article in the *Journalist* magazine (organ of the USSR Union of Journalists) calling on my colleagues to treat the subject cautiously, and write about the prostitutes' ruined lives, wretched souls and miserable unfed children, rather than about their seemingly carefree existence.[7] Such an existence was a myth, in any case, if we remembered how often whores were beaten or even murdered by clients or by pimps, how easily they contracted venereal diseases, how empty their lives were. And the danger of AIDS couldn't be overlooked either.

I'm not sure whether my article had struck home or whether the press was just fed up with the subject, but soon the fuss about prostitution in the mass media started gradually dying away. New, no less important, topics became the order of the day.

Letter-Box

In his story, Vitaliev touches upon a very crucial problem. In vain! Why do you poke your nose into our youthful interests? It's none of your business! Crying bloody murder: prostitutes, metallists, punks. You don't like it? Don't like our music? Don't like our clothes and conduct? Good for you! There you go! I personally like to dress provocatively, I like to be stared at. Whoever beckons me – I will follow him. I am attracted by an easy life. I like (I adore, do you hear me?) sexual intercourse. Leave us alone, would you? Cheers,

Laura and her friends, Gorky.

Prostitutes won't make good wives for our workers and engineers. It's better to sleep with a dustbin than with such a woman. Whores should be hanged by their legs on a birch tree, or exiled to the taiga to do hard labour.

P–va, Perm region.

After graduating from the institute, I worked in Italy and France and used to frequent brothels there. It hasn't made me any worse, has it? Many of our embassy people accompanied me there and no one was inclined to think of himself as an evil man . . . Could you explain to me why the Western countries where prostitution is lawful are economically more developed than we are? Real perestroika will start only when the girls of easy behaviour are free to practise their trade under the supervision of a doctor.

Respectfully yours, F–V, Naltchik.

These female beasts must be isolated from society and forced to work hard. We all are to blame for their existence since we couldn't educate our youth properly. And if we fail to eradicate prostitution, let's open parlour houses for these bitches to earn dollars for our country.

Kh–Va, and all normal people from the city of Gorky.

Dear Comrade Vitaliev! Your article provoked the following feelings with us career women. When shall we be able to earn enough not to have to count the copecks before pay-day? When shall we stop looking for the cheapest clothes for our children, because their working fathers and mothers haven't got enough money? And what do we women actually see in our lives? We get up at 6 am, cook breakfast quickly and rush to work, taking a sleepy child to the nursery school on the way. After the office – to the shops. We stand in long queues and come home loaded with purchases. There, we start washing up and doing our flats, to our husbands' constant grumbles and reproaches. After that, you are so exhausted you can hardly reach your bed, and tomorrow it starts all over again. No time for books or films, let alone the theatre, no time for yourself. Eternal shortage of money, and of time, and no hope for improvement whatsoever. And we all have higher education, serious jobs, and are all honest women. We love our poor, honest, hard-up husbands. But is that a real life? We will never see as much money as your prostitutes have. In fact, we don't need that much, but just want to live like human beings. Those are the social roots of prostitution. They do exist . . . Prostitution is bad, of course. But is our life good?

P.S. Perhaps you could explain how it has happened that you can't earn good money by honest labour in our society. To achieve a kind of well-being you have to trade in your body, your convictions, your conscience. You would probably find it difficult to provide an answer. So would we. But still there is nothing more important than that . . .

K–va, Moscow.

Having collectively read your article on prostitution, we express our profound indignation at these Soviet girls' behaviour. We wives and mothers think our society doesn't need such girls. They are traitors to our motherland. Fines are not enough for them. We, the collective of women, demand capital punishment!

Workers of the semiconductors factory (12 signatures), the town of Prokhladny.

On reading 'The Plague of Love' I got envious of these girls. They earn 20,000 roubles for a short time, and I have been working all my life for 87 roubles a month. I live with my daughter, and what do we have? Coats, dresses, underwear, footwear – all from second-hand shops, at reduced prices. My daughter wears clothes after me. Then we mend them, patch them, restore them and wear them again. In two months, I'll be retired, and still living like a beggar, working since I was sixteen. If I were nineteen or twenty now, I wouldn't hesitate to go to Sochi and become a prostitute. Maybe this is bad, but it's money. And money is life! Only prostitutes, salespeople and thieves live well in our country.

I–va, Kiev.

Dear Comrade Vitaliev, If you come to our city of Zaporozhie, you will see our young girls with Komsomol cards in their handbags parading along Lenin Avenue with Negroes as their escorts. The Negroes embrace them and the girls stick to them like lice to dirty clothes. I am no racist, but when I see such couples, or rather tandems, in the streets I feel like I'm living in a nightmare. If you do come to Zaporozhie you could prevent the spreading of AIDS in our city.

Your reader L–v, Zaporozhie.

I know one young and rather attractive blonde living nearby without a husband, and with three children. Once I saw her talking with young Armenian guys round the corner. I am sure that she is a prostitute, though I've got no facts to prove it.

M–ka, Sochi.

My mother died when I was eight. My father was a drunkard. He died when I was eighteen. He would take away from me all the money I earned and spend it on vodka. Often he would beat me up . . . I became a prostitute when I was fourteen and tried to support my father. His last words were: 'Thank you for everything, daughter. I've brought you a lot of grief. I'll answer for that to God. Forgive me if you can . . .' I got married at eighteen and gave up prostitution. But my husband turned out to be no good. I couldn't satisfy all his perverted desires. And he walked out on me, after taking everything from the house but the child. No alimony! I don't need his filthy money. Here I want to thank our State for the free kindergarten and a lot of help. But my monthly salary is the same 80 roubles – hardly enough to feed us two. So I had to return to prostitution. What else could I do? Now I'm 'Laura from under the sofa' – there is no fixed price for me. Everybody pays as much as he can. I am still beautiful, though dowdy. And I'm clean too . . . Sooner or later, I'll change my lifestyle, I'm sure. Only the utmost need has put me in the way of prostitution. Believe me please, brother . . .

A. Kh, Tashkent.

I am a former militiaman. We were always told by our chiefs we had no prostitution in this country, and in statements we were ordered to write 'the woman of easy behaviour' instead of 'prostitute'. We often got complaints from foreigners, asking us to shield them from our women. It was very painful for me to think they could conclude that all our women were prostitutes. We militia were quite helpless and could do nothing but compile lists and file complaints. Once we detained two Putanas, and they complained to the very top. Next day I was put on the carpet by ex-Minister of the Interior Shchelokov himself! He was very angry. Thank God, we had entered the case in our register . . . otherwise . . . These girls have very high connections. They all have cars and buy things in Beriozka shops. Work, family, home, love, honour – these concepts are nothing but words to them . . . This social disease is spreading. We need an anti-prostitution law – strict but just . . .

P–n, Moscow.

How do you do, Comrade Vitaliev? This is a 'Laura from under the sofa' writing to you. You haven't frightened us a bit. I laughed at your article. Our government will never restrict our rights. We have matriarchy now . . . Men are miserable alimony-paying stooges. You pay alimony and we'll be having a good time in the South, increasing our savings every day. Put that in your pipe and smoke it! [A stream of curses follows.]

V–va, Cheboksary.

All prostitutes in our country should be imprisoned for life, in Siberia only. Their foreheads should be branded for everyone to see who they are. We mustn't allow them to spread infection all over the country . . .

Tractor plant workers (38 signatures), Vladimir.

I am a research worker at a major Moscow institute. About two years have passed since my wife died tragically. I have a daughter of six. Being a widower, I often mix with the girls you wrote about and have come to the following conclusions: 1. I don't see why prostitutes cannot be given licences by the State in the light of the new law on individual working activities. 2. I think it necessary to introduce weekly medical examinations for them. 3. Prostitutes' relations with foreigners must be validated by appropriate administrative practices. These will make it possible to achieve the following: on the one hand, it will help the State to cover a budget deficit caused by restrictions on selling spirits. The money would flow to the State's treasury. On the other hand, it will contribute to preserving both the physical and moral health of our compatriots. And, lastly, the democratisation of our society will be promoted. There will be the right to choose – to take the licence or not. If a woman is above it – OK. Want a mink coat? Good luck! The right to choose is the greatest right of all.

Respectfully, V–v, Moscow.

You've ruined my life! I had been dreaming of going to Tuapse to enter the culinary technical school for three years. But my mother, having read your article on the Tuapse prostitutes, has strictly forbidden me to go. Where shall I study now when I finish secondary school? It all happened because of your article.

Elena Shch., 17, Saki.

I am furious at the fact that our prostitutes go with foreigners – not with our Soviet men. They must be used solely in the interests of our own society. Prostitutes are able to help many Soviet families. Wouldn't a wife be pleased when her husband comes home from a working trip in high spirits, morally and physically healthy? He will be like that if he meets a good prostitute while he's away. You may think I am immoral . . . Nothing of the kind. I am a good family man and never use four-letter words . . . Prostitutes must serve not some foreign moneybags, but our simple Russian proletarians. Again, don't think I am a dirty man, please. I am simply a patriot of my country.

P–ko, Lipetsk.

My dear correspondent Vitaliev! I liked your article very much. Our press hasn't mentioned prostitution before, and I think we should publish a special newspaper to carry articles solely on that subject, and to create a strict law against it, so as not to disgrace our country in the eyes of foreigners. Some words about myself. I am fifteen now. When I was fourteen, I made friends with some foreign students from Jordan. They were nice guys – kind, modest, gentle – no comparison with our Russian blokes who are generally rude, drunk and foul-mouthed. They took me to restaurants, gave me flowers, presents.

Once in winter I went to their hostel just to warm up a little because it was freezing outside. They gave me some wine with sleeping powder in it. What happened next? You can guess for yourself. I wake up in the morning, and there they are sitting and smiling – these two Jews [? – V.V.] from Jordan. I got pregnant. When my father got to know that, he nearly killed me. Somehow the neighbours found out too. Rumours reached my school. I was ostracised: no one would talk to me. So I made friends with the girls of easy behaviour, got to smoking and drinking with them. And 'worked' too. Not for money, but out of stupidity. I had nothing to lose. Even on the walls of my house, my former friends wrote that I was a prostitute. They were right of course . . . My parents haven't spoken to me since, they just beat me up from time to time . . .

Why do I write to you? I want to warn other girls not to follow in my footsteps. It just takes one ill-considered step, and you are finished. You are lost. You'll never make a good wife with such a past behind you. The law against prostitution must be very strict to frighten away the young ones. A foreigner once said to me: 'You Russian girls are so cheap. Women in my country do not sell themselves for money.' I want my country to be pure, not cheap! And the ones like myself must be put in prison. No, we must all be shot. Not to torture ourselves with sad memories . . . Write more about us! Write about our miserable lives, venereal diseases, disrupted pregnancies. This is bound to impress pure girls . . . As to myself and the girls like me . . . We are not impressed. We are finished. And we know that. We cannot live without money, restaurants, rich foreigners . . . Old habits die hard . . . Please excuse me for this letter. I shouldn't have written it. But I liked your article so much. Do write more articles! And then I will always buy *Krokodil* with the money I've 'earned'.

With the utmost respect, Angela, Moscow.

Your article fights! On reading it I was so disgusted by Putanas that I felt an urge to join in combating this vice. I think this is the best article ever published by *Krokodil*.

P–va, 18, Novotroitsk.

I am not surprised that we are facing some vices characteristic of the Western world – prostitution among them. It couldn't be otherwise when the Western way of life has been publicised in our country for the last fifteen years. The cult of the West is on our TV screens. The sounds of our national folk music are drowned by thundering Western rock groups. This is not such a trifling thing as it may seem. The atmosphere of profit-making and easy entertainment, characteristic of our country at the end of the Seventies to the beginning of the Eighties as a result of aping the West, has created prostitution. Instead of formulating new laws, we must recreate the moral atmosphere of the pre-war years when the young people tried to imitate heroes of the Revolution and not some Western singers as happens now.

V–v, a worker, CPSU member, Kuibishev.

To eradicate prostitution, the demand for it, if we follow the logic of a pistol, it's necessary to castrate all male foreigners coming to our country – provided they don't mind of course. If we are to be guided by different, more realistic logic, it's advisable to open brothels in every port, to enable these popsies to work lawfully under medical supervision. Then venereal diseases wouldn't spread to our towns and villages.

Ts–ky, Krasnoyarsk region.

My name is Christina. I am seventeen and getting on a bit. I'd like to say a few words on why our young girls become prostitutes. It often happens that a girl falls in love with a guy and he turns out to be a pig, and on getting what he wanted, just throws her away like an old toy. This is the start. Pregnancy, abortion, loss of respect among her friends follow. She is accosted by every boy in the vicinity: so you've obliged one of us, why can't you do the same for the rest? If she refuses, they beat her. Only a few can resist. The outcome is obvious: the girl turns into a prostitute . . . A few words about myself. Though only seventeen, I have seen a lot: fear, pain, humiliation, shame. I fell in love with a married man. I know I'll never give birth to a healthy child. That's the fate of all prostitutes. I also know I won't last long: either I'll be killed or I'll take my life myself. It's the best way out of the fix I'm in . . . Our town is small. Everyone knows everyone else. To survive, you must have connections with the militia, who are always ready to arrest you. But they're in no hurry to arrest the real villains and crooks. They prefer to shake hands with them. And these young bastards roam the streets at night, looking to catch some helpless girl . . . I want this letter to be published and read by those girls who are on the verge of becoming prostitutes. My dear girls! To hell with such a mockery of life! Real life is beautiful. Don't despair because of your first failures. You are future mothers, and you must find strength to fight down your baser instincts. You must live – not just exist.

Christina M, Donetsk region.

I'd like to expose the roots of present-day prostitution. They date from the time, ten to fifteen years ago, when 'Lauras' were little girls. Where was the school and the Komsomol then? The girls are not to blame. Bureaucracy was tsarring it everywhere – jackals in black limousines with servants and huge salaries. The girls couldn't fail to see this. As to perestroika, I haven't felt it yet. We have forgotten what ham or salmon is. Our existence is miserable. We are sick and tired of stupid cartoons depicting life in the West. Show us our life instead. Bribes, drunkenness, speculation are everywhere. Life is expensive and salaries are low. I will refer to Margaret Thatcher (a bright woman who made mincemeat of the three Soviet journalists during her TV interview), who said that we wouldn't publicly admit our short-sighted domestic policy and the rest of it. The girls are OK. They just crave for better lives . . .

P–n, Surgut.

I am an ex-convict. Seven out of the twenty-seven years of my life have been spent behind bars. I saw lots of filth and I am fed up. For two days I have had your article on my mind. I think it's great. Prostitution is filth and it must be condemned publicly. The morals militia is a good idea but it should be supported by regular publications in the press as realistic as yours. I offer you a helping hand in your struggle: I've got lots of experience. We must act.

P–v, Voroshilovgrad.

I am a militia colonel in retirement. At the end of the Sixties I was dealing with prostitutes in Tbilisi preventative prison. We couldn't say they were prostitutes and had to call them tramps. I am in agreement with the author that not all of them are lost to society. When you treat them humanely, they often react in the same manner, looking at you with these sad eyes of theirs. A tactful and intelligent militiaman must work with prostitutes. Then some of them will be saved and will avoid the final downfall. Thank you for your journalistic courage.

V–sky, War and Labour veteran, Tbilisi.

Prostitution must be treated as a criminal offence. Whores are worse than thieves. Thieves steal money and clothes from people. Prostitutes steal honour and dignity from us, Soviet women. Many foreigners judge us all by them. They must be poisoned like rats with strychnine. They must be sent to the taiga to cut wood for seven or eight years. If she fulfils her daily norm – feed her, if not – don't feed her! They are worse than thieves, robbers and even murderers.

D–kaya, Chelyabinsk region.

I'm not inclined to treat prostitutes negatively, they are just smart women who don't want to work for miserable salaries. It's a common view in our country that a woman must be a work-horse. No one wants to know about her female spiritual and psychological peculiarities. I was struck when your correspondent in his article offered the girl Astra the cheapest, most stinking cigarettes, fit only for a man. This is the example of how a woman's nature can be ignored. Our slogans say 'All for the good of man'. And where can you get these goods? I don't even have higher education and cannot buy anything for my small salary. And who wants to live in poverty? I am just like a Dostoevsky heroine – poor and hopeless. When I was at school, I had bright visions of my future life, but as soon as it came to reality, all the dreams dispersed. I don't even want to read modern books or watch TV. I feel repugnance at the sight of well-to-do people on the screen when real welfare and social justice are nothing but slogans.

A–va, Irkutsk.

Prostitutes, especially Komsomol members, must be caught in the act and shot on the spot. Then, in a year or so, we'll observe a 50 per cent reduction in prostitution.

    T–vich, War and labour veteran, Electrostal.

If it were up to me, I would send all these bitches to the North Pole.

    P–va, Stavropol region.

All the whores must be put in 'putanatoriums' – special places like leper colonies. There they will be supervised by medical people and the militia. All the sailors and other foreign visitors craving for a woman must be sent there to be stripped of their dollars, marks and pounds. This hard currency must be used to finance programmes to combat AIDS and prostitution. These 'putanatoriums' must be on a self-accounting system – that's my proposition.

    Z–v, Krivoi Rog.

Kuprin* in *The Pit* wrote that prostitution would exist as long as marriage existed. Why did he say so? Probably because marriage in its essence is nothing but a transaction. A modern woman sells herself for a stamp in her passport. Isn't there an analogy between marriage and prostitution?

    D–va, librarian, Volgograd.

'Make laws natural, and prostitution will disappear as a social pheno-menon,' Tolstoy said. What's to be done to 'make laws natural'? To open medical institutions for natural copulation, like in the West, and to make them easily accessible to everyone – just like toilets and cafés. The women working there will be hetairae – mistresses of pleasure. They will have good salaries – not lower than those of engineers. Women will find suitable mates there, and formal families will be strengthened by these natural relations. 17,000,000 lonely women who will work there, given freedom of sexual satisfaction, will be able to do much more than our boasted Party. The country will be renewed beyond recognition and all negative phenomena will die away.

    A–v, Kiev.

Have you ever given thought to why the majority of women still prefer an eight hour working day at the office to the easy life of a prostitute? Although anxious to dress well, to be merry and attractive, they still refuse

---

*Alexander Kuprin (1870–1938) – a prominent Russian writer.

themselves the lives of Putanas. That happens not because of any moral principles, but because of the sheer impossibility of overcoming the feeling of disgust. Only innate innermost culture stops them from crossing this invisible line.

P–va, Moscow.

Esteemed Comrade Vitaliev! I have been working for thirty years, since I was fourteen. I have a medal as a socialist emulation winner and another medal as a labour veteran. Seventeen years ago I divorced my husband. Now I'm living with my daughter in an unheated terrace. Having chronic bronchitis, I can't stand the cold, but what can I do? Earning 85 roubles a month, I can't afford to rent a decent flat. What awaits me? Nothing but miserable old age. No savings, no flat, no nothing. So why do you condemn these girls, the prostitutes? For a few years, they can earn more than I am able to earn in three lifetimes. They will enjoy a comfortable existence and a place to live in. Eventful youth and comfortable old age are better than honest youth and miserable old age.

E.P., Leningrad.

Prostitutes' contribution to international friendship is indisputable. They sell themselves not to spies, saboteurs or invaders but to those who come on friendly visits. As to foreigners, it is their own business whether they use the benefits of our country or not. As a matter of fact, in the West men are also accosted by publicity-makers and dealers of all kinds. And here they must think themselves lucky to be approached by a girl without a revolver and with a nice proposition to forget about their aggressive imperialist plans for an hour or so.

K–n, Kiev.

We are not against women. We are against the evil force sitting inside them.

S–ko, Kislovodsk.

Ballet must be prohibited together with prostitution. These ballerinas show our youth some private parts of their bodies when dancing and thus contribute to perversion.

B–ky, the Crimea.

Let a miserable hen-pecked husband find some respite from his ever-nagging, stupid, fat, 120-kilogram wife in the embrace of a cheap and beautiful 'Laura'. Then our wives will remember they are women, will stop eating so much (an immediate solution to our food shortages problem), will learn to think and to look after their appearances, will cease grumbling at their husbands. Universal prosperity will set in.

P–v, Yaroslavl.

5

Parabellum Jeans

The country was awakening from many years of slumber. The sleep was lethargic, but thank God, not lethal. In 1986, we were just at the beginning of a long road but our pace was increasing. Thanks to Gorbachev's reforms, political prisoners were freed, Academician Sakharov was returned to Moscow, emigration and foreign travel were boosted, Stalin's crimes were exposed anew, and some long-established apparatchik privileges were abolished. In the economic field, cooperatives were formed and the tight grip of the administrative command system on the country was loosened.

But the main achievement of the first two years of perestroika was glasnost'. People were no longer afraid to express their opinions openly, to speak up in public. The term 'dissident' fell out of use. It was really a tremendous achievement after years and years of lies and forced silence.

The press found itself in the vanguard of glasnost'. Everyday, newspapers and magazines were carrying something new. People came to realise that drug addicts, prostitutes, organised criminals and the homeless existed in our country. This news was embarrassing for many. The Stalinists, conservatives and inveterate bureaucrats were vehemently opposed to the revelations and were falling over themselves to contain glasnost'. The magazines *Nash Sovremenik* (Our Contemporary) and *Molodaya Gbardia* (Young Guard) and the newspaper *Sovietskaya Rossiya* became their strongholds. The mass-media were unofficially divided into 'conservative' (see above), 'progressive' (*Ogonyok, Moscow News, Novy Mir* etc) and 'centrist' (*Pravda, Izvestia* etc).

It is not the aim of this book to analyse the political processes of the time. My sole interest is to show how they were reflected in the daily routine of a journalist. And the one which had the foremost effect on my future life and career was Gorbachev's courageous drive against high-level corruption. Shortly after coming to power, he removed from the Politburo such influential figures as Grishin and Romanov, the Moscow and Leningrad Party chiefs, notorious for abusing their powers. Then it was the turn of Kunayev and Aliyev, Party leaders of Kazakhstan and Azerbaijan respectively. Only under Gorbachev was a thorough investigation begun into the so-called 'Cotton affair' in Uzbekistan, which involved massive padding of the real figures for cotton production in this Central Asian republic. Almost all of the Uzbekistan Party chiefs were mixed up in the case. By means of systematically inflated statistics, they accumulated millions and millions of roubles. At the centre of the whole affair stood the then powerful Sharaf Rashidov, the first secretary of the Uzbek Party committee and a favourite of Brezhnev's. When the case came under investigation, he committed suicide. Nikolai Shchelokov, the former Minister of the Interior of the USSR, followed his example, shooting himself at his luxury dacha in Serebrany Bor on the outskirts of Moscow. Shortly after his death his first deputy, Yuri Churbanov, was arrested. Churbanov was Brezhnev's son-in-law and was connected with the Uzbek cotton dealers. Having accumulated absolute power in his hands he was corrupted absolutely. (Recently he was tried by the Military Court, together with nine high-ranking militia bosses from Uzbekistan, and was sentenced to twelve years' imprisonment.)

All these people seemed invulnerable under Brezhnev, but with Gorbachev in power their time was up.

The process of combating corruption was under way. I was eager to become a part of this process, to play even a minor role in the purification of the country. In the summer of 1986 I was in Riga (the capital of Soviet Latvia), investigating a quack woman doctor who fleeced gullible people by claiming to cure them of every imaginable disease with injections of raw eggs. In fact, it was just a kind of hypnosis on her part, but she was very popular and was earning lots of money. My task was to find out what makes people go to a quack instead of to a hospital. The answer was seemingly simple: the quack was probably considerate and attentive to the people's complaints, whereas at a hospital they were likely to find an aloof and distracted doctor constantly engrossed in filling in numerous bureaucratic forms and anxious to receive as many patients as possible.

Of course, egg injections couldn't do any good to a sick person. They could only aggravate his or her condition, which actually happened to the reader whose letter had launched me on this mission. I already knew the title of the would-be feuilleton: 'The Fateful Eggs'.[1]

I decided to pose as the woman's prospective patient, a candidate for an egg injection, though my *Krokodil* bosses had strictly forbidden me to undergo any paramedical procedures. They didn't have enough special correspondents to run such a risk.

The elusive quack was constantly on the move, changing the flats where she received her patients, and I had to ask the Riga militia to help me locate her. I found her on the outskirts of town, in a shabby wooden hut guarded by two burly men who didn't look like patients at all. Several rows of shoes and high boots were standing near the porch like soldiers at attention. Inside there were lots of people waiting to be injected, all of them bare-footed and all carefully holding *avoskas* (just-in-case string bags) full of eggs. It looked like some weird witches' sabbath.

I didn't have to invent an ailment: 'luckily' I had my ulcer – a souvenir from the university. 'So you've got an ulcer, my young friend,' the quack said, patting my stomach lightly. 'OK, go to the next room and I'll give you an injection.' I was rather taken aback: 'But . . . But . . . I don't have any eggs on me,' I muttered in an attempt to postpone the execution. 'Never mind,' the quack said cheerfully, 'I've got some extra ones. They'll cost you just thirty roubles.' There was nowhere to retreat to. I sighed and started towards the neighbouring room. 'Wait a moment,' the woman said. 'Have you taken any pills for your ulcer recently?' It was a ray of hope. 'Yes,' I said hurriedly, 'an hour ago I took five tablets of Belalgin.' 'Then you'll have to wait a week for your injection. Come this time next week, and God forbid, don't take any medicines at all, that's my rule. Eggs don't go with drugs, you know.'

I was saved, though I had a feeling that the real reason for the delay was different: the cunning quack had probably just smelt a rat and felt suspicious of me . . .

At any rate, I had a week to kill in Riga, and practically nothing to do. To while away the time, I decided to drop in on the Latvian Procurator's office* and ask whether they had any interesting cases for me to write about. I didn't know that I would find there one of the most interesting stories I had ever come across.

At the grey old building of the Procurator's office which had housed the Republican Police Department under Ulmanis†, I was cordially received by a good-looking middle-aged woman, the head of the investigative section.

'Yes, we've got a very interesting case under investigation,' she said. 'But there's still a lot to do, and you could help us.'

'How come?' I wondered.

'You could look into the case yourself, speak to people and try to find out who is behind it all. We know who it is, but they are too powerful for us to deal with, they have connections both here and in Moscow. You'll see

*The Procurator's office in the USSR not only supervises the militia and the courts, but is also entitled to investigate the most serious crimes – rape, murder, big robberies etc.
†Carl Ulmanis (1877–1942), a pre-war Premier and President of Latvia.

for yourself . . . You journalists are allowed everything nowadays – much more than we are . . . But you must take courage.'

Of course, I was intrigued. That very day I started looking into the case, which was indeed very unusual . . .

I am going to spare the reader the details of my small investigation and the names of people I met. Every journalist has his own professional secrets, and besides, a blow-by-blow account would only be tedious. Instead, I shall just recount the case in the form of a story.

I

The beginning of the story goes back to the early Eighties – an era of acute jeans shortages in our country . . .

Ivan Petrovich Shishkin, an assistant construction worker, was standing by the second floor window in one of Riga's old houses which was being repaired by his crew.

Ivan Petrovich was a heavy drinker, a bottle-a-day man. Today, he had a hangover as usual, and his pale, wrinkled face brought to mind a handkerchief retrieved from a washing machine. He felt as if he had a brick inside his head, one rather like the heavy, stuccoed stones that he was removing one by one from the old houses' wall . . .

Under one of the stones there appeared an empty space where Ivan Petrovich was surprised to find a small parcel carelessly covered with some old rags. He unwrapped the parcel with trembling hands – and nearly dropped it from the second floor window. He was holding a gleaming, well oiled pistol. There was also a clip with eight rounds in the parcel . . .

Who had hidden the pistol under the stone, and when, is still unknown. Probably it was an Ulmanis officer, sometime in 1940, who was hoping for a rapid end to Soviet power in Latvia. Or it could have been a valiant fighter from the anti-fascist underground movement during the German Occupation.

Anyway, the militia experts would eventually conclude that Shishkin had found a 'Borhardt-Luger P-08' pistol, made in Germany in 1936. Pistols of this type are sometimes called 'Parabellum', which in Latin means 'get ready for war'.

Certainly Shishkin had found the pistol quite by chance. But isn't it Queen Chance who often proves the vehicle of history? This incidental finding was destined to play a fatal part in our story . . .

After some hesitation Shishkin decided to keep the pistol and to swap it for vodka when an opportunity arose. Thus he had broken the law by which he should have delivered the gun to the militia. Anton Chekhov stated in one of his letters that if a rifle is hanging on the wall in the first act, it must fire by the end of the play. This was said in the slow-moving nineteenth century. Now the situation has changed, and speeds have increased considerably. So our gun will fire not at the end of the story, but in the next paragraph.

At noon, on a sunny May day three shots sounded in apartment number 27 in Alauksta Street, Riga. The tenants of the house heard them but remained unperturbed, as if these were not gunshots but the sounds of the radio world weather forecast predicting heavy rainfall somewhere on the African coast. One could be forgiven for thinking that pistol shots rang out in the house at least as often as rubbish was removed from the dustbins, that is twice a day . . .

Emma Vasilievna Bourilina, the head of the commercial department of the Riga Trade Union Committee, and her lover had been murdered in their apartment. The unknown killer used the same pistol that Shishkin had found some time before. Certainly Ivan Petrovich, that constant drunk, had nothing to do with the crime, and before becoming a weapon of murder the Parabellum had travelled a long way. But I will expand on that later.

'*De mortuis aut bene, aut nihil*', either speak well or say nothing about the dead, the wise ancient Romans used to say. I shall have to break this antique rule in connection with the late Emma Vasilievna and stick to another (thank God, the Romans seem to have proverbs for every occasion): '*De mortuis – veritas*': about the dead – truth.

Twenty-four hours after the murder, the bodies were found by Bourilina's niece, who had come from Leningrad to visit her aunt. The investigation team from the Procurator's office discovered in the apartment many pieces of expensive jewellery, articles of gold and silver, and precious stones. They were scattered all over the flat. The cupboard was full of bottles of French perfume. In one dark corner, heaps of Western-made clothes and footwear were piled. Many more expensive things were found in the flat of the youngish trade union leader whose monthly salary, by the way, amounted to the astronomical figure of 130 roubles – hardly enough for one pair of decent high boots. This murder proved to be the first thread which helped investigators to unravel the intricate web of fifty criminal affairs . . .

But back to apartment 27. A parcel of Western clothes ready for delivery was among other things found there during the search. It carried an address written in Bourilina's hand: Lvov, 18 Pushkin St, Flat 39, V. A. Dembovich.

In a matter of hours, the addressee of the parcel was arrested in Lvov on suspicion of murder.

For Vladimir Dembovich, a resident of the west Ukrainian city of Lvov, Riga was a special festive place, like Paris for Hemingway. There (in Riga, not in Paris) he studied at the Institute of Aviation Engineering, there he often went on trips when he worked as an engineer at Lvov airport. He was married to a beautiful woman with an imported name, Elvira. She worked as a stewardess, but to Vladimir's regret, not on international lines. Why did he regret it so much? Because for a long time he had cherished a dream of . . . a pair of Western-made jeans. In his eyes, jeans were not just mere trousers but a symbol of the chic Western life for which he yearned. At that time (and nowadays too, though to a lesser extent) Western jeans were an object of luxury, and the dream of every young person. In his student years, Dembovich just couldn't afford them: in 'The Centre' – a kind of speculators' Hyde Park in down-town Riga – they cost nearly 250 roubles a pair ('two and a half' as speculators put it). Of course, in ordinary State shops there was no sign of jeans whatsoever.

Now, being an engineer, he could afford a black market pair by splashing out two months' salary on it, which though problematic was not utterly impossible. But there were no jeans in Lvov at all. The epoch of acute jeans shortages was in full swing . . .

Dembovich's jeansless life came to an end suddenly in 1981 when, on a mission to Riga, he met a friend from the institute who had a reputation as a Don Juan among the students.

'I hooked an incredible girl,' he boasted to Dembovich. 'Besides being a good-looker, she's a high flier in business and can "*dostat*' "* anything – from caviare to a car, through the shop's back door.'

'Could she possibly "dostat' " a pair of jeans?' asked Dembovich, shivering wth anticipation.

'Sure she can – any brand: Wranglers, Levis, just name it . . .'

'Please introduce me to her,' Dembovich implored.

And he was introduced to Emma Bourilina, who took a liking to him at first glance, seeing that he was weak-willed and easily manipulated.

Bourilina decided to make Dembovich her 'representative' in Lvov, since it was becoming more and more dangerous for her to deal on the Riga black market. Her high position on the Trade Union Committee

*"Dostat' "– a peculiar Sovietism, meaning to wangle things that are otherwise hard to get.

stood in her way, and she desperately needed new outlets, preferably at a distance from Riga. Lvov was ideal for that.

Thus Dembovich acquired his very first pair of jeans. Bourilina sold them to him at a friendly discount – not for 250 roubles, but only for 180 (the State price for jeans would be no more than 100 roubles).

Having climbed into the jeans, a happy Dembovich went back to Lvov. Soon he got a letter from his new lady friend asking how the jeans fitted, and whether he could "dostat'" a few cured sheepskins to be turned into fashionable winter coats. Vladimir managed to get the skins, and brought them to Riga, where Bourilina sold them at 'The Centre' for a huge profit.

To repay Dembovich for the skins, Bourilina (a) promised to get him a rare carpet and (b) made him her lover.

Bourilina's flat startled Dembovich, with its piles of imported clothes, footwear and other goods, it resembled the store-room of a Beriozka hard-currency shop.

'Where did you get all this gear, Emma?' Vladimir would ask.

'You're being inquisitive, silly,' Bourilina answered playfully.

For equally inquisitive readers, I must explain that in her office, Bourilina was in charge of all foreign travel by Riga's salespeople. A foreign trip was a rare privilege at that time, and only a chosen few were allowed to travel abroad. Bourilina's duties were to form tourist groups and to approve the character references which had to be provided by everyone wanting to see the outside world. She was also supposed to instruct the would-be tourists on how to behave in the West: not to indulge in clothes-hunting, and to maintain the high moral standards proper for a Soviet citizen. At the same time she considered herself free of all these moral obligations. 'I feed on what I fight' – this was the motto of her life. In keeping to it, she had no scruples about receiving 'souvenirs' from the lucky ones whom she sent abroad. 'Bribes taken from 9 am till 6 pm' was the inscription on the invisible plate displayed on her office door. Now you understand why it was so easy for Emma Vasilievna to buy goods in short supply in all the shops in Riga: all the salespeople wanted a chance to see the world. She held the whole globe in her powerful hands. Or at least it seemed so to Riga's business community.

Bourilina's romance with the feeble Dembovich was progressing. Vladimir was always anxious not to let his wife find out about his Riga love affair. He was afraid of scandal. It was just this fear that Emma Vasilievna decided to play upon.

'Listen, my dear,' she said once in bed, 'don't you think it's high time for you to pay your debts? I'll give you some gear to peddle in Lvov . . .'

'Are you suggesting I should go on to the black market, Emmochka?' Dembovich protested weakly. 'But it's a crime!'

'Crime? And what have you done to poor me? Seduced me – that's what! Isn't that a crime, to ruin a poor woman? I think I'll have to write to Elvira about your behaviour and let her know what a bastard her husband is . . .'

So Dembovich started peddling clothes on the black market. All the profits he sent to Bourilina, who was very strict about it: love is love, but business is business!

She did repay Dembovich, but in her own way, by doing him favours. 'I'm the top of the heap in Riga, Volodya,' she kept telling him. And indeed, through her connections at the city council, she helped Dembovich's sister to get an illegal Riga registration. She also invited Dembovich and his wife to spend the summer at her gorgeous dacha on the Baltic sea coast, allowing them to use one of her cars. Dear 'Emmochka' had become the apple of Elvira's eye. On top of all this, Bourilina solemnly promised Dembovich to arrange a trip for him somewhere in the Bahamas, or at least to Bulgaria. He was so dependent on her by now that sometimes, if he failed to sell an item in time, he preferred to send Bourilina his own money rather than provoke her.

Bourilina's parcels to Lvov were going in a steady stream. They reached Dembovich by post, or arrived by special messengers, among whom there was a dining-car waiter on the Riga–Lvov train, who had travelled abroad by courtesy of Emma Vasilievna and was eager to repay her.

Dembovich turned into an expert speculator, selling 20-rouble shoes for 50 to his own sister, profiteering from his neighbours and colleagues. A couple of times though, for fear of arrest, he attempted to rebel: no more black-marketeering for me! But Emma Vasilievna, using the stick and the carrot alternately, always managed to repress these small rebellions, and two days before she was murdered, she telephoned Dembovich to inform him that another parcel was on the way.

Did Dembovich have sound reasons to kill Bourilina? No doubt about it. Jealousy (he was not her only lover at the time), fear of exposure to his wife, the danger of being a collaborator in a crime – each of these taken separately, as practice shows, can constitute a good motive, and may easily become fatal.

But Dembovich didn't murder Bourilina. On the day of the assassination he was in Lvov.

While the Lvov militia were checking his alibi, an unexpected thing occurred in Riga. A neatly bejeaned young man peeped into the office of the senior criminal investigator at the Riga airport militia station.

'Do you want to know who murdered Bourilina and her lover?' he asked. 'I have some information.'

The double killing in Alauksta Street was already the talk of all the city.

'Who are you?' the investigator asked.

'Riga airport technician Viktor Lisenko,' the young man responded, military style. 'Both Bourilina and her friend were killed by a student named Valery Dolgov. He used a pistol borrowed from Viktor Kuznetsov.'

From Lisenko's not very consistent account, it emerged that Kuznetsov and Dolgov were known to him from 'The Centre'. Lisenko claimed to have broken away from this lot some time ago. He alleged that Dolgov had been threatening to kill Bourilina for a long time.

'He said she owed him a packet,' Lisenko went on. 'Valery is generally not a bad fellow, but unpredictable and vain. He craved a luxurious life. That's why he planned to rob Bourilina and then to hijack a plane with hostages and skip the country. He said he wanted nothing to do with the Soviet Union.'

Lisenko reported that a woman speculator by the name of Anishchenko had witnessed the murder and could confirm his words. As to the pistol, a 'Centre' thug called Kuznetsov had been boasting of owning a Parabellum, which in the end he lent to Dolgov. This Kuznetsov reputedly was a dangerous sort of character: he didn't work, but he was tough, and earned his living by beating money out of the wealthy 'centroviks',* debtors and skimming part of the payment as a 'royalty'.

The Procurator's office to which the report was forwarded checked Lisenko's alibi first. His girlfriend Inna stated that on the day of the murder, Viktor had been with her all the time. This 'alibi', as you will soon discover, cost Lisenko two pairs of imported high boots bought from a hard-currency shop. But being as yet unaware of this, the investigators approached Dolgov.

But pay attention! From this point our story goes into the restrospective, almost until its end.

Valery Dolgov was born in a small Siberian town. His father was a construction worker, and his mother a lawyer. (The zodiac, if it is to be believed at all, placed him under the sign of Aries, carrying such mutually

*'Centrovik' – in local jargon, a speculator from 'The Centre'.

contradictive traits as practicality and extravagance. These two qualities did seem to co-exist in him strangely.)

As a teenager, he went into wrestling, and after school was drafted into the Army, where he earned excellent reports as the military radio station chief. After two years of active service he returned to his native town, but not for long. He couldn't stand provincial life, and went to Riga to study. His main ambition was not just to become a student but to conquer this famous beautiful city.

On arriving in Riga in 1982 with his good military record, the young Napoleon from Siberia easily passed his entrance exams at the aviation engineers institute (by coincidence, the same one from which Dembovich had graduated some years before). Dolgov studied hard, was a Komsomol activist, and was eventually appointed the course leader.

At this point, his rosy career made a sharp turn. 'Power corrupts,' the saying goes. Being vain and self-centred, Valery failed the test of power – even such a small amount as a course leader can wield. For some trifling offence, he severely beat up one of his fellow students, and this was the end of his leadership. It was a tragedy for Valery suddenly to become a rank-and-file student, losing all the privileges that went with the position. Out of his contradictory (remember the horoscope) nature, instead of studying even more diligently, he gave up attending lectures and consequently failed several exams. As a result, he was deprived of his student's allowance (only those with good marks are entitled to it) and found himself living on money sent by his parents. He was also evicted from the hostel because of his drinking bouts, which were occurring more and more often. In the end, he decided to take a year's academic leave from the institute, which can be granted to bad students to enable them to catch up with the curriculum.

Thrown out of the hostel, he had to rent a room in a flat, since he couldn't afford to rent a whole apartment. The other room in this flat was rented by Liliya Anishchenko, a woman in her forties with two children and a criminal record.

Once, a loitering Valery smelt the distinctive corpse-like stench of burnt sugar coming out of her room. He peeped in and saw his neighbour boiling something on the electric stove. Red-faced and dishevelled, Anishchenko looked like a wicked sorceress from a children's movie.

'What are you brewing in there?' he asked, pointing at the sizzling pan with the dark-brown, gluey contents.

'Sweets to make you ill,' she joked.

From sugar and rice-powder for babies, Anishchenko was making nauseously sweet candies which she sold to gullible sweet-toothed children in the street for a 100 per cent profit. The sweets were indeed causing illness and skin disorders in her little customers, but this didn't worry her at all. By rapidly concocting over 100,000 of these phoney sweets, she illegally earned 10,000 roubles.

Valery Dolgov was fascinated by this prosperous private enterprise which could compete with Riga's famous 'Laima' sweet factory – in output, at any rate, if not in quality. He was even more impressed by the amount of money it was bringing in. So Valery struck up a relationship with his neighbour and became a constant visitor to her workshop of a room. Anishchenko's interests were not confined to sweets. For hours on end, she would rattle on about her all-inclusive connections in Riga business circles, often mentioning an influential domineering woman with whom she allegedly was on friendly terms. To prove that, she would show Valery Western clothes acquired with the help of her powerful friend and intended for sale on the black market.

To while away the time, the extravagant (horoscope) Valery was drinking heavily, and the money sent by his parents was dwindling fast. He made an attempt to earn some cash honestly by unloading freight at railway stations, but the pay was so low that he gave it up and started visiting 'The Centre' where shrewd black-marketeers peddled clothes. He liked their life style and the way they dressed, but in his conspicuously plain provincial outfit he was looked down on by the 'centroviks' and suffered from an inferiority complex. To my mind, every other crime is bred by this kind of complex. So Valery was ripe to break the law. He asked his neighbour to get some jeans for him to put on sale.

'That's a good boy, at last,' Anishchenko rejoiced, and thirty-seven pairs of brand-new Syrian 'Simon' jeans materialised out of nowhere. Out of the kindness of her heart, she sold them to Valery for 100 roubles apiece (the State price was 80), thus earning a tidy 740 roubles.

Practical (horoscope again) Dolgov peddled the trousers in the city of Rostov-na-Donu for 130–150 roubles a pair, and raised about 2,000 roubles, not including his aeroplane fare. (Rostov-na-Donu was a 2.5 hour flight from Riga). He could now afford to buy Wrangler apparel for himself and thus subdue his inferiority complex.

Gradually, Dolgov became a prosperous, self-made young man. He was no longer dismissed as a hick at 'The Centre' and was fluent in speculator's jargon: 'What's the weight?' instead of 'What's the price?', 'to push' instead of 'to sell', 'one rouble' instead of '100 roubles'.

It was here, in summer 1983, that he first met Viktor Lisenko. It was a business meeting: on that very day the two of them 'pushed' some 'pants' (jeans), 'slippers' (cross-country shoes) and 'batniks' (shirts) which

Lisenko had previously bought from a foreigner. The newly-made friends had thus earned 535 roubles – not too much but not too little for a start to the joint 'operations'.

Viktor Lisenko was far from being an innocent lamb. He started speculating when still a schoolboy, and at the technical school where he came to study afterwards he was constantly fleecing clothes from his fellow students. By the time he came to work at the airport, Lisenko was an old hand, inveterate speculator. He didn't try to conceal his status as a 'centrovik' – on the contrary, he was permanently advertising his illegal business and used every opportunity to sell Western jeans, perfumes or sunglasses to his colleagues. This didn't prevent him from being elected the Komsomol leader of the airport.

But frankly speaking, Lisenko was a lousy dealer. People say that a gifted person is gifted in everything. The same is probably true of a good-for-nothing. Being a lazy student and later an incompetent technician he was a poor speculator too. Good at talking and making plans, he was rarely able to translate them into life and was always in debt up to his ears. For an attempt at stealing luggage about two years before, he had been expelled from the Komsomol, but not prosecuted. Since then his belief in his lucky speculator's star had increased greatly.

Soon after he made friends with Dolgov, Lisenko fled from his parents' house, or rather was thrown out of it for his 'unworthy' way of life. Together with Valery, he rented a flat in Meistaru Street. The boys became very friendly and were inseparable, like two legs of the same pair of jeans.

'Don't you see, Valera,' Lisenko was lecturing Dolgov over a bottle of wine in the Luna cafe where 'centroviks' used to get together, 'that a speculator is a very respected man? He helps the population to overcome shortages in shops . . .'

'But why don't the militia like us then?' Dolgov inquired.

'As for me, I have no problems with the militia,' Lisenko answered enigmatically. And this was really so: he had numerous militia friends.

Gradually, Dolgov found himself totally dependent on Lisenko. In Valery's eyes, Viktor was a big swindler, a hard-currency dealer, a well-connected 'centrovik' and so – a real man.

As to the hard currency, it was a dangerous racket, since it involved the risk of capital punishment. But some 'centroviks', Lisenko among them, dealt in foreign money from time to time. The militia preferred to look the other way. Why? Patience, my reader, you will know everything pretty soon.

At one point, 'The Centre' was overflowing with so-called 'samopal'.

'Samopal' (literally a self-shooting gun) meant home-made jeans imitating Western brands. They were produced from Soviet fabric, supplied with all the corresponding labels and sold as Western merchandise at enormous prices. It was pure counterfeit, since the quality of the fabric and the cut itself were very inferior. Such jeans usually fell apart in a matter of days. The price of 'samopal', though high, was a little lower than that of genuine Western jeans; that's why they were much easier to sell. Suddenly it became unprofitable to deal with the real imported trousers and all 'centroviks' started peddling the fabric. Its State price was 17 roubles a metre, but at 'The Centre' it cost 50–65 roubles.

Lisenko and Dolgov, keeping in step with progress, decided to switch to the fabric business as well. Needless to say, as soon as the 'samopal' boom began, the fabric disappeared from the State shops.

The 'samopal' boom was evidently created artificially. The honour of bringing it about belonged to a young Riga hairdresser, Boris Shapiro.

The tenants of 4 Ganu Street were puzzled by strange goings on taking place behind the closed door of apartment 16a. Each time they passed by, they stopped, laid an eager ear to the door and listened intently. Apart from natural human curiosity, their queer behaviour could be explained by the fact that all round the clock the clatter of a sewing machine, slightly muffled by the door, was reaching them from the flat.

'It must be the new tenant sewing,' some of the listeners guessed.

'But why at night too?' the others quite reasonably objected. 'It definitely smells fishy.'

Had they listened more attentively, they would have been able to discern that there were at least two sewing machines in the flat, working together. This ruined the theory of an ever-sewing lonely tenant, since even Pierre Cardin himself is unable to work at two machines simultaneously.

The secret was quite a simple one. The flat had been rented from the owner for 40 roubles a month by a bearded young man named Boris Shapiro.

Riga Film Studios have their own stereotype of a positive hero: he must necessarily wear a beard. This stereotype is evident in all the pictures they produce. The flat-owner was probably misled by these movies. In flat 16a, Boris founded an underground workshop specialising in counterfeit Western jeans. Two tailors hired by him were working day and night and got 30 roubles each for every pair.

The hairdresser was a businessman by nature. In 'The Centre' he had the reputation of being a devilishly crafty guy. The Wizard, that was his nickname.

The main wisdom of The Wizard lay in the fact that he never sold clothes himself, hiring smaller 'centroviks' for that purpose. He was afraid of arrest, though such a danger at 'The Centre' was practically non-existent. He even had his own bodyguard, the iron-fisted Viktor Kuznetsov, nicknamed Kuzya (you have already heard this name from Viktor Lisenko).

As an exemplary businessman, Boris kept a diary where he worked out his daily accounts. This diary – a handwritten monument of a speculators' culture – was found in his flat during the militia's search. It abounded in seemingly enigmatic entries like 'Fact – 307, pushed 513, gained 206.' This, translated from 'The Centre' speculator's language, means 'Bought – 307 roubles' worth of clothes, sold them for 513 roubles, with a profit of 206 roubles.' No wonder with such earnings he didn't much care about his official job at the barber's shop, where he seldom gave a shave without bloodshed. With haircuts it was no better: there were rumours that once Boris accidentally cut off a client's ear with the hair. He was just too immersed in his business plans to be attentive.

The idea of faking Western jeans occurred to Boris when he was visiting his mother in the Ukraine and saw piles of denim fabric sold openly in the shops. He calculated that it would be much cheaper to imitate Western jeans than to buy real ones: he was planning to sell these fakes at a somewhat lower price, thus undercutting the real jeans peddlers. His profits should sky-rocket, due to the low production cost of 'samopal' trousers. So he bought loads of fabric, zips, labels etc, hired two underpaid young tailors, rented the flat – and Boris Shapiro & Co Ltd was set in motion. At first glance the jeans they produced resembled real ones just as Holland resembles the Netherlands, and would even fit a customer like a glove. The only difference was that in about a week all their seams came apart like Leningrad bridges on summer nights. But this didn't worry Boris and his employees.

Comparatively cheap 'samopal' trousers caused a panic at 'The Centre' that was comparable to the uproar at London's Stock Exchange when pound, yen and dollar rates start to fall simultaneously. Western jeans were no longer the 'soft currency' they used to be in 'The Centre'. They were replaced by the fabric as a raw material for 'samopal' jeans manufacturers.

Here is the final touch to the portrait of Boris Shapiro. Having earned more than 6,000 roubles on 'samopal' trousers, he remained a petty thief. From his native barber's shop, he filched seven bottles of Red Moscow perfume (7 roubles a bottle), three bottles of For Men Eau-de-Cologne (1 rouble 40 copecks a bottle) and three bottles of Anteus Eau-de-Cologne (2 roubles a bottle). Six thousand as opposed to 1 rouble 40 copecks – an eloquent proportion!

I have nothing more to add to the image of Boris Shapiro, but one thing: in the events which led to the double murder in Alauksta Street, his trade was destined to play quite an important role.

Back to our bosom pals Lisenko and Dolgov, who had decided to speculate in fabric.

For a start, Valery asked his former neighbour Anishchenko to get the first supply of jeans fabric for them. He solemnly promised to pay her no less than 30 roubles a metre, knowing only too well that in 'The Centre' they would be able to push it for at least 50 roubles. Anishchenko agreed.

Emma Vasilievna Bourilina now comes back on stage again. It was she whom Anishchenko, as a friend of hers, asked to help with the fabric.

'OK, I'll try,' said Bourilina.

That same winter evening in 1984 she paid a visit to the Tradesmen's Palace of Culture, of which she was officially in charge. With her slim leg clad in an Austrian high-boot she kicked open the door of the director's office and ordered him to write an official letter to Riga's Central Department store, asking to buy one hundred metres of jeans fabric for the needs of the Palace's amateur drama society.

The director was so startled by his boss's unexpected visit that he didn't hesitate to write this odd letter and to seal it with the Palace's big saucer-like stamp. Of course, he realised that an amateur drama society would need such an amount of fabric only if it planned to stage a play about 'centrovik' life, which was clearly not on the repertoire.

Coming home with the letter, Bourilina took one of the trade union's forms and drew up a warrant in Anishchenko's name, giving the latter the right to buy the fabric on behalf of the Palace. She wrote that Anishchenko was the drama society's artistic director. Armed with the letter and warrant, Anishchenko had no problems in buying the material – not 100 metres, but only 36: there was no more at the warehouse. Having cleared the department store of the fabric, she paid 17 roubles a metre – State price – to the cash-desk. Afterwards she sold the fabric to Dolgov, not for 30, as agreed, but for 40 roubles a metre, 'so as not to upset her influential friend'. Valery had to accept the new price – he had no alternative. Together with Lisenko, they pushed the fabric in 'The Centre' for 50 roubles a metre – the demand was great.

The speculators' 'drama society' thus earned 1,188 roubles: the 'stage director' Bourilina gained 568, the 'artistic director' Anishchenko 260, and the 'actors' Lisenko and Dolgov 180 roubles each. This was very similar to the wage distribution in a real Soviet theatre!

Lisenko felt grossly underpaid and made up his mind to get rid of Dolgov as a partner and to set up on his own. He went to Anishchenko and asked her to get some more fabric through her powerful woman friend.

Liliya Nikholaevna was in great need of money at that time: she was planning to rebuild her house in the country.

'OK,' she said, 'get one and a half "things" quickly.' (In speculator's language a 'thing' meant 1,000 roubles.)

Lisenko, being as usual all in debt, didn't have that much cash. So he went to the well-to-do Boris Shapiro, who agreed to lend the money (at interest, of course) but warned that he wanted a quick return.

'Don't you know me, Boris?' Lisenko tried to sound insulted.

'I sure do,' the far-seeing Shapiro answered. 'That's just the point.'

Viktor took the money to Anishchenko, dead sure that she would easily get hold of the fabric. Probably it would have really turned out that way had Anishchenko asked Bourilina to help, as before. But this time, Liliya Nikholaevna, too, double-crossed her partner, and hurried to spend the money on her house without a word to Bourilina.

Time passed, but there was no fabric. Shapiro was becoming more and more insistent in his demands to get the money back.

'Wait for another month, Boris, I'll be rich soon,' Lisenko implored.

'I can't wait,' the unyielding Wizard answered. 'I'm transferring your debt to Kuzya.'

The director of an old Japanese film found an interesting means of getting rid of a hero whom he didn't need any longer for the development of a plot. At some point, a huge bear, a *deus ex machina*, appeared on the screen and ate up the unnecessary personage. The role of such a bear was performed in 'The Centre' by Viktor Kuznetsov. For a 'royalty' of 300 roubles Kuzya would make any debtor see reason. A 'centrovik' approached by him was risking not just his health but also his business prestige: he lost both his clout and his contacts. Like the hungry bear from the movie, Kuzya could eat anyone, having first beaten every last copeck of debt out of the target. There were rumours that he even owned small-arms.

What did Kuzya do when he was not occupied with reclaiming debts? As an exemplary 'centrovik' he was involved in various schemes. He peddled radios and tape-recorders, hard currency and Western cigarettes which he bought in Moscow and sold in Riga for double the price.

But his special interest was pornography, or rather porno-business.

Kuzya was one of Riga's first video owners. In his flat in Malienas Street he ran an underground video salon where he showed to trusted people Western thrillers of King-Kong type for 5 roubles and pornographic films like *Emmanuelle* for 10 roubles per person. (The price for the latter was doubled because of the higher risk involved.) Kuzya's video salon was prospering: no less than twenty people at a time watched the 'naughty' pictures.

The day after Shapiro lost his patience, in accordance with 'The Centre's' unwritten bylaws Kuzya met Lisenko in the street and said: 'Mind, Vitya, if you don't return the money in three days, I'm switching on the meter.'

'Switching on the meter' meant that with every passing day the debt would grow. This was another of 'The Centre's' ruthless rules.

Lisenko was seized by panic, and not without reason: to lay his hands on one and a half 'things' in three days was far from easy in itself.

He rushed to Anishchenko.

'You'll get the fabric – just wait a little,' she sang looking the other way and stirring the bubbling brown mixture in the pan with a dirty poker. 'As to the cash, I haven't got a copeck . . .'

She explained that there was no way of retrieving the money from Bourilina, because she was bound to have put it to work, and it was not fair anyway. This was the first time Lisenko heard of Bourilina.

He went to 'The Centre' hoping to borrow some cash there. But Shapiro had already warned all the 'centroviks' that Lisenko was 'naked' – that is penniless – and he was refused a loan.

Viktor was cornered. He didn't have even any personal spending money, because his airport salary was already reserved for a colleague to whom he owed a big sum.

Three days elapsed and the meter was switched on.

Lisenko was wriggling like a fish on a hook. Trying to avoid the ubiquitous Kuzya, he escaped to the town of Panevezhis, and attempted to borrow money from local 'businessmen'. But bad news has wings: 'No loans for the naked,' local dealers said bluntly. The escape attempt failed, and Lisenko returned to Riga, having wasted his very last roubles.

To crown it all, suddenly, like a bolt from the blue, a large consignment of denim fabric was delivered to the Riga shops and was on free sale there. To speculate in fabric now became senseless . . .

Lisenko was furious with Bourilina, who he thought had double-crossed him.

The days went by, and Kuzya promised bloodshed if the money was not repaid in the near future. The debt was hanging over Lisenko like a sword of Damocles.

The idea of robbing Bourilina suddenly occurred to him for the first time. 'Being a bigshot in trade, she must have lots of expensive things in her flat,' he ruminated.

Lisenko understood that he wouldn't be able to carry out the robbery on his own. So who else should he share his plans with than Dolgov, who was also permanently hard up and desperately needed money.

'You know what,' Lisenko began circumspectly, 'fabric isn't going to bring us profits any longer, Valera. We're in a mess. But we can overcome the crisis. I've got a plan – to rob one wealthy bigshot. For that we'll probably need a gun . . .'

'What do you mean? Murder?' the frightened Dolgov asked.

'Are you mad, or what?' Lisenko was genuinely furious. 'We'll use the gun just to scare the bigshot out of her pants, if necessary. It's our last argument, you might say.'

'Well, generally speaking, I'm in favour,' Dolgov said as if he was voting at a Komsomol meeting. 'But where on earth shall we get this so-called last argument?'

'I'll take care of it myself,' Lisenko answered patronisingly.

One more week passed. The meter was ticking away not only the roubles of Lisenko's increasing debt, but the last days of Emma Vasilievna's life.

Viktor Lisenko devoted all his unlimited energies to getting a gun. This was a far from easy thing to do. He couldn't possibly just advertise for a pistol in the evening newspaper. Neither could he get it in a shop: in the Soviet Union arms are sold only to hunters with special licences, and must be registered by the militia.

Having borrowed some cash from Dolgov, Lisenko again went to Panevezhis and nearly succeeded in buying a gun on the local black market. But at the very last moment, the seller of a 5.6 mm Colt pistol took fright and the deal was not completed. Back in Riga, Viktor tried to get a gun from an African student but failed again.

The plan was falling apart at the seams like 'samopal' jeans. To rob Bourilina without a gun was senseless: Lisenko realised that she would not be easily scared. To make matters worse, if Anishchenko's words were to be trusted, Emma Vasilievna had just got a new lover – a strapping blond guy who was living in her flat.

No, a gun was a must. And he decided to stake his all on Kuzya, to go into the lion's den. It was common knowledge in 'The Centre' that he had some connection with arms, and Lisenko ventured to call on him.

Kuznetsov, sporting his usual jeans uniform, was recumbent on the sofa and was watching a porno movie on his video. He was menacingly combing his hair which, by the old superstition, predicted a storm.

Naked bodies were intertwined on the screen. Casting a glance at them, Lisenko forgot the aim of his visit for a moment, and just stood there staring.

'Getting a free eyeful,' Kuznetsov growled. 'You're supposed to pay if you want to look . . .' He got up from the sofa and switched off the video. 'Or maybe you've brought the money, my little friend?' he went on mockingly. 'If so, mind, my darling, the meter is ticking and you owe me not one and a half "things", but two already. At this rate, I'll be able to afford a car very soon.'

'L-listen Kuzya.' Lisenko was stammering with fear. 'To get square with you I must frighten some money out of a big wallet. For that I need a gun. Have you got one, by any chance?'

At that moment, Kuzya had the gun indeed. To understand how he had got hold of it, let's leave Kuzya's video salon of a flat for a while and recall the miserable Ivan Petrovich Shishkin, suffering from a hangover, who found a Borhardt-Luger P-08 (Parabellum) pistol at the very beginning of our story. He was not plotting robbery or murder but decided to trade the Parabellum for some liquid currency. And a customer appeared soon – let's call him Slavsky. He offered 100 roubles for the pistol. For Shishkin, it was an astronomical sum, enabling him to buy a whole crate of vodka. In his heart of alcohol-sodden hearts he didn't expect the sum to be that high and agreed hurriedly. The 100-rouble note travelled to the money-beaten palm of a vodka store saleswoman.

'History is but a succession of absurdity and incidents,' Nietzsche once said. And though officially we do not accept his philosophy in my country, he cannot be denied some common sense. In the history of the pistol in question, as in some human biographies, Queen Chance played a decisive role. The Parabellum was destined not to be corroded by rust and time in an obscure hiding place, but to become an instrument of murder.

Slavsky stored the gun in the stoke-hold where he worked. He boasted of his acquisition to a friend, Pertsov, who occasionally visited 'The Centre' and knew some of the 'centroviks' – Kuznetsov among them. Pertsov was aware of Kuzya's interest in arms and offered to take him to Slavsky's stoke-hold. On seeing the gleaming, well oiled weapon, Kuzya bought it on the spot, together with the clip, for 150 roubles. He planned to push it profitably to a foreigner or to swap it for some grass (another of his 'hobbies').

'So how about a gun?' Lisenko asked again.

Kuzya thought. By lending Lisenko the pistol for a short time he could kill two birds with one stone: earn some money for the hire and help the idiot (Lisenko) to raise the cash and pay his debt, which in the long run meant a 'royalty' – that is, more money – for himself. The reward promised by Shapiro was to be good. 'Anyway, the risk is minimal,' Kuzya figured. 'Viktor is too much of a coward to fire at someone.'

'No more beating about the bush,' he said aloud to Lisenko. 'Just give me seven roubles, then we'll discuss the whole thing further.' Of course by seven roubles Kuzya meant seven hundred. He was just using his beloved 'Centre' dialect.

Driven by hope, Lisenko hurried to the airport, where by some inhuman effort, and a good deal of begging and imploring, he managed to borrow the required sum from his colleagues. ('Back by tomorrow, I swear.') Kuzya solemnly produced the Parabellum, symbolically wrapped in a piece of greasy jeans fabric.

'As soon you return the gun,' he explained to Lisenko, 'you'll get six roubles back. One rouble I'll deduct for the hire.'

Over the moon with joy, Lisenko rushed to see Dolgov. He couldn't wait to boast of his deadly acquisition. In his jeans pocket, cooling his leg pleasantly through the fabric, lay the Parabellum. Not realising fully that he had got a lethal weapon, Lisenko felt as though he had successfully bought a pair of the most modern, most fashionable jeans of the most prestigious Western brand.

'Parabellum jeans,' he thought and smiled at his pun, deciding to insert it some time in his talk with Dolgov.

'I've got it,' he blurted out as soon as Dolgov answered the door.

Lisenko carefully unwrapped the piece of fabric. The slim pistol's body was dappled with sunlight coming through the window.

'Wow!' Dolgov's eyes widened with admiration. 'There it is: our "last argument". Look, Valera, does it work?'

Lisenko inserted the clip into the pistol, lowered the safety catch with his thumb. Aiming the gun at the wall, he pressed the trigger lightly . . .

A deafening sound broke the stillness of the room, filling it with the thunder of death. Dolgov covered his ears with his hands. Lisenko, having dropped the smoking pistol on the couch, did the same.

A dark, neat hole was gaping in the wall. It smelt of powder and stucco. The first shot from the Borhardt-Luger pistol had been fired. Three more were to follow.

The robbery date was set for next Saturday, May 26, 1984. As it approached, the cowardly Lisenko felt more and more reluctant to participate. He decided to use Dolgov as a cat's-paw. By that time he was able to boss him around as much as he wanted. He told Dolgov a phoney story about the money Bourilina allegedly owed him. That's why, he explained, she avoided meeting him: as soon as she noticed him through the peephole in her door, she locked it even more thoroughly.

'So, Valera, it's useless for me to go to her flat: it could ruin the whole thing from the start,' he intoned to Dolgov. 'You'd better go there with Anishchenko, and I'll wait downstairs in case of any emergency.'

Dolgov wouldn't dare object.

'I think it would be sensible to reconnoitre the place first,' he suggested, 'just in case . . .'

'Brilliant! You've got the head of Henry Ford.' Lisenko was quick to flatter.

The reconnaissance was necessary. It meant a preliminary (or rather preparatory) visit to Bourilina's flat. For that they needed a pretext. And they found it in the form on an old ten-rouble gold coin – a tsarist chervonets. The coin had been given to Lisenko for sale by an ageing uncle now in retirement in the countryside.

'Offer the coin to Bourilina,' Lisenko instructed Dolgov, 'and while she's thinking about whether to buy it, make sure you have a good look around the flat.'

After the briefing, Lisenko telephoned Anishchenko and asked her to introduce Dolgov to Bourilina and to enquire at the same time about the promised fabric. That same evening, Anishchenko took Dolgov, who was sweating with excitement, to the door of the apartment 27 in Alauksta Street. The door was answered by Bourilina herself.

'Hello, Emmochka,' Anishchenko twittered. 'Please meet my former neighbour Valery Dolgov, the student.'

Bourilina stretched out her palm – soft and wet as a jellyfish. As a result of a timid Dolgov's handshake, the numerous rings on her fingers made a soft clanking sound like railway carriages' buffers when coupled.

Emma Vasilievna showed the vistors into the living-room. Dolgov felt dizzy at the sight of the carpets, the crystal, the fine Finnish furniture.

He produced the coin for Bourilina to see.

'I must examine it,' she said, and together with Anishchenko retired to her bedroom.

The cunning Liliya Ivanovna later told Lisenko that she had questioned Emma about the fabric and the latter had promised to get it very quickly. Dolgov, she said, could testify to their talk in the bedroom.

And he did confirm it, though of course he couldn't hear what the women were talking about.

While they were conversing in the bedroom, Dolgov lowered his frame into the armchair, which was so soft and deep that it lowered a sitter's sense of self-respect. Valery wished that Bourilina lived somewhere in Georgia, where there is a tradition of presenting a guest with anything he likes in the host's house. If that had been the case, he would have needed a truck to carry the gifts.

He was so carried away by his dream that he didn't notice Emma Vasilievna reappearing in the living-room. Playing with the gold chervonets in her palm she said: 'I'll keep the coin for a while, though I personally don't need it. I shall talk to my friends; maybe someone will be interested. Call on me in a couple of days.'

The goal of the visit was achieved.

'Well, Vitya,' Dolgov told Lisenko an hour later, 'she is extremely rich – no question of that. The flat is stacked with foreign knick-knacks, furniture, clothes, electronics. There is a Sharp tape recorder – the latest model. And the hostess herself just jingles with jewellery, like a New Year's tree with toys. I can imagine how much more of the stuff is hidden in the drawers.'

'Great!' exclaimed Lisenko joyfully. 'Tomorrow is our day.'

He gave Dolgov his last instructions: 'Now look, you go with Liliya just like today and ask about the coin. Then you take out the gun and demand the cash. When she brings it, warn her not to go to the militia, just to be on the safe side. She won't go anyway, being a swindler herself.'

Lisenko then phoned Anishchenko, asked about the fabric first, and on hearing there was none (which he expected) pleaded with her to go to Bourilina with Dolgov again next morning to settle the problem once and for all. He was afraid that without Anishchenko, the cautious Bourilina might not let Dolgov into the flat.

Next day, at about noon, the armed gang (that's what they actually were by now) consisting of Lisenko, Dolgov and the unsuspecting Anishchenko approached Bourilina's block of flats. For Emma Vasilievna, this Saturday morning had started with minor business. She was awoken by a telephone call from a friend asking her to find a room at a hotel. As you know, this is quite a problem in the Soviet Union, with its great shortage of hotel accommodation, especially in big cities like Riga. But for Emma Vasilievna it was a mere trifle and took just a phone call to another friend – a hotel manager. For this small favour, she would take her cut – it went without saying . . .

Near the entrance to the house, and out of Anishchenko's sight,

Lisenko surreptitiously passed the Parabellum to Dolgov, who stuck it in his jeans pocket.

'Good luck,' Lisenko whispered, and remained as agreed in the street, near the doorway.

With the 'last argument' weighing heavily against his leg, Dolgov followed Anishchenko up the stairs. His head was whirling. He felt like a student before an exam for which he was totally unprepared.

'Valery?' Bourilina was genuinely surprised when she discerned Dolgov trying to hide behind Anishchenko's back on the landing. Through a partially open door Valery could see inside the flat where a half-dressed man appraised the unexpected visitors with a quick glance before disappearing behind the bathroom door like a big puppet behind the curtain.

'I . . . I just . . . about the coin . . .' Dolgov stammered. 'You said I could come over.'

'But I said in a couple of days,' she interrupted, 'and here you are the next morning trying to burst into the flat when I and Imant are still in bed.'

Bossy, metallic notes sounded in Bourilina's voice. Valery was ill at ease: he couldn't help feeling that he – an incompetent student – was being scolded by a strict professor. He didn't know what to do next. Unexpectedly, Anishchenko offered him a helping hand. 'If we do leave now,' she thought, 'Valery will tell Lisenko that I didn't speak about the fabric with Emma.' She had to provide an alibi for herself.

'Emmochka, could I have a few words in private?' Anishchenko murmured in a candy voice. She winked at Bourilina, hinting at some very confidential talk.

'All right. You're here now, so come in,' Bourilina agreed with a sigh of reluctance. 'You too,' she nodded to Valery.

The women immediately hurried to the 'conversational' bedroom, where Anishchenko, using the opportunity, decided to ask Bourilina for a consignment of wrapping paper for her home-made sweets. The door closed behind them.

Valery was silently suffering in the corridor, wishing all this to be finished as soon as possible.

Eventually, Anishchenko and Bourilina reappeared from the bedroom. There was a frown of fake disappointment (designed for Dolgov) on Liliya Nikholaevna's face.

'So long. Imant!' Bourilina cried suddenly in a high-pitched voice, 'Liliya is leaving.'

' "Liliya is leaving" – she doesn't want to acknowledge my presence at all,' Dolgov thought with sudden anger. 'Just wait, I'll teach you how to treat the guests properly.'

Imant Purin'sh – Bourilina's youngish boyfriend – came out of the bathroom. He was holding a shaving brush in one hand and his face was covered with blobs of lather.

Dolgov realised that in a moment it would be too late. He snatched the Parabellum from his pocket.

'Stand still!!!!' he shouted at Purin'sh in a dreadful, alien voice. Imant froze. Even under the lather it was evident how pale his face grew.

'Come aside, Liliya,' Dolgov ordered Anishchenko, and pointed the pistol at the petrified Bourilina.

'I want your money, stones and gold, and quick, you bitch!' he croaked. 'Don't try to double-cross me: the pistol's loaded' – words that he must have heard in a detective film. 'If she stalls, fire into the ceiling to persuade her,' Lisenko had advised in the morning.

Valery expected any kind of reaction but the one that followed. Bourilina was taken aback, but she was in no hurry to obey. Instead, she peered into his eyes, and suddenly burst out laughing.

'What a fool! What a miserable little fool you are! Put your toy away, and get out of here fast! Imant, will you see the student off?'

Later, he would be unable to explain what came over him at that moment. Probably it was his contradictory spirit (horoscope!) – 'So you don't believe, me. All right, I'll show you I'm not joking . . .' But more likely, it was his deep-rooted inferiority complex that prompted his further actions. His swollen vanity forbade him to admit that he was a constant loser. And a miserable fool, as Bourilina had just put it . . .

Valery flicked off the safety catch and pointed the gun at Purin'sh, who was walking towards him. Bourilina suddenly realised he was not bluffing. She gave a shriek and rushed for the front door. Her scream brought Valery back to reality. He caught her by the hand, and simultaneously shot Purin'sh in the chest.

All this happened within less than three seconds.

Dolgov didn't hear the sound of the shot. He saw Purin'sh collapse, and the shaving brush fall. The dark red stain spread fast on his white vest.

Anishchenko burst out wailing behind Dolgov's back, caught totally by surprise. She sidled towards the door. Dolgov tried to block her way, but she was as spry and slippery as a bar of wet soap. She broke his grip and slid out of the flat, slamming the door in Dolgov's face.

Meanwhile Emma Vasilievna had fled to the living room, but Dolgov had grown satanic at the sight of blood. In two leaps he caught up with her and clubbed at her head with the butt of the pistol. Bourilina sank onto the floor, and Dolgov fired at her point-blank.

At that moment, the dying Purin'sh gave a moan in the corridor. Dolgov rushed to him and hit him on the head three times with the butt of the Parabellum. Purin'sh sank back. With the last blow, Dolgov accidentally pressed the trigger and the third bullet pierced the parquet floor.

A deafening, all-pervading silence fell. Like a glass of ice-cold water, it made Valery's teeth ache.

Stillness was ringing in his head. He put an ear to the front door: everything was quiet. The neighbours didn't seem to have heard anything.

He felt like an outsider, like a spectator at a strange play in which he himself was performing. Multicoloured spots were dancing before his eyes and pictures from his short, young life were reflected in them: school, institute, 'The Centre'. The pictures appeared and vanished, bursting like soap bubbles . . .

He looked into the mirror hanging in the corridor. An alien, unknown face with the murderer's mark of Cain was looking back at him . . . Then, moving as if exhausted, he dragged the two dead bodies to the bathroom, put them into the tub and having filled the bath full of water, sprinkled it thickly with washing powder. He would never be able to explain why he did this.

Meanwhile, Anishchenko, pale as chalk, descended on Lisenko from the black gape of the doorway. 'What's happened, Liliya? Have you had too many of your famous candies, or what?'

'There . . . Valery . . . murdered . . .'

In his heart of hearts, Lisenko had been expecting the tragedy. A powerful motor of self-preservation now started up inside him. He grabbed Anishchenko by the lapels. 'Listen, you old bitch, if you let slip to anyone that I was here, remember, your children will be finished. Go home and eat a sweet, but be careful not to get poisoned . . .'

This was too much for poor Liliya Nikholaevna. As soon as Lisenko let her go, she broke away from him and scurried off along the street.

'No, she won't inform,' Lisenko thought.

First he locked himself in a public telephone box and dialled – whom do you think? – Kuznetsov! He made a date with him for the evening, saying that he was ready to settle the accounts. Then Lisenko produced one more coin, and dialled Bourilina's number. No one answered for some time, then the receiver was lifted but with no Yes? or Hello, just silence and heavy breathing . . .

89

'Valera, it's me, Viktor,' said Lisenko. 'I know everything. Are they both . . .?'

'Both,' Dolgov echoed at the other end of the line.

'Calm down, and listen to me. Search the flat thoroughly. Take the money, the stones and the rest. Don't forget about the tape recorder.'

Lisenko was planning to give the Sharp to Kuzya as part of his debt.

Made calmer by Lisenko's call, Dolgov began to rummage through the flat. He took some money, hard currency cheques, some jewellery, silver and the tape recorder, of course. Having quietly left the apartment, he took the loot to his flat in Meistaru Street. Lisenko was waiting for him there.

'I didn't want to kill them,' Dolgov exclaimed as soon as he came in.

'Shut your bloody trap!' Lisenko hissed. 'What's done is done. I'll see to it that no one suspects us, and we'll put the militia on Kuzya's trail.'

Lisenko took the pistol and part of the spoils and advised Dolgov to go and lie low with his friend Zinoviev, who lived in Kengarags, a Riga suburb.

'The jeans you wore to Bourilina's you'll have to get rid of,' he said. 'But don't worry, tomorrow I'll buy you some new ones as a reward for your courage.'

Lisenko understood that the murder couldn't be kept secret for long. So he had to denounce Kuzya as quickly as possible. For that, he had to return the Parabellum to him first.

But Kuzya proved brighter than Lisenko thought. He accepted the tape recorder but utterly refused to take the pistol. 'You've bought it from me, haven't you?' he said.

It was pointless now to inform on Kuzya, and that left only one alternative for Lisenko: to blow the whistle on his pal Dolgov. But he had to do it cleverly, in case suspicion should fall on himself.

So he hurried to see Anishchenko and ordered her to say, if she was picked up, that the money for the fabric had been given to her not by him, but by Dolgov, and that Bourilina had known Dolgov for a long time and had dragged him into her schemes. Lisenko had quarrelled with Dolgov, she must add, and they hadn't seen each other for a long time.

Scared and confused, Liliya Nikholaevna couldn't work out what to say if arrested. She decided to wait until the heat was off in the safest shelter of all – a psychiatric asylum. Having a psychiatrist friend, she found no difficulty in simulating mental disease, and was accepted into the republic's psycho-neurological hospital.

The next morning, using Bourilina's cheques, Lisenko bought the boots as a pay-off for his girlfriend Inna for providing him with a false alibi.

Only one thing remained – to plant the Parabellum on Dolgov, having sweetened him first with the new jeans. With Bourilina's money, Lisenko bought the new Wrangler jeans at 'The Centre' and set out for Kengarags, where Dolgov was in hiding.

'Here's a present for you,' Viktor said, giving Valery the trousers, 'beautiful Parabellum jeans.'

They both laughed.

Lisenko produced the pistol. 'Keep it,' he said to Dolgov. 'We'll probably need it again soon.'

'What for?' Dolgov wondered. 'To rob someone else?'

Lisenko stared at him intently. 'You know what?' he said after a pause. 'As soon as this Bourilina story dies down, let's defect to the West. Bright guys like us have nothing going for us here. We'll hijack a plane with hostages and fly over the border. Don't forget, I work at the airport.'

Here, our two would-be hijackers parted company. But they were destined to meet again in ten day's time at the Procurator's office, where they were brought face to face. We saw at the beginning of our story that what Lisenko did immediately after his visit to Kengarags was to denounce Dolgov to the militia. He felt completely safe: Anishchenko wouldn't have guts enough to report him, his girlfriend Inna would confirm that he was with her on the day of the murder, and as for Dolgov, he would never blow the whistle on his tin god, and even if he did, who was going to believe a murderer?

As they say in whodunnits, Lisenko miscalculated.

Valery Dolgov was caught cold, with both the loot and the pistol. He didn't hesitate to say that it was Lisenko who was the real murderer. Then Anishchenko was fished out of the psychiatric asylum. When she found out that both Lisenko and Dolgov had been arrested, her mental health improved immediately and she started singing like a canary.

But for some reason, the militia were in no hurry to complete the job and to arrest the other heroes of our story – Shapiro, Kuznetsov, Shishkin, Slavsky etc – though each of them had been definitely involved in the crime. Why this reluctance?

To answer the question, we must ask another: why had 'The Centre' been prospering in full view for so many years? And yet another: why was Dolgov so quickly executed by firing squad, although in the end he sincerely repented?

And that's where the main part of my investigation started.

II

It was obvious from the start that someone in the militia (and in the local judiciary too) was not interested in the thorough investigation of Bourilina's numerous connections, which led not only to 'The Centre' but to the top as well. As I have said already, eventually more than fifty separate criminal cases originated from the murder in Alauksta Street. There would definitely have been many more had the investigation team from Moscow not been suddenly dispersed.

On a Saturday morning in January 1987, I had two successive telephone calls. The first was rather ominous: 'Vitaliev?' asked the husky voice with a noticeable Baltic accent. 'Take care, journalist . . . Don't forget about your son . . .'

Before I could reply the line was disconnected. And what on earth could I answer? . . .

My little son Mitya, aged six, was listening to the record player in his room: he was enjoying 'The Kolobok', a Russian fairy tale about a round loaf that goes for a walk in the forest. Every animal he meets there wants to eat the Kolobok up, but the cunning loaf always manages to escape. The high-pitched falsetto of the actress playing the Kolobok was reaching my ears . . .

Threatening calls had become quite routine of late. They started after the first parts of my 'Parabellum Jeans' story were published by *Krokodil* magazine, and now (for the third time already) I was thinking seriously of changing my home telephone number . . .

The last part of the story was to appear in the next issue of the magazine. It was a crucial piece, in which I mentioned the names of some Latvian mafiosi.

I looked around my small two-roomed flat; the typewriter on the table, the books on the shelves . . . My wife was staying with her parents for the weekend, and there were just the two of us in the flat: my son and I. And the voice of the brave Kolobok from the record player: 'I escaped from Granny, escaped from Grandpa, escaped the hare, the wolf, the bear . . .'

In the end, I have to admit, the wandering loaf was eaten up by the fox . . .

'How long will it be before someone eats *me* up?' I thought ruefully . . .

The telephone was ringing again. 'Vitali Vladimirovich?' a smooth and pleasant voice enquired.

'Yes,' I answered cautiously, ready to hear more threats.

'My name is Major Mikhailov. I am a senior investigator with the Ministry of the Interior. I'd like to talk to you in private.'

'All right,' I said with relief, as the introduction and the voice itself didn't seem dangerous. 'You can come to my office some time next week.'

'No, I'm afraid it's an emergency, and it can't wait. We must meet today.' My interlocutor was being insistent.

'You see, I'm looking after my son, and I can't leave the house for the time being,' I said.

'Don't worry. I'd prefer to come to your place in half an hour, if you don't mind. See you soon.'

'Write down the address,' I said, but too late: there were short buzzes in the receiver, signalling that the talk was over . . .

Strange, I thought. How is he going to find my house without knowing the address? I had forgotten that the man worked for the Ministry of the Interior, which is in charge of the entire Soviet Militia.

Major Mikhailov did appear in exactly half an hour. He was a smallish, stocky man in his forties, and kept looking round like a frightened rabbit.

'Is there anyone else at home?' he asked anxiously.

'Just myself and my son,' I replied to his obvious satisfaction.

We proceeded to my desk. The Major was panting heavily, reeking of cheap tobacco.

'We are all reading your novel* with great interest at the Ministry,' he began.

'Thank you, but I guess you didn't come here just to say that.'

'No. The fact is, I was the head of the Moscow militia team investigating these Riga affairs you write about. We had spent a year and a half in Riga, and then all of a sudden our team was called back to Moscow and dispersed.'

'Was it?' I asked with genuine surprise.

'Tell me please, have you mentioned any high-ranking officials from the Latvian Ministry of the Interior in the last part of your story?'

'Yes, I have. And former Deputy Minister Pauls among them. I have proof that he was the man behind organised crime in Riga.'

'We had such proof too,' Major Mikhailov interrupted. 'That's probably why our team was dismissed. We must have gone too far . . . This Pauls has many connections, not only in Riga but in Moscow too. If you do mention him, it would mean a certain relief for us, but you would be asking for trouble . . . Tell me, has anybody approached you yet with similar questions?'

*A fictionalised account of this story, *Parabellum Jeans*, was published in the Soviet Union in 1987.

'No. There were some hostile telephone calls with threats, but they were all rather vague. That's about all.'

'Someone will approach you soon. It will be the most unlikely person – the one you'd never suspect of being mixed up in it all. And you must let us know immediately . . . It was real hell, this Riga case. We were being got at all the time – either threatened or offered bribes. Do you know how they deal with people who stand in their way? These people just disappear into thin air, without a trace. There are plenty of swamps in Latvia, you know . . . You never find a corpse. And sometimes, by our law, where there's no corpse, there's no crime . . .'

I shuddered.

'We never had the chance to complete our investigation,' Major Mikhailov went on. 'Pauls had connections with some bigshots from the country's Procurator's office. They must have got at our bosses at the Ministry, and we were ordered to stop. That's why I chose to come here, rather than invite you to my office.'

'What's Pauls doing now?' I asked, just for the sake of asking.

'He is comfortably retired, and dreams of returning to the Ministry some time. All compromising evidence has been destroyed. And he would return all right, if it weren't for your novel . . . Now it would be difficult for him. Tell me, are you positive his name won't be removed at the last moment?'

'I've read the proofs of the last piece already. Nothing short of an earthquake can change it now . . .'

'Let's hope there'll be no earthquake, though he could have easily arranged one.' Mikhailov smiled wryly. 'OK, Vitali, I'm leaving . . . Here are my telephone numbers. Feel free to call any time, if anything happens . . . And take courage, my friend, you've done a good job . . .'

The door clicked shut behind the Major. 'I've escaped the Granny, escaped from Grandpa, escaped the hare, escaped the wolf,' sang the carefree Kolobok. Mitya was playing the record again . . .

I couldn't say that I was really frightened: you tend to get used to everything, threats included . . . but of course I felt uneasy. This was a complicated sensation: natural fear for myself and my family was mingled with, if not obliterated by, a wild hatred towards those insolent crooks, mafiosi, blackmailers – those who rejected the laws of human existence and were trying to introduce instead their own perverted rules of behaviour. Somewhere in my heart of hearts, I felt that this time the danger was a real one . . .

Late that same night I was awakened by a throbbing sound coming from behind the window. I looked out through the dim, frost-etched glass onto the quiet street, submerged in darkness, and in a while was able to discern a big black van parking just outside.

I glanced at the clock: it was 3 am. Our street is usually deserted even during the day, so this truck looked very alien in it – especially at night . . . The van was parking loudly, and to my horror I saw that it carried no number plates. I remembered the Italian film on the Mafia shown on TV a couple of days before. The sad-eyed mafiosi in the film had used a very similar van to dispose of the dead bodies of their rivals . . .

Suddenly the full recollection of that morning's talk with the frightened Major came down upon me like a hammer on an anvil.

'They've come to get me,' I thought, feeling drops of ice-cold sweat break out on my forehead.

The truck came to a halt. The doors were flung open and three men in dark clothes jumped out one by one. They started towards our house . . .

My son was sleeping placidly in his bed, making soft sucking sounds with his lips – an atavism showing that not so long ago he had been a baby . . .

I rushed to the kitchen, and without switching on the light, groped for the axe behind the stove. With the heavy axe in my hand, I felt a bit safer, though I still had a vague hope that they wouldn't enter the house, or would make for another doorway. Standing in the corridor clutching the axe, I told myself that probably I had been over-impressed by my talk with the Major . . .

The entrance door slammed, and I heard heavy steps climbing the stairs, coming closer and closer.

I hid behind the door. Should I call the militia? Too late . . .

I have read somewhere that at the moment of extreme danger, your whole life passes before your eyes in a few seconds. And indeed, standing there in the dark corridor behind the door, I felt that in my mind, all my life was flashing past me . . .

Meanwhile the steps were coming closer and closer and I started to picture how I would strike down the first intruder, then the second . . .

But what was this? The heavy feet were receding. They definitely were . . . The killers (or whoever they might be) were climbing the stairs past my flat, higher and higher. In half a minute, they were several flights away. I felt absolutely drained . . . My son was still sleeping peacefully in his cot, making muffled sucking sounds in his sleep . . .

Five minutes later, I peeped out of the window to see the van moving away. As it passed beneath a solitary street-lamp, I made out the weathered inscription on the side: 'Moscow Water-Pipes Repair Service'.

I remembered that these kinds of trucks do not always have number plates on the back . . .

On the next day, the tenant from the fourth floor told me how a hot water tap had come off suddenly in his bathroom in the middle of the night and he had to call the emergency repairs team . . .

In accordance with Major Mikhailov's prediction, I was indeed soon approached by someone whom I hadn't expected: the press officer from the Ministry of the Interior. He wondered whether I had mentioned Pauls' name in my novel. I answered yes, and he insisted I cross it out. I refused point-blank, and he didn't press the point. There were no repercussions for me . . .

Anyway, my life was spared for further stories and further threats.

By the time 'Parabellum Jeans' was fully published[2] I had managed to provide just some general facts testifying to 'centrovik' connections with the corrupt bosses of the Riga militia. The ring leader was certainly Pauls, but he was far from a lonely figure. And some time after the publication, I made another trip to Riga which resulted in the postscript to the novel, also serialised in *Krokodil*.[3]

So what did I dig up? Under the direct supervision of Pauls, the gang of top-ranking militia people had a free hand. At the head of it was Spulgys, the chief of the Riga Criminal Investigation Department. He was responsible for fighting speculation, black marketeering and illegal hard currency rackets. Bourilina's motto, 'I feed on what I fight', was his motto too. He was part and parcel of the criminal world. In return for bribes and 'favours' Spulgys took care of Riga's black marketeers, peddlers and other 'centroviks'. Just one speculator named Logvinova presented him with a crystal ashtray, an imported fur coat for his wife, and a Western-made jacket for his son. Spulgys, you see, was a good family man and he didn't hesitate to take bribes of spirits and foodstuffs – again for family consumption. All he kept for himself was the money, contributed by the criminals. For that, he gave them carte-blanche to speculate in 'The Centre' and turned a blind eye to the reports of their illegal activities coming from his subordinates.

Greed and corruption have no limits and tend to expand in the course of time. Spulgys went so far as to start speculating in clothes himself. Of course, it was not practical for a lieutenant-colonel of the militia to appear at 'The Centre' in person, so he gave his merchandise to Logvinova and she sold it for him. By that time, Logvinova was openly taking him bribes and presents, and she readily informed her neighbours that she supplied her militia friend with cognac and caviare.

Another of Spulgys' clients was a woman called Driomova, who ran an undergound brothel and abortion clinic. In return for bribes, he shielded her from arrest, tipped her off about impending raids, and did various other favours.

Spulgys' other duty was to supervise personally the concern that specialised in buying precious metals from the population. This odd kind of supervision was limited to squeezing money from speculators and hard currency dealers operating in the vicinity of the shop.

On top of all this, he attempted to steal the cache of old treasures found by an honest citizen who, in full accordance with the law, brought it to the militia.

This was the service record of Lieutenant-Colonel Spulgys – the man who had swapped his crystal spirit for a crystal ashtray . . .

In the court to which he was eventually brought, he behaved in a rude and insulting manner. When the verdict of eight years in prison was announced, Spulgys leapt up from his chair and screamed in a paroxysm of fury: 'I'll put you all behind bars some time, and if not, then I'll kill you!' Doesn't it give you the creeps just to think that for so many years a person like that was one of the chiefs of the Riga militia?

Spulgys' authority was based on his corrupt surbordinates, among whom I could name several heads of criminal investigations sections, senior investigators and militia inspectors. The woman directly respons-ible for working against 'The Centre' was also sentenced to prison for bribe-taking and corruption. Her name was Gurkovskaya, and for many years, under the wise leadership of Spulgys, she headed the counter-speculation section. She was also a close friend of Bourilina.

Now, you can see why the 'centroviks' and people like Bourilina and Anishchenko found the going so easy.

As to the 'centroviks' themselves, they were not as innocent as they may seem. Speculation in our country, with its constant shortages of many important goods, is a grave crime. Lisenko was wrong to say that speculators helped to overcome the shortages. On the contrary, more often than not they artificially created them (remember the story with the fabric). As a matter of fact, 'The Centre' lived by gang law, if a gang can live by any laws at all. Money was beaten out of debtors, 'meters' were switched on and off, drugs and arms changed hands. And as you have seen, murders were also arranged there. As to Dolgov, to my mind he was more of a victim than a criminal. I'm sure there was no need to execute him.

Lisenko, who thought up the whole thing, 'got away' with fifteen years in prison. I was told by a militia official some time after the story was published that Lisenko was having a very hard time in correction camp, where everyone treated him as an informer (which of course, is what he was). There were even several attempts to murder him, and the militia had to keep on moving him from one camp to another.

Shapiro, Kuznetsov and the others were arrested in the long run too, but 'The Centre' itself, though on a smaller scale, exists in Riga to this day. Probably, it will come to an end only when our shops are saturated with high-quality goods and thus speculation and black marketeering are undermined economically. I'm sure it's just a question of time.

As to the egg-injecting quack thanks to whom I came across the 'Parabellum Jeans' story, I did visit her again a week later, accompanied by the militia. Her profitable business designed for gullible people was brought to a stop and her patients went to polyclinics. Perhaps they were not received there so politely, but polyclinics were much safer for their health in general. And free of charge, besides.

So I didn't have an egg injection, but I'm not inclined to regret it.

$$\boxed{\text{Letter-Box}}$$

The detective documentary 'Parabellum Jeans' by V. Vitaliev has stirred up a storm in Latvia since the first two episodes were published. Many readers tend to think *Krokodil* won't be brave enough to continue the story. But it is. Our local press still prefers to sit on the fence. No changes in our everyday life have come as yet. The case of Bourilina and her high-ranking patrons is still being hushed up. Bourilina herself is buried in a luxurious cemetery for the élite. Former Deputy Minister of the Interior Pauls is sitting pretty as a lawyer at the State farm near Riga. He got off scot-free and says he doesn't mind having a whiff of fresh country air. Many are inclined to think that he will be OK, since he comes from the family of Pelshe, the late Politburo member. Pauls's brother is the Minister of Health in Latvia. I am not bloodthirsty. I just wonder whether changes will ever come to Riga. We have a lot of corruption. Our house is near the special government residence. Drunken parties, boisterous scandals, rows – that's what keeps its occupants busy. We have written lots of letters asking for them to be stopped, but all in vain . . . When we started reading 'Parabellum Jeans', we were struck by Vitaliev venturing to tread upon such big shots' toes. Some are sure that he will lose his job soon. Our public opinion is split into two camps. The first predicts that Vitaliev will go on a long, long mission and 'Parabellum Jeans' won't be completed. The second thinks that *Krokodil*, being just a satirical magazine, won't be able to expose all the facts seriously and to find the real culprits. But we still hope very much that it will.

Respectfully, G–ve, Riga.

Our former Deputy Minister of the Interior Pauls, while drunk behind the wheel, got into a road accident and nearly killed a woman, but wasn't even detained. *Pravda* has covered this incident. Where is justice? As to the mild sentence given to Spulgys – one of the corrupt Riga militia chiefs – it's again a trick to divert attention from Pauls, who is related to Pelshe himself.

K–ts, Riga.

6

Once Upon a Time in Amur

Receiving official replies to his articles is part of a Soviet journalist's daily routine. As a rule these replies are very general and formal. They usually start with the phrase: 'As a result of checking the facts described in your article the following measures have been taken . . .' The measures may differ. As a rule, some petty boss is 'reprimanded' or more seldom 'severely reprimanded'. He can also be stripped of his bonus pay. Sometimes the official reply, signed generally by a secretary of this or that Party committee, announces that Tom, Dick or Harry (or all three together) have been removed from their posts. Every journalist considers it an achievement when he succeeds in dislodging an incompetent bureaucrat as a result of his article. That is why after my 'Sufferings of a Young Vet' was published, in whose aftermath both the rector and the Dean from the agricultural institute were deprived of their posts, my colleagues hurried to congratulate me. When glasnost' enabled me to start writing about more crucial topics, the official replies became lengthier and more concrete. For instance, the reply to the 'Plague of Love' which came from the Ministry of the Interior stated that after the publication 383 prostitutes had been exposed and registered in Sochi. As to 'registered' the meaning was clear: at the Sochi militia headquarters I was shown such a register, or rather an album, with the photographs and names of the prostitutes. So 'registered' in this context meant that 383 more photographs were added to that compact portrait gallery of heavily made-up and usually blank-eyed women. But the word 'exposed' definitely puzzled me. I just tried to imagine the procedure for such an 'exposure' . . .

But the official letters on five or six typed pages which came in after my second documentary novel 'Amur Wars'* surpassed all previous records. You can judge for yourself: 'The facts described in the publication really took place,' said the reply sent by the secretary of the Dnepropetrovsk

*First published in the Soviet Union in 1987.

Party committee. 'As a result of it, 138 people were condemned and sentenced to different terms of imprisonment, and 75 militia men were punished – 18 of them imprisoned, 66 expelled from the Party, 32 sacked from the ranks of the militia. All the chiefs of the regional and city militia and the Procurator's office have been removed from their posts – including the head of the Dnepropetrovsk militia department with all his deputies and the regional Procurator and all his deputies . . .'

In the second reply – this time from the Minister of the Interior of the Ukraine – it was stated that about 60 firearms, 300 kilos of drugs, about 1,000,000 roubles and two dozen cars were confiscated from the criminals mentioned in the publication. Impressive figures, but far from complete. The story of the Dnepropetrovsk mafia which I was the first to investigate did not end with the appearance of 'Amur Wars'. It continues up to the present day. Moreover, this country's largest criminal organisation is gaining power. As one of the foremost Soviet investigators put it in *Ogonyok* magazine, 'The Dnepropetrovsk family has recently gained control over Moscow and Leningrad.'[1]

Now, in 1989, our readers are no longer shocked by such words as 'Soviet mafia' and 'Soviet racket'. But when I started investigating into the 'Amur Wars' in the summer of 1987, these words were still unheard of and did not even appear in the press. Back in 1987, I had to explain to my readers what 'mafia' and 'racket' meant in general and what was special about their Soviet versions. I could not forsee the great boom in racketeering now taking place in the country with the growth of cooperatives. I could not imagine that the Dnepropetrovsk mafia would grow so powerful. Frankly speaking, had I known then how far this investigation would lead me, I would have probably given it up – not through fear, but because of the sheer impossibility of having the story published. But here I am. And the story which I thought would never see daylight appeared at the end of 1987 in 5,300,000 copies (the circulation of *Krokodil*). I was awarded a Journalist of the Year Honorary Diploma for it (together with 'The Plague of Love' and 'Parabellum Jeans'). *Sotsialisticheskaya Zakonost* (Soviet Legality) journal – organ of the USSR Procurator's office – called the novel 'this shining example of a publication showing the relations of traditional criminals with the so-called "tsekhoviks" [owners of underground factories and workshops] and their connections with some State officials in Dnepropetrovsk'.[2] And on top of that, the story is to be put on the screen by Lenfilm, the second largest Soviet film studio. Who could have expected all this to happen? But it's happening all right, in the spirit of glasnost', openness, truth.

Nowadays our 'progressive' (or 'left-wing') press is often rebuked by its 'conservative' counterparts for its dominantly negative approach to life. But listen: haven't we had enough of the overwhelmingly 'positive' approach when the press used to publish nothing but panegyrics, eulogies and false figures and was bursting with the spirit of 'profound satisfaction' (the cliché from many Brezhnev speeches). A 'negative' approach breeds shame and the desire to improve – so it can become a vehicle of progress. The kind of inflated optimism that pervaded our mass media under Brezhnev breeds nothing but irritation and disbelief, which could not lead the country very far. It was just this exclusively 'positive' approach that brought our land to the verge of an economic and spiritual abyss.

Of course, no journalist must see nothing but the dark sides of life. But I'm sure he must see them *for the most part*. And not just see for himself, but show them to all his compatriots, to all his readers. Good things are usually on the surface, bad ones are usually hidden. And the main task of a journalist, especially an investigative one, to my mind, is to expose these hidden things and to fight them.

Besides, a *Krokodil* journalist is supposed to be critical, if not altogether iconoclastic. I do love my country and I think there can be no real criticism without love. Without it, criticism is just nagging. Without it, laughter is just a mere carping. Critics are generally much better patriots than eulogists.

Anyway, back to 'Amur Wars'. How did I learn about the story? I was returning from my native Kharkov after visiting my father's grave, and on the train I got into conversation with a fellow-traveller who was an engineer from Dnepropetrovsk. When he found out that I was the journalist who had written 'The Plague of Love', he grew excited. The story was very popular and the black market price of the *Krokodil* issue containing it was 10 roubles (the State price of an issue is 30 copecks).

'You journalists now write about almost everything – prostitution, drug addiction, the homeless,' he said.

'Why "almost"?' I asked.

'Because I haven't read a thing about the Soviet mafia."

'Does it really exist?'

'Come to our Dnepropetrovsk and see for yourself.'

I couldn't go to Dnepropetrovsk on such short notice, and decided first to try and find out something from Moscow. For that I telephoned an old friend, who happened to live in Dnepropetrovsk.

'Have you heard anything about the local mafia?' I asked.

'You mean the Sailor and his gang? They're the talk of the whole city. But this is no telephone story. Come here and see for yourself.'

It was my second invitation to Dnepropetrovsk, and I was definitely intrigued by the enigmatic Sailor. So I set off, sure that all I would find in this smoky industrial city would be an ordinary criminal group – probably with some southern Ukrainian overtones. 'Mafia' must be an exaggeration, I thought. People like to abuse this foreign word without properly understanding what it means: someone whose purse has been stolen screams bloody murder and claims that he is a mafia victim. Even in Riga I didn't find any mafia in the proper sense of the word. Mafia, as I understand it, is not just a crime, nor is it simply organised crime. It's a kind of family business, involving clans. Certainly we could speak of the Uzbek mafia, headed by Rashidov: he and his henchmen's sons and relatives were mixed up in criminal affairs. But in Dnepropetrovsk?

What is 'mafia' in general? This word appeared in Sicily in the middle of the nineteenth century. In Sicilian dialect, it means 'shelter'. Indeed, the first mafiosi readily sheltered Sicilian peasants from tax-inspectors and policemen. At the end of the nineteenth century, the word 'mafia' came to America with Italian (Sicilian) emigrants. It began to denote particular kinds of criminal activities: Italo-American family gangs connected with corrupt authorities – first in New Orleans, then in Chicago. La Cosa Nostra – a pre-war Chicago criminal group headed by the notorious Al Capone – can serve as a good example. It comprised mainly Americans of Italian origin. The *Guinness Book of Records* defines the present-day American mafia as the world's 'largest syndicate of organised crime . . . which has infiltrated the executive, judiciary and legislature of the United States'.[3] It consists of some three to five thousand individuals in 25 'families' federated under a 'Commission' with an annual turnover in vice, gambling, protection rackets, tobacco, bootlegging, hijacking, narcotics, loan-sharking and prostitution which was estimated by *US News and World Report* in December 1982 at 200 billion dollars, and a profit estimated in March 1986 by the attorney Rudolph Giuliani at 75 billion dollars.[4]

The difference between the Soviet and American mafia is considerable. As A. Gurov wrote in *Sotsialisticheskaya Zakonost'* monthly, 'Mafia, in the international sense, is associated for the most part with a semi-legal business organisation, having its own stocks and transnational connections. Our [Soviet] criminal groups, despite their high organisational level and far-flung network of corrupted connections, are still primitive in their economic aims and foundations if compared to, say, La Cosa Nostra.'[5]

Soviet mafias are also limited geographically, seldom crossing the boundaries of a region or republic. Their sole interest is power, unlimited power within their sphere of influence.[6]

It goes without saying that mafiosi are opposed to perestroika. The administrative command system initiated by Stalin and strengthened by Brezhnev suits them perfectly, because it breeds economic chaos with resulting corruption. For the slow progress of Gorbachev's economic changes we usually blame some nameless bureaucracy. But practice shows that many of the most conservative top bureaucrats were – and are – mafia members. Hence, to expose mafia these days means to promote perestroika.

I

I went to Dnepropetrovsk in July 1987, and at first was at a loss where to start. Usually I begin an investigation with paperwork, studying court files, militia reports and other documents. In this case it proved to be extremely difficult. On the one hand, I guessed that the Dnepropetrovsk mafia (or whatever it was) had connections in the courts and militia, so I didn't want to arouse any premature suspicions as to my interests. On the other hand, the heyday of the Sailor's gang was at the beginning of the Eighties, so the documents from those years were stuck in dark and dusty archive corners and took some effort to excavate.

But the main difficulty was that the information on the gang's activities (scarce as it was) was scattered in numerous files and volumes of court proceedings and criminal cases which at first glance had nothing to do with the subject. Dnepropetrovsk is a large city, with a population of more than a million, comprising eight districts – each with its own court, Procurator's office and militia department – not to mention the corresponding institutions of the city and the region as a whole. Each of these thirty (!) establishments had archives of its own, and to find anything there was like locating a needle in a haystack . . .

But there was a ray of hope. In 1984–5, thanks to the heroic efforts of the special investigation team from the USSR Ministry of the Interior, the nucleus of the Sailor's gang was smashed. Nineteen criminals were arrested, tried and sentenced to different terms of imprisonment. The proceedings of this case occupied thirty-four thick volumes, which I scanned very carefully, but that only added to my confusion: they were just a collection of disconnected episodes, though it was evident that something really big was behind this long list of seemingly trifling offences.

At some point I grasped that this time mere paperwork was not going to lead me very far, and I switched to the second stage of my routine of investigation, that is meeting people. I visited bars and restaurants where the Sailor and his men had been salting away the loot, I went to hospitals, prisons and hotels, I had long talks with those few militia people who had been trying to contain the Sailor (though with little success) at the most difficult time. I spoke to the young judge who was presiding over the hearings of the Sailor's case. As you will see, it required a good deal of courage on his part. I also managed to get hold of some rare gang photographs.

At this point, I received a sinister telephone call at my hotel . A husky voice with a Ukrainian accent advised me to go back to Moscow if I wanted to avoid grave consequences. I tried to forget about the call, but was reminded of it when coming back from my friend's house late one night. The street seemed utterly deserted, when suddenly I was struck from behind by an object which was probably a stick. A split second before the blow, some instinct made me duck and the stick, instead of hitting my head, struck my shoulder. It was a close shave. When I turned round, there was no one in sight. The bushes planted thickly by the road-side gave a quick soft rustle and that was it.

At first, I thought they had broken my shoulder-blade, but I was wrong: next morning I was OK, despite the big violet bruise under my T-shirt. I already knew enough about the Sailor's boys to get the message. These thugs were playing in a tough game. And I still needed my health to write the story. So it was a signal for me to go. To parade one's courage in such a situation was stupid. What I feared most was that they would break into the hotel room and destroy my notebooks, bulging with facts and figures. They were not complete, but the whole affair seemed boundless – the deeper you delved, the more there remained to be discovered. So I decided to call it a day and return to Moscow. Having taken a month's leave from the office, I escaped to my small out-of-town dacha and started writing.

'Quiet is the Ukrainian night,' Gogol once wrote . . .

For some, yes. . .

Along the winding suburban streets of Dnepropetrovsk move three Zhiguli cars, ripping up the darkness with their headlights. The procession comes to a halt near a private house partly hidden behind acacia trees. Six young men in white shirts and impeccably ironed trousers emerge from the cars and saunter towards the house. In a moment its heavy shutters and iron-clad doors are shuddering from the impact of their hefty fists and shoulders.

'Come on! Open up and receive your guests!'

The sleepy owner is already busy with an intricate Japanese lock. With trembling hands, he opens the door. The six invaders burst in and pass through the rooms examining the contents with quick, expert glances. They are satisfied with their quick appraisal: carpets, crystal, bronze – everything in its place, as it should be in the house of a food store manager.

'We'll have a feast here,' one of the unwelcome visitors declares to the host. In no time, the frightened owner's wife has laid the table: cognac, smoked salmon, caviare – delicacies never to be found in the host's food shop, but always available in his home.

At some point, the nocturnal visitors notice the white grand piano in the corner, covered with a thick layer of dust.

'Can you tickle the ivories?' the newcomers' leader demands.

'My daughter used to . . .' the host makes an awkward, apologetic gesture.

'Wake her up! Make her play!'

'For God's sake! Can't you do without music?'

'Wake her up, I tell you! Or I'll bury you under the asphalt!' The leader displays the barrel of a shot-gun, short as a four-letter word.

In a minute, the house is ringing with music.

'Play, "Sailor's Dance"!' the bandits cry. '"Sailor's Dance" for our chief, the Sailor!'

The daughter, wearing a dressing gown thrown over her nightdress, prods at the keys. The guests swig cognac from crystal glasses.

'Bring more food!' they shout to the host.

But the owner and his wife have slipped out, leaving their daughter at the gangsters' mercy. Unnerved by this sudden evacuation, the thieves produce shotguns and open fire on the stocks of crystal in the sideboard. The girl screams.

The Guys from Amur are enjoying themselves . . .

Amur is a working-class suburb of Dnepropetrovsk (formerly Yekaterinoslav). The name goes back to the times of Catherine the Great, who often holidayed here, on the banks of the Dnieper river, and whose playful ladies-in-waiting chose these then deserted places for their trysts with black-haired Ukrainian 'parubki' (youngsters). The descendants of these 'parubki' are still dwelling in neatly white-washed Amur huts, nestling among cherry trees and acacias.

What else is interesting about Amur? Only one thing: from the earliest days it had been notorious for its high crime rate. The reason probably lay in the hot temper of the locals, typical southerners, or maybe in the cheap and plentiful local wine – no one knows exactly. But the fact is that here in these tiny, shadowy Amur courtyards the Sailor's Guys were born and grew up to become for almost a decade the unofficial kings of the whole of Dnepropetrovsk.

Their line was robbery and crime, but of a slightly unusual nature (at least for our country at that time). I take from a bookshelf the bulky volume of the *Soviet Encyclopaedic Dictionary*. Here on page 1149, between the Russian historian P. I. Richkov and the English physicist Rayleigh, we find the imported word 'racket'. The entry says: 'Racket (in the USA) – blackmail, extortion conducted with threats and violence by gangsters (racketeers).'[7]

Everything is true in this laconic definition, except for the bracketed 'in the USA'. But this is not surprising: the dictionary was published in 1983, when there was a habit of projecting on to the West all our social vices, as if we thus guaranteed ourselves against them all.

But even back in 1983, rackets were not confined to the USA alone. During the 'sweet' stagnation years of 1972–82 when underground factories, black marketeers, wheeler-dealers, speculators and doubtfuls were prospering, racketeering couldn't help but appear in our country. And it did appear as an inevitable companion of the black economy and privately owned wealth. The illegally earned fortunes of crooks and dealers were private property indeed, though they lived in the socialist State.

I need not explain to my Western readers what 'racket' means, but when I was writing this story in Russian I had to provide some explanations, since the word was practically unknown in the Soviet Union. Certainly, the Guys from Amur didn't know it. As a matter of fact, most of them (the Sailor included) were hardly literate at all, though this did not prevent them from racketeering in its classic form.

It is interesting to note that criminal proceedings against them had been periodically started since 1976, but none was ever completed. It was not till 1984, when Brezhnev's era came to an end, that a special investigation team headed by Major S. Serebrennikov, the senior investigator of the major crimes squad, was sent from Moscow. It comprised detectives from all over the country, who started to repair the abandoned and rusty machinery of investigation.

In one of my notebooks, I made a list of those who were subjected to racketeering by the Guys from Amur. I deliberately refrain from calling them victims. Why? You will see from their occupations: barman, barman, beer-seller, butcher, waiter, money-lender, drugs peddler, store manager, underground factory owner (tsekhovik), thief, barman, butcher, waiter, salesman and so on and so forth.

This list probably won't mean anything sinister to a Western reader, but in Soviet society, alas, barmen, waiters, butchers and the like are notorious for having big illegal incomes. To get a job as a butcher or a barman, you must as a rule pay a big bribe, which quickly repays itself with the help of customers who, exhausted from standing in queues and consequently not very attentive, are frequently cheated.

The Guys from Amur didn't touch anyone who was definitely not a swindler, not because of any noble principles, but through mere common sense: honest people do not tend to be very prosperous – neither in Russia nor, I guess, in the West . . .

It all started spontaneously, from a kind of inferiority complex (as in Dolgov's case). The future racketeers all grew up in Amur and went to the same school, like the ones in the film *Once Upon a Time in America*. Only this time it was not in America, but in the Ukraine.

By the mid-Seventies, Dnepropetrovsk was swarming with shady groups of various kinds. These people led luxurious lives, eating in the best restaurants, riding in smart cars, sporting Western clothes. The Guys from Amur, who had not yet been organised into a gang, were very envious of such a lifestyle. But what could they do? They were not sophisticated enough for the black market business. All they had were iron fists and criminal records for petty hooliganism. Being physically strong, the Guys from Amur had only one means available to overcome their inferiority complex, and that was to assault the higher class of crooks.

The Sailor's gang passed through several stages in its evolution. Having started as a bunch of Robin Hoods, at some stage the Boys from Amur changed. In trying to establish their own rough justice, they turned into an indispensable part of the huge machine of injustice. Just another proof of the fact that there cannot be two different kinds of justice in one society.

The Amur wars, like any armed confrontation, started with conflicts of local importance. But little by little, newer and newer forces were dragged into the battle. And shots sounded more and more often in the winding lanes running down the hill towards the River Dnieper.

'Oh, Odessa, pearl of the sea coast . . .' The band in the Kalina restaurant was singing, or rather bawling, the popular song.

Near the little stage, people in various states of intoxication were dancing. They jerked, clapped and waved their hands to the lively Jewish tune. At times, it seemed they were not actually dancing but mutely pronouncing a passionate speech in defence of their lifestyle . . .

'Oh, Odessa . . .' Oh, the golden middle of the Seventies. Golden for crooks and criminals, for those who cheated Peter to pay Paul, stealing money in one restaurant and spending it in another.

> 'Oh, Odessa, pearl of the sea coast,
> Oh, Odessa, you've known too many woes . . .'

That very evening, at that very moment, the same song sounded in so many restaurants and cafés, so many legs were drunkenly pounding dance floors that all our huge land was swinging rhythmically and even the stars on the Kremlin towers – in a dark-brown, cognac-coloured sky – were rocking slightly to the tune of 'Oh, Odessa . . .'

At the table nearest the band sat three young men and two women. They were not dancing, but drinking and eating. One of the young men was Viktor Shapkin, whom the Guys from Amur and Matross (the Sailor) called Shapa. He was staring at the dancers and boiling with fury. For him, who had grown up in Amur and had twice been prosecuted already by the age of twenty-five, the dancing big spenders were a repugnant sight. His companions Kukuruza (the Corn) and Komar (the Gnat) shared Shapa's indignation.

Having downed his glass, Shapa suddenly sprang up from his chair, snatched a shotgun from under his coat and pointed at the musicians.

'Oh . . .' The music stopped abruptly. Women shrieked.

'Play! Or I'll fire!' Shapa roared hoarsely to the musicians, who tentatively picked up their instruments. The pianist, who wasn't sure whether Shapa knew the notice in a nineteenth-century American bar, 'Don't shoot the pianist, he's doing his best,' struck the keys with stiff wooden fingers. 'Oh, Odessa . . .'

'Dance!' Shapa bellowed. 'Everybody dance!'

Obeying his order, the dancers started twitching puppet-like under the muzzle of the gun.

And here the shot came – Shapa inadvertently pressed the trigger, and the piece of lead struck the floor in front of the stage. The musicians abandoned their instruments and fled. The dancers followed their lead. Shapa was laughing out loud.

By the time the cloud of smoke over the gangsters' table had dispersed, Shapa and his friends were already in the street on their way to Amur.

This was the rowdy, stupid way in which the Guys from Amur

109

established their reputation in Dnepropetrovsk. One day they would beat up a swindler, the next they would open fire at the bar in a restaurant . . . The rumours of these feats spread all over Dnepropetrovsk, gaining more and more colourful details and snowballing to bizarre dimensions.

They started to be feared. Some barmen began serving them with free booze, which was readily accepted, and after the booze came free meals. As criminal investigations practice proves, the next step in bribery is money. This step was made.

It is still not known which of the illegal dealers was the first to pay for his safety. But a quiet existence could be bought at least for the moment – that soon became clear to all the town's 'businessmen'.

At first, the Guys from Amur were too shy to extort money in the open, which proves that they were not programmed to become criminals. They lured the underground millionaires into fixed card games – the Boys from Amur were excellent gamblers, (gambling is illegal in the USSR), palmers and jugglers too. They made the wealthy punters bet on absolutely hopeless matters. This is how they worked some of the tricks:

With the card games, the procedure was as follows: three gangsters would come to a bar or pub and invite a barman or manager to play with them. To refuse could mean trouble, so the crook had to agree. One of the bandits would be appointed as his partner, but this was just a manoeuvre, of course. They let the 'big wallet' and his 'partner' win a couple of games, and then a card-sharp who was always part of the team, would start switching cards adroitly and the crook was finished in no time. His 'dolist' (partner in Amur slang) would ostentatiously fork out his own share of the loss, so willy-nilly the crook had to pay too. It was pure chicanery, since the dealers' money was then shared among all three bandits – 'dolist' included.

In the gangsters' repertoire, there was also a home-town game which they called 'Amur handkerchief'. A crook was asked to guess the denomination of a banknote tied into the corner of a handkerchief. This was a set-up too: in another corner of the handkerchief, a banknote of a different denomination was hidden. If the first was guessed rightly, the second was artfully produced, so the crook was bound to lose in any case.

When there was no clean handkerchief to hand, the simplified version of this game was used. It was called 'Shmen', and was limited to mere guessing. The banknote in this case was simply produced from a gangster's pocket.

But the most primitive and effective trick was the so-called 'birth year bet'. The Guys from Amur would tell a waiter or a barman, 'We bet five thousand roubles you won't name the year of your birth correctly.' 'Why, that's simple,' the puzzled dealer would answer. 'Forty-eight.' 'You lose, mon cher, not forty-eight but nineteen forty-eight. Pay up.'

Often, the fooled 'lokhs' (that's what they called the wealthy crooks) were reluctant to cough up. Then the bandits had no scruples about beating the money out of them.

The Guys from Amur were getting rich. Every restaurant or café manager in Dnepropetrovsk considered it an honour to receive them for a grand dinner or supper – free of charge of course. The Boys frequented restaurants every day, thus gradually overcoming their old inferiority complex. They were using drugs too. Dnepropetrovsk is one of the centres of poppy-growing in the Ukraine, and a drug called 'kuknar' is made from poppies. It's a hard one, like heroin, injectable and very expensive. The area is also famous for its hemp – a well-known hallucinogenic plant.

They had their favourite haunts like the Jubilee Restaurant, where they drank, or the Icicle Café, where they 'worked' ie played cards, Amur handkerchief and so on with the wealthy swindlers. The Icicle was an ice-cream café, though spirits were also sold there to the Boys from Amur by the barmen Pekurovski and Chertok, who were gang members themselves. The last fact, as you will see, was not a guarantee of their safety.

It was in the Icicle that Matross caught out the barman, Vikentiev. The cautious barman didn't feel like playing cards with the Guys from Amur at first. He knew that they were always up to some trick. But when they said that they were going to play not for money but for ice-cream, he consented: you can't lose much playing for ice-cream, can you? Matross himself was to be his 'dolist'.

The poor lokh was terribly mistaken. After ten minutes of the game, it turned out their opponents Yura the Red and the Weaver, had won forty-four thousand portions of ice-cream.

'How will you cough up, in ice-cream, or in cash?' Yura the Red demanded.

'You won't be able to consume so much ice-cream, boys,' Matross reasoned, 'so we'll pay in cash.'

After a brief calculation, Chertok, one of the other barmen, declared that the debt in cash amounted to 41,360 roubles: the café had high ice-cream prices.

'I'll pay my half tomorrow,' Matross sighed, and with a quick wink at his companion left the café. Vikentiev, being not only wealthy but clever, did not hold out: he paid his half, 20,680 roubles, in four days.

This was the classic example of the 'quiet' racket – sadly more the exception than the rule. They couldn't help seeing that the quiet style was much less effective than the ruthless one. Their ways were becoming more and more vicious, more and more like pre-war Chicago. The Amur Wars had started. These are some of the early skirmishes.

Once, when a thief refused to pay his 'debt', Shapa, whom we have already met, took some pliers and tried to tear the gold crowns off his teeth.

The Pole (Polevoi), the Boar (Luniov) and the Pickpocket (Zaishlo) once dragged Varnavsky, an obstinate black market dealer, out of his house and drove him to the cemetery, where they stood him beside a vacant grave. A thug called Dimenstein picked up a faded wreath from the ground, put it on Varnavsky's neck and pushing the dealer – more dead than alive with fear – towards the grave, kept saying: 'Think where you can get the money!' It was only here that the moneybags did start thinking, and agreed to pay.

Being an avid reader of Stevenson, the Greek (Grek) came to collect a debt from an underground factory owner called Fyodorov. The smart operator was not at home, and the Greek left his small black-and-white photograph with Fyodorov's wife, asking her to show it to her husband as soon as he arrived. The 'Greek gift' worked all right: on seeing the familiar face on the photo, Fyodorov grasped that resistance was useless and surrendered. He met the Greek at the central market entrance and gave him a stack of banknotes, carefully wrapped in newspaper.

As to the petty tsekhovik Goldberg, the Guys from Amur didn't threaten to beat him up, they just 'borrowed' his car as security against his debt. The car was returned unharmed after Goldberg paid the required 4,500 roubles – the result of a card game.

The Sailor's boys had another means of extortion called a 'fine for unreceived profits'. It can be illustrated by the case of Bosenko, the butcher. One day he was asked by the Sailor for the keys to his flat: the Guys from Amur claimed that they planned to play cards there with some rich lokh. Bosenko promised to think it over. In a couple of days, the Sailor came again, and explained to the butcher that because of his refusal to hand over the keys on the spot they had lost the wealthy client, so Bosenko must pay a 5,000 rouble fine. 'We'll throw you into the cellar to feed the rats if you don't cough up,' Matross promised. Bosenko tried to flee to the Black Sea town of Kerch, but the Boar went on a mission there and caught him.

At the end of the 1970s, the Guys from Amur were at the height of their fame. There were about 200 people in the gang. They had cars, drugs, arms, influence. The heyday of the gang coincided (not by chance, as you will see) with the height of the Brezhnev era. They were the talk of all the city. Via the grapevine, everyone knew about their achievements. Many were inclined to think of the bandits as the only force which could contain the prospering crooks and dealers. The city militia at that time was very corrupt, and hopelessly unreliable. In fact, most of it was in the pocket of the Guys from Amur.

And if common people knew they had nothing to be afraid of, and even pronounced the word 'Matross' with a certain respect, the swarms of speculators, swindlers and other lokhs were terror-stricken. The very mention of the word 'Sailor' inspired animal fear in them. Oppressed by constant extortions, they were suffering insomnia and nervous break-downs. Tranquillisers didn't seem to help any longer. For hours on end, they lay looking through their windows into the thick darkness of a southern night. And as soon as they managed to catch a nap, they saw one and the same nightmare: Red Dimenstein's Zhiguli braking near their house, and brawny men in white shirts with knives and shotguns coming out to get them . . .

Some years ago, any citizen of our country who was planning to go abroad – even to a socialist State, and even for just a week as a tourist – was supposed to submit written character references from his or her place of work to the visa department of the militia. These references had to describe his qualities as a worker, and as a human being, and were signed by the so-called 'troika': the director, the Party secretary and the trade union leader. As a rule they were purely, sometimes even terribly formal. They were terribly hypocritical too.

Let us interrupt our narrative to quote from one such reference: 'Shows initiative and organisational abilities . . . Is able to co-ordinate his activities well and to solve all problems quickly . . . Politically mature, principled . . . Correctly understands and translates into life the policies of the Party . . . Is able both to educate the masses and to learn from them. Friendly with colleagues, responsive . . . Is capable of accepting criticism and drawing the necessary conclusions from it. Well balanced and persistent in reaching his aims. Energetic, neat, accurate, courteous, modest, self-demanding and disciplined. Well respected by the collect-ive . . . Communist-way worker. Good propagandist . . .' The signatures of the 'magic triangle' follow.

This glowing reference was given to Alexander Fyodorovich Mil-chenko, born in 1948, a worker at the trade machines repairs factory, for his trip to Bulgaria. Who is this man? A saint? And why do I quote this document so extensively?

Simply because Alexander Fyodorovich Milchenko, by the time he got the reference, had been the leader of the Amur bandits for many years. He was better known in Dnepropetrovsk as Matross, the Sailor.

Years later, the factory director, trying to justify himself to the investigators, would say that he had given good references to a bad man only because the latter was planning to go abroad . . . Sound logic indeed. Though in the director's shoes, I wouldn't totally disown my signature under this document. At least as to 'organisational abilities' and 'persistence in achieving his aims' the reference was completely true to fact. But it does require some additions.

Alexander Milchenko was born in the Caucasian town of Maikop, the eldest child in his family, which moved to Dnepropetrovsk soon after his birth. In school he did not do very well, and remained twice in the same class for a second year.*

After the Seventh form, Milchenko left his secondary school and went to PTU – a vocational school for training workers. There he was attracted by football, and soon, having shed all his learning by the side of the football pitch, he was playing for the Ukrainian Youth Team.

And here he suffers a split that is characteristic of our major sports, which were officially amateur, but in practice purely professional. In theory, he worked at a factory, but in reality he played football, appearing at his official place of work only to collect his salary. It was probably then that Milchenko came to believe that his exceptional status gave him the right to unearned money. He didn't like working, and didn't want to. 'Let the Turks work' was his favourite Ukrainian saying.

The invitation to play for Dnepropetrovsk Dnepr, the first division football club, was the peak of his soccer career and a test he did not pass. He was recognised in the streets of Dnepropetrovsk, and in his native Amur he became a real idol, with everyone eager to treat him to a beer or a vodka or even to some grass. In order not to upset his fans, Milchenko never refused. Beer, vodka and grass undermined his footballing skills, and soon he was thrown out of the team. His soccer career was ruined, but fame remained. For Amur, it was enough.

Very quickly Milchenko managed to unite round himself a flock of young bullies who desperately needed a ringleader. He was a born commander and craved for power. The young hoodlums started calling him 'Matross' – the 'Sailor'.

Why this nickname? Some say that once, when still a boy, Sasha (a diminutive of the name Alexander) went to the River Dnieper with some

---

*In the Soviet Union, a pupil who studies badly and gets bad marks during the year can be left in the same class for yet another course.

older boys who jokingly pushed him into the water, even though he couldn't swim. But Sasha did not drown. After some struggling and flailing the water with his pudgy little hands, he swam. From then on, the boys in Amur started calling him 'the Sailor'. There was a touch of a joke in this nickname, but it stuck.

His house was the only dwelling in Amur to have a telephone, which was installed with the help of an official letter signed by the same factory director. Addressed to the chief of the Dnepropetrovsk telephone exchange, this letter, contained the plea: 'In order to maintain the uninterrupted operation of the meat and dairy industries of Dnepropetrovsk region, we ask for the telephone to be installed at *engineer* [!] Milchenko's house.'

Strangely enough, even after the installation of the telephone in the house of the newly created engineer, the meat and dairy industries of the region continued to work in fits and starts. It was only the Sailor's gang that started operating smoothly. Thus the football forward had become the criminals' 'coach'.

When his last job at the factory started to annoy him and to stand in the way of his criminal activities, Milchenko quit. Since by Soviet law every healthy citizen must work, he decided to buy a certificate of mental handicap, and managed to do this rather quickly for 40,000 roubles.* Some of the leading city psychiatrists proved to be easily bought.

Several years later, when Matross was on trial, he was subjected to psychiatric examination at a Kharkov hospital and the legend of his lunacy was exploded. No matter how theatrically he sobbed on seeing a physician, and despite the hunger strikes he staged at the hospital (at night he made up for the daytime fasting by eating his food under the blankets), the Kharkov psychiatrists were not so easily misled (or bought) as their counterparts in Dnepropetrovsk. Matross was declared sane.

But this happened only some years after he obtained the certificate, and 90 roubles monthly invalid allowance to go with it. It was probably just with this pension – his official source of income – that he bought the luxury Volga sedan for 15,000 roubles, registering it thoughtfully in his mother's name. He acquired it from his friend and bodyguard Sultan Rakhmanov, the Olympic weight-lifting champion. His other bodyguard was the world amateur boxing champion Viktor Savchenko, who was sometimes taken on raids by the Amur Guys to act as a frightener. 'Look who's sitting there in the car,' they would say to a lokh, pointing at Savchenko, whose face was familiar to everyone in Dnepropetrovsk.

*In terms of comparison the average annual salary of a *Krokodil* journalist is no more than 3,000 roubles a year.

With bodyguards like these, Matross no longer had to strive to be physically fit. He grew obese and domineering. Every week he used to collect his closest henchmen for a conference in a sauna establishment. Every other day he frequented restaurants and cafés.

There is a smallish café popularly known as 'Skovorodka' (The Frying Pan) near Dnepropetrovsk Central Market. Roasted meat is served there in sizzling frying-pans. I got into conversation with its manager.

'Sasha knew how to relax,' he told me. 'When he entered the café all his boys stood up and no one started eating until he gave the word . . . he was always the first to taste the meat from the frying-pan. If someone got there before him, the guys would throw him out of the café. And Matross, being fastidious, wouldn't eat from that frying-pan again.'

In his criminal methods, he was not so fastidious. Remember poor Varnavsky standing at the edge of a vacant grave with a withered wreath around his neck. And it was not unusual for Matross to order his boys to throw an obstinate lokh into a dark cellar swarming with rats. The Sailor knew no clemency. He could do to a crook anything short of killing him. 'Thou shalt not kill' was a commandment he very much respected, though being an ordinary Soviet man Matross was probably hardly aware of the existence of the Bible, nor was he a believer in any God but Mammon. Yet his boys had never murdered anyone, even when crooks driven to desperation retaliated by murdering them. The reason? You will soon find out.

II

While researching into the Sailor's activities, I kept being reminded of Mario Puzo's novel *The Godfather*. Matross definitely hadn't read it, though he could if he wished, since the novel was published in the Ukraine at the end of the Seventies by the Kievian monthly *Vsesvit* (The World). The Ukrainian version was for some linguistic (or rather censorial) reasons much shorter than the original, but the resemblance between Puzo's Italo-American gangsters and the Guys from Amur is striking. The American mafiosi were equally devoted family men. They had the same strong team spirit and were similarly ingenious in their crimes.

As for Matross himself, he had certain features in common with the quiet and reasonable Don Corleone. Like him, his favourite verb was 'to reason'; like him, he had created a kind of criminal brotherhood. At first (I stress, only at first), the Guys from Amur were always together, in battle and in leisure, at wedding parties and at funerals.

Among the photographs which I managed to obtain in Dnepropetrovsk is one of the wedding of Yaryoma, one of the gangsters from Amur. The newlyweds are surrounded by smiling hoodlums. Third from the left is Matross in a white shirt with a large collar. On the left of the bride is our friend Shapa – 'the Minister of Strange Affairs' in Matross's 'government', the one in charge of ruthless enforcement by threats and beatings. Here is the Gnat (first from the right sitting), Cabbage-Head (first from the left standing) and other guys. Among them are some girls. No prostitutes whatsoever, just busty Ukrainian working girls from the suburb. Everyone is happy, everyone is smiling. This photo was taken in the mid-Seventies when the gang was just starting. Its evolution is evident from the other wedding photograph taken several years later. On it, the guys and the girls are looking much more bossy and self-confident. Matross's hand with the heavy ring is resting on his wife's shoulder. Shapa, with his face scarred by a razor blade, is standing nearby. Viktor Savchenko is squatting in the foreground. It is clear from the photo that the guys had won many battles which had made them tougher and more brash.

There is another photo which I did not succeed in getting hold of – I only saw it in the album. It is a family portrait of the Milchenkos, taken in their house. The interior is plush: carpets, Victorian chairs with spiral-turned legs. On the Sailor's shoulder is his little baby daughter; his blonde, beautiful wife is standing beside him. Igor, his teenage son, neatly dressed and well combed, is also there, looking good as gold and resembling a youthful Komsomol leader. In fact, he could have become one if it were not for his early addiction to drugs . . .

One more detail that made Matross resemble Mario Puzo's Godfather was the clan system. Don Corleone's sons followed their father's criminal path – it was a tradition of La Cosa Nostra. So Sailor's son Igor, aged sixteen, gathered a flock of teenagers around himself, and despite being the youngest of the gang, became its leader. He was nicknamed Matrosyonok – little Matross – and his gang members were 'matrossyata' – little sailors.

Igor's gang was engaged in what you might call mini-racketeering. Like their elders, they extorted money from wealthy lokhs. Their demands were a little lower though: they counted their loot not in thousands like the Guys from Amur, but in hundreds. But the message was the same.

The youthful gang even boasted the Soviet Union's first female racketeer. Her name was Natasha and she was Igor's girlfriend. She was clever, thin, pretty and quickly found her place in the gang. She would break into a wealthy crook's flat with a hammer – alone! – and would start smashing everything around her until the occupier coughed up. So persistent and beautiful was she in her anger under the influence of drugs, that no one could resist her. Later on, she tried to sue me for libel when I named her in my novel. But I won the lawsuit.

The Sailor's clan was far from the only one in Amur. The sons of several other bandits (Shapa, for example) also had gangs of their own.

'Where am I?' Anzor Avetisyan separated his leaden lids with an effort. A hangover was playing snooker in his head. He was lying on the back seat of his own Zhiguli parked opposite the city's main department store. Anzor had never been inside the store, since he bought everything on the black market. Now his cream-coloured Belgian suit was as rumpled as if he'd slept not in a car but in a washing machine.

Anzor was frantically trying to recollect the previous evening. This was not an easy thing to do: a black hole was gaping in his memory. After half and hour of feverish attempts he recalled just one word 'Rama' – 'the frame'.

Rama was a colloquial name for the bar of the Icicle café.

Trying not to extinguish this tiny spark of recollection he started his car and carefully drove it to Rama. On the way he struggled frenziedly not to hit the kerb, since some unknown force was constantly dragging him to the right. He was not afraid of the GAI – the road militia – where he had good connections . . .

He went warily into the bar, prepared for any surprise.

Barman Lona (Pecurovoski) was counting money at the cash desk. The second barman Chertok was sitting at the counter sipping coffee.

These two had directed the previous day's performance, also starring Avetisyan. They had put a sleeping powder in his drink, and when he passed out they had bundled him into his Zhiguli and driven him to the department store car park. The second act of the performance was to follow.

'Here he comes, the poor gambler.' Lona greeted Anzor without looking up from the cash-desk. He didn't even stretch out his hand in greeting.

'He must have brought the debt,' Chertok added sardonically.

'Guys, w-w-what happened yesterday?' Anzor went stiff with apprehension.

'The less you drink the more you earn,' Lona remarked didactically. 'Here, have the hair of the dog – it's on me – and try to remember.'

118

He poured some vodka into an empty glass and gave it to Anzor. This gesture of generosity frightened Anzor even more. 'If Lona offers you a free drink, it means he's up to something', he thought, but took the glass nevertheless.

'Stop playing host,' Chertok grumbled to Lona. 'Let him bring the money first.'

'Yeah, Anzor, when are you going to pay your debt?'

'W-what debt?' Avetisyan choked on his vodka. His question sounded as a night-time phone call in an empty office.

'There he goes again!' Chertok feigned indignation. 'How much did he lose in the card game yesterday?'

Lona produced a sheet of paper crumpled as if chewed by someone and spattered with brown brandy spots. It was covered with spidery scribbling.

'Thirty-nine thousand six hundred roubles,' he declared, pretending to tot up the sheet. 'As little as that.'

'By God, fellows, I didn't play, I swear,' Avetisyan implored, but Chertok interrupted him:

'If the two of us agree you played it means you played,' he pronounced solemnly, then took the suspicious piece of paper from Lona, tore it into shreds and threw them in Anzor's face.

Avetisyan took his curly head in his hands and moaned: 'Oh God, they've double-crossed me . . .' Suddenly he had a distinct recollection of Lona giving him a glass of something. He downed it – and darkness fell . . .

In the back of his mind Anzor had been expecting to be fleeced by the Sailor's boys. His friends, the dealers, had told him a lot about the merciless racketeering Amur guys. 'It's useless to resist them,' they would say. 'One way or another they'll get what they want. It's better just to pay on the spot.' If it was only a question of three to five thousand roubles, he would have paid up. But nearly forty thousand – and not to Matross himself, but to small frys like these two barmen . . . Out of the question.

To be frank, Anzor had the forty thousand roubles, and even more. Much more . . . Later the prosecution would maintain that he had embezzled about half a million roubles from the State. Anzor's business was quite an unusual one. In his motor shop he sold glass cleaning fluid in place of methylated spirit. These two substances look and smell alike, but they differ substantially in price: glass-cleaner costs twenty copecks a litre, methylated spirit one rouble. Calculate for yourselves, my readers. Anzor subdued his remorse at cheating with the thought that as a drink, the glass-cleaner's taste and bouquet were very similar to those of methylated spirit – or so said the alcoholics who had tasted both. Besides, as the Romans said 'Non olet' – money doesn't smell.

All the same, Anzor wasn't going to give away forty thousand roubles to just anyone. He wasn't that simple . . . 'I'll give them three "things",' he thought, 'then they'll probably leave me alone.' He searched through his suit and produced about three thousand roubles in pocket money . . .

'Too little!' Lona said, when he finished counting.

Subsequent events developed as follows. Seeking protection against Lona and Chertok, Anzor approached the Sailor. 'Matross is a reasonable man,' his friends assured him. 'He won't allow such an outrage.'

'Be reasonable,' Matross told Avetisyan, and demanded ten thousand roubles, promising to speak to the barmen and settle the whole affair.

On learning this, Lona and Chertok approached the Boar and the Greek, who had broken away from Matross some time before. They promised these two a big slice of the profits for their help in beating forty thousand roubles out of Avetisyan.

When the Sailor and the Boar ran into each other in a restaurant called the Dnepropetrovsk, they got into an argument, but then made a quick peace and developed a plan of coordinated action. Poor Avetisyan found himself caught between two fires.

Having paid ten thousand to Matross for his peace of mind Avetisyan came to Rama, where he had been invited by Lona over the telephone. There, besides the barmen, he found the Boar, the Greek and two of the Sailor's men – Rickets and Stas.

'Begin!' the Greek commanded, and waved his hand.

Under the impact of the Boar's blow, Avetisyan opened the cellar door with his head. The second blow sent him rolling down the stairs. Down there, he took a severe kicking and was beaten with boards, bottles, empty crates. Half dead, and barely conscious, he heard someone exclaim: 'Finish him off!' Only then did he whisper. 'Don't. I'll pay . . .'

The execution stopped immediately. Anzor was dragged upstairs to the bar, and they poured a glass of cognac down his throat. And here the businessman saw a grinning Matross standing in the doorway and watching him with keen professional interest – a similar interest appears in the eyes of a prostitute leafing through a porno-magazine. Only now did Anzor realise the full extent of the plot: that now he had to say goodbye not only to the ten thousand given to the Sailor, but to the original forty thousand as well. 'One way or another, they'll get what they want' – his friends had proved quite right.

This episode didn't end with Anzor's forcible contribution. When he learned that Lona and Chertok had had three thousand roubles out of

The first year of my life.

Celebrating 7
November at a rally
in Kharkov, the
Ukraine, 1961.

With my mother at a
puppet theatre in
Kharkov, 1961.

Aged seven, 1961.

RIGHT: Writing at my dacha, 1984.

BELOW: National Service at the Military Training Centre, 1975: I'm the one with the cigarette . . .

My father, Vladimir.

RIGHT: At a Press Conference with colleagues, 1983 (Ch 3).

A Soviet Black Market, this one in Moscow, 1981 (Ch 5).

A typical Soviet Court in session (Ch 5).

The Guys from Amur at Yaryoma's wedding, 1979 (Ch 6).

Matross's 'Volga', acquired for him by an ex-Soviet Olympic weightlifting champion (Ch 6).

Yaryoma's wedding party:
Matross is third from
right, Shapa in the middle,
1976 (Ch 6).

An example of the much-
hated hard currency
berioska shops (Ch 7).

A gunman takes aim (Ch 5).

The art of queuing: a typical Leningrad food queue (Ch 7).

The memorial commemorating those killed by the Germans during the Second World War outside Leningrad: it has been vandalised by modern Leningrad Nazis, 1988 (Ch 8).

Special Correspondent, Vitali Vitaliev, at work in Moscow.

Avetisyan in the beginning and hadn't informed him, Matross grew furious, and when he remembered how they had tried to turn the Boar against him, he lost his temper and decided to put the screws on his personal barman Chertok. Together with Marmura he walked into the Icicle and said to Chertok: 'Bring me two "things", Boris, and mind, I don't ask twice.'

Chertok knew Matross too well to hold out, but not wishing to be the loser he decided to turn against his friend, barman Davidenkov. Together with the Boar and the Greek, he beat Davidenkov unconscious in his bar, The Malachite Box, took the whole of the day's takings and fled.

All these events marked the next stage in the evolution of the gang. The Amur 'brotherhood' created in the old days was coming apart: the left hand didn't know what the right hand was doing. The Sailor's men tore up their former rules, and the absence of norms became the only norm. To get money by all possible means – that was the only principle from now on. Friends and foes became interchangeable, as in a bad spy thriller. Having gained the support of the city's militia and élite, Matross lost his legendary sense of 'justice' and came down upon his own gang members: Chertok, the Pole and others. All hell broke loose.

Such lack of principles made the Amur Guys no different from dealers, their alleged enemies. The latter had long ago shed any moral inhibitions. Avetisyan, robbed and beaten by the gangsters, remained friendly with the Guys from Amur in spite of this. Once he even asked the Sailor to help him to cool off some nosy militia investigators who had grown suspicious of his glass-cleaner business. He gave Matross ten thousand roubles for that, and the matter was settled, though the Sailor in fact didn't give a rouble to the militia: he simply telephoned his best friend – the chief of the Dnepropetrovsk Militia Department.

In the course of time the gangsters and the dealers came to resemble each other more and more – just as two brothers, different in appearance in childhood, may get more and more alike as they grow older.

The methods of extortion also evolved. No more elaborate schemes, card games, exquisite cheating. No more 'quiet' style. Torture, terror and blackmail came in their stead.

One lokh was tortured with a hot iron. Another paid extortion money under threat of seeing his house blown up and his baby daughter's head battered against the wall. There was a tragic case when the Guys from Amur victimised one of their former friends – a thief with a long criminal record. He had just come out of prison having made up his mind to get married and go straight. The Sailor's Guys didn't let him: they demanded twelve thousand roubles of an alleged debt. Under their pressure the recent jailbird had to rob a wealthy tsekhovik to raise the money and wound up in prison again. It is interesting to record that this underground factory owner stored his loot at his summer cottage under the fifth brick from the left in the fourteenth row from the top. If you pressed this brick, it sprang out and exposed the hiding place with stacks of banknotes.

So now the Boys from Amur were not only preying on each other, they were spawning new crimes, and eventually the inevitable happened: unable to keep up with the Sailor's growing despotism, the dealers realised that no one could help them but themselves. The first sign of resistance came quite unexpectedly.

One summer night in 1979 a group of gangsters broke into the flat of a dental technician. They pointed their pistols at his chest and demanded the gold which he was supposed to possess.

No one knows what prompted the technician's actions. Maybe he had no gold at that moment, or maybe he just lost his temper, but the fact is that he grabbed a kitchen knife and stabbed one of the robbers, the Pickpocket. For some reason the rest of the gang did not attack the technician, they just took their bleeding comrade and left in a hurry. They had strict orders from Matross not to use weapons under any circumstances, probably as a result of the Sailor's deal with one of his high-ranking militia friends. 'No murders which could mean trouble for me, no problems for you and your boys' – that's how the conversation may have sounded.

The stabbed gangster died. For a fortnight the technician didn't dare to leave his flat, certain that the Sailor's revenge was bound to strike. But the Guys from Amur never came. Revenge never came. Matross didn't like making much ado about anything. Besides he was tied by his deal with the militia. He threw a luxurious funeral for the fallen comrade, when the bandits marched along the main street of Amur dressed in black suits and white shirts and holding the coffin in their outstretched hands. Matross followed the procession in his luxury Volga.

Rumours of the brave technician's feat spread all over the city, reaching bars, markets and underground factories. A month later two of the gang who had come to extort money from a bar were met with axes and killed. The barman and his two brothers also thought that Matross would be back. They started buying arms on the black market and formed their own resistance unit. Matross didn't touch them either.

My readers often ask me if the valiant technician and the barman were brought to court for murder. No, they were not. And I can give the assurance that if by any chance (fingers crossed) your house is broken into at night (or even in the daytime) by several (or even one) armed robbers (or robber) you can do with them (or with him) anything you like. You won't be prosecuted, believe me. At least not in the Soviet Union . . .

In 1978 in Dnepropetrovsk there was a battle. Some of the locals still remember it well, though there is no official record. It took some effort to find any witnesses, but find them I did. It was from their accounts that I reconstructed the episode.

The clash was between the men from Amur and the so-called Caucasian mafia who traditionally control the local markets. The cause was that the Sailor's people had tricked a Caucasian bicho (this means 'boy' in Georgian) into the 'birth-year bet.' When he lost and refused to pay, they called some of their faithful militiamen and had him arrested. The proud, touchy and well organised Caucasian mafiosi couldn't stand for such an insult. They called in support from all over the country. The Moscow and Leningrad 'Dons' came to Dnepropetrovsk in Volgas and Mercedes, bringing their soldiers with them.

A small stretch of the Dnieper embankment outside the Dnepropetrovsk Hotel was chosen as a battleground. Fighters from both sides, armed with automatic weapons, lay behind the parked cars and the parapet. An exchange of shots followed, until the firing was stopped by Matross himself, who hurried to the battleground to make peace. The 'Peace Treaty' was signed at a Chile-length table in the Dnepropetrovsk Hotel restaurant. A silver tray passed around and the boys and the bichos threw banknotes onto it. The collection was invested in bribing the arrested Caucasian out of the hands of the militia.

There was another case of organised resistance to the Guys from Amur when they decided to extend their influence beyond Dnepropetrovsk. They had had some experience of racketeering in other towns, but those were just small episodes. Now a posse of bandits took the bus to Krivoi Rog, the second largest city in the Dnepropetrovsk region, with a population of about 800,000 and a large mining industry. They came back battered and bruised, when they tried to harass local people at a bar and were thrown out not only from the bar but from the city too by local toughs. Adding insult to injury (in the literal sense of the word), the Sailor's house was fired at a couple of times during the night and his famous Volga car was burnt by unknown assailants.

Matross would not have made a gang-leader without his strategic brain. He quickly grasped the danger of the situation. It was senseless and even dangerous to fight the dealers any longer – this could lead only to further financial losses and casualties. His boys, tough as they were, couldn't overcome organised resistance: they themselves were no longer as friendly and united as they used to be. So Matross began to seek an alliance with the most powerful illegal operators – the tsekhoviks. This bunch had appeared in Dnepropetrovsk on the threshold of the Eighties and was gaining power quickly. The tsekhoviks' small underground factories produced fake Western jeans and T-shirts, knick-knacks, plastic bags, and so on. These were passed off as imported goods and sold at enormous prices. The business flourished and soon the tsekhoviks – representatives of the so-called shadow economy – became much better-off than the ordinary cheating shop-assistants and barmen. They probably had more money that Matross himself. It was with them that the head of the Dnepropetrovsk racketeers – the man who started off as the hater of profiteers – decided to make friends.

There is a children's joke: two swollen, sated bed-bugs met on the wall above the bed. 'Let's make friends!' the first suggested. 'But what have we got in common?' the second one asked. 'Don't you understand? We are of the same blood!'

The Amur Wars could have only one possible result – the alliance of gangsters and tsekhoviks – since, if we think of it, they shared the same blood, the blood of common Soviet citizens. Both were parasitic on society at the expense of ordinary workers, peasants, intellectuals. So what if the gangsters had damaged the 'businessmen' in the past? The black marketeers paid off the racketeers with money stolen from someone else's pockets. These thousands of roubles were made up of swindles, thieving and deceits. They were fleeced from the people in return for ersatz jeans and shirts, fake Western plastic bags – that is for clumsy imitations of those products not yet mastered by the Soviet economy, which is good enough to produce spacecraft but fails to provide the population with decent trousers, or plastic bags strong enough not to come apart under the weight of a matchbox.

The symbiosis of gangsters and 'businessmen' typical of any mafia was gradual. It so happened that the Boar and the Greek, who had rejoined the Guys from Amur after the 'operation' on Avetisyan, got interested in an underground manufacturer of plastic bags called Ostorozhenko. Old habits die hard, and the bandits occasionally felt nostalgic for their former ingenious methods. They took several Ostorozhenko-made fake Western plastic bags and put them into the tsekhovik's storage shed, standing in his courtyard. The bags were made of stolen Soviet raw materials but were covered with foreign inscriptions – 'Ku-Klux-Klan', 'King Kong', 'Demis Roussos' and the like. On each bag there was a blurred face which was so badly printed that it was not clear whether it belonged to King

Kong or to Demis Roussos. The face together with the foreign lettering usually came off after the first rain and left dirty grey patches on the plastic surface.

Having planted the bags in the shed, the Boar and the Greek caught up with Ostorozhenko in a pub and said: 'We bet you a thousand roubles there are bags with faces in your shed.'

The manufacturer fell for it, and was promptly forced into a Zhiguli and given a lift to the shed. Never before had Ostorozhenko looked at his own products with such repugnance. The gargoyle of a face seemed to be grinning at him from the bags, as if to say: 'What a fool you are!'

'So you owe us a "thing",' the gangsters said, leaving Ostorozhenko face to face with King Kong–Roussos. Since he was in no hurry to pay, a week later the Boar and the Greek met him in a deserted street and expertly broke his jaw. So Ostorozhenko paid his 'debt' straight after having been discharged from hospital.

This 'jaw operation' was applauded by the bigger tsekhoviks Razin and Sevagin, also engaged in the plastic bags business. They were happy with their competitor's loss, and decided to trace the gangsters and make them their allies.

They made some inquiries and found out that the Guys from Amur had recently blackmailed such big-shot tsekhoviks as Guzhenko and Goldin. Guzhenko had been grilled into talking about his underground business in a restaurant. His revelations were tape-recorded and the tape became the gangsters' trump card in extortion. Goldin was threatened with a slander campaign in 'business' circles and agreed to buy the bandits two Mercedes cars in exchange for his 'spotless' reputation. Razin and Sevagin liked these methods. They wanted to make the bandits their bodyguards and to use them as a weapon against their rivals.

To begin with, they asked the Amur Guys to collect a fine from their former colleague Shwarts, who had recently founded his own 'firm' and was trying to compete with them. They said Shwarts had stolen a big consignment of plastic bags from them and promised the Sailor's Boys a percentage. (In fact, Shwarts did steal fifty roubles' worth of plastic bags, but the 'fine' he was supposed to pay for that amounted to five thousand roubles – one hundred times more.) The Boar and Dimenstein invited Shwarts in to Razin's car and took him on a guided (or rather guarded) tour around the city. The trip might have been a pleasant excursion for Shwarts if the thugs had not been brandishing an axe in front of his face, with remarks such as: 'Pay up or we'll break your backbone.' Razin and Sevagin sat on the back seat and assisted by alternating reasonable interventions with the gangsters threats. The tour ended in a dark echoing gateway, where the thugs proceeded from words to actions. Beating Shwarts mercilessly with whatever came to hand, Dimenstein kept repeating: 'I'm ruthless with people who don't obey my orders.'

Razin and Sevagin watched from a safe distance – who knows what might occur to these gangsters? 'You'd better pay, you'd better pa-ay-ay!!!' they kept wailing. This whining was almost as bad for Shwarts as the thugs' own blows. He couldn't stand it any longer and gave away a thousand roubles. Both the bandits and the tsekhoviks understood that this was the maximum they could squeeze out of the close-fisted Shwarts. The sum was shared fairly among the Guys from Amur and the 'businessmen'. This was the beginning of their long friendship, and a new phrase crept into the local tsekhoviks' jargon – 'to switch the bandits' ie to call gangsters for help. So you see they had no illusions as to whom they 'switched'. The formerly independent Amur Guys had turned into some sort of strong-arm assistants to tsekhoviks. And for their part they had no longer to waste their time searching for a wealthy lokh: they were put on the track of one tsekhovik by another. Nevertheless, to give some 'credit' to the gangsters, they did not renege on the principle of thou shalt not kill, though the tsekhoviks often incited them to murder. It is a good illustration of the point that the crooked businessmen were still less morally bound than the gangsters themselves.

There came a moment when a real boss was singled out from the ranks of Dnepropetrovsk's black marketeers. He was a former photographer by the name of Arkady Semyonovich Vokal. Photography had not made him a fortune, so he started a much more profitable line, an underground factory to produce fake crystal. It was made of ordinary glass. Glass knick-knacks were sold in sleepy Ukrainian small towns under the name of rock crystal. The only thing about them remotely connected with rocks was their mountainous price.

Vokal was also involved in plastic bag production and in the manufacture of large quantities of drawers-type pants, peddled to provincial dandies and fashion-crazy dowdies as Western-made jeans or baggy 'bananas' – depending on the demand.

But the main capital to elevate him above rank-and-file status Vokal gained by the production of carpets, which were then in very short supply. In Dnepropetrovsk he established a clandestine workshop where old flannelette blankets were miraculously turned into new 'Persian' carpets, stencil-printed with elaborate 'oriental' patterns.

When Vokal felt that his workshop was not safe enough in Dnepropetrovsk he transferred it to the town of Chernigov, where it occupied the cellar of Public Bath Number Two. The perspiring bathers upstairs could not imagine that right underneath, Vokal's employees were making lots of money for their boss with no less sweat.

After his arrest both his Volga and Zhiguli cars (the rarest phenomenon in this country) were confiscated from Vokal, and his wife was deprived of rings worth 15,000 and 10,000 roubles, ear-rings worth 8,000, a 3,500 rouble gold chain, and much, much more. By that time Vokal had prudently divorced her and married a sixty-year-old Muscovite (he was forty-two). Her Moscow registration was the most appealing feature of his new wife: in fear of arrest, Vokal had decided to become a Muscovite himself. (The same marriage-escape to Moscow was undertaken by Matross when the militia started to investigate him in earnest. Kindred souls!) His Moscow marriage did not stop Vokal from leaving his elderly sweetheart for periodical reunions with her younger predecessor at the seaside resort of Sochi.

In the long run Vokal was sentenced to death for the embezzlement of two million roubles. (Don't worry: he wasn't executed and in five years' time he was released altogether – I'll come back to this in a moment.) But in the meantime he continued to drive his two cars – the Volga on even dates and the Zhiguli on odd ones, just for a change. He also enjoyed unanimous respect not only among restaurant and market managers but also among some of the city's fathers. Suffice it to say that he called P. Stuzhuk, the Dnepropetrovsk militia chief, 'Dad', though they were not related. But then business ties often prove stronger than family ones.

Matross too was friendly with Stuzhuk, and though he did not call him 'Dad', he never missed an opportunity to kiss the city's militia chief in public, Brezhnev-style. It goes without saying that Matross and Vokal had a lot in common. Moving steadily towards each other from opposite directions, they were destined to meet, and so they did, like two fat bugs on the wall. 'Let's make friends!' bug Vokal suggested. 'But what have we in common?' bug Matross asked. 'Don't you understand? We be of one blood, thou and I.'

These words by Kipling became the motto of the alliance between gangsters and tsekhoviks. The two bugs – the two bosses – had reached the summits of power and prosperity. Like two superpowers in the nuclear era, they couldn't afford confrontation.

Matross began investing his racket money in the profitable Vokal enterprises. Having become one of his principal 'stockholders', he then forbade his boys to interfere with tsekhoviks and members of Vokal's clan. 'If someone touches you or your people, just give me a ring, I'll reason with him,' Matross advised Vokal trustingly.

This was the end of the Amur Wars. But not the end of the Dnepropetrovsk mafia.

The main weapon against the mafia all over the world, as I have already said, is openness, truth, glasnost'. Mafia abhors all these. To have a full picture, let us recall that at the beginning of the Eighties in Dnepropetrovsk the dealers, the gangsters, the city militia and some members of the authorities merged into one unique Soviet criminal organisation, a real Palermo-like mafia.

As to the dealers and the gangsters all is clear. But what about the militia and 'some members of the authorities'? It is here that many questions arise. Some have remained unanswered to this day.

When the team from the Ministry of the Interior came to Dnepropetrovsk to look into the Sailor's activities, no one would help them. On the contrary: the investigators were harassed, their hotel rooms searched, and they were watched and followed. Three times they arrested Matross and each time he was miraculously set free. His criminal case was started twelve times and eleven times the prosecution was stopped.

There was a man in Dnepropetrovsk who had started to fight Matross as early as 1976. Practically alone and at his own risk, he opened a file on the Sailor and began collecting evidence. This courageous man is D. R. Adamov, the former chief of the city's Criminal Investigation Department. Why former? Because shortly after Matross's final arrest he was relieved of his post with no plausible explanation. He remains unable to find a job with the militia, receives constant threats over the phone and has recently suffered a severe heart attack. He is absolutely worn out now, and sometimes when he telephones me in Moscow he starts sobbing uncontrollably over the phone.

For many years the Dnepropetrovsk militia and the procurator's office had been turning a deaf ear to all complaints about the Guys from Amur. No wonder: almost all of them had been bribed by Matross.

Some militia were bought quite cheap. The deputy head of the Zhovtnevi district militia, Barvina, was bribed by the Boar with the watch 'Orient'. The senior investigator from the Babushkinsky district militia, Sakharov, was happy with a 500-rouble back-hander from the Greek. The witty gangster stuffed the banknotes into a volume of the Criminal Code of the Ukrainian republic, on the page containing the article on 'bribe-taking', and gave it to the corrupt militiaman. There were many similar examples of bribery, so it becomes even clearer why the battered Shwarts and some other racketeer targets who ventured to ask the militia for protection met with a cool reception and no help.

Back to Stuzhuk, the city's militia chief and the friend of Vokal and Matross. There was a photograph in existence that showed Matross kissing Stuzhuk at the airport. The militia leader, just back from the Ministry of the Interior session, was met off the plane by the leader of the city's gangsters. 'What's the news at the Ministry?' he probably asked. Then they kissed to the stupid tradition initiated by Brezhnev, who wass in the habit of kissing passionately on the lips every foreign statesman arriving in Moscow.

Several people (Adamov among them) saw this historic photograph with their own eyes. But after the Sailor's arrest it vanished into thin air, together with the Sailor's file on the militia. The devious gangster had every bought militiaman listed there. Where did these documents go? Another unanswered question.

Now we can only guess who was on the Sailor's list. It is highly probable that it included the deputy chairman of the regional court, Boganets; the deputy head of the regional militia department, Tokar; the chiefs of the city and regional fraud squads, Bilik and Zdelnik; and many more. And shortly after Matross was arrested another deputy head of the regional militia department, Kovalenko, hanged himself in his flat. The reasons are still unknown. Though perhaps one can guess.

Matross was detained by members of the Moscow investigation team disguised as GAI – highway militia. Drunk and self-confident as he sat behind the wheel of his Volga, he refused to believe his eyes when he was stopped. 'You are asking for trouble, boys!' the Godfather shouted. 'Your boss is my best friend. I drink with him every day!' But this first time the militia people were not frightened away and the mafioso was hand-cuffed . . .

We have seen that this was not the last time the members of the special team had to arrest Matross. So who, or what, kept springing Matross out of prison? For the main part it was probably his sea-chest full of money. Guess how much money was confiscated from him after his arrests. Fifteen roubles and seventy-three copecks, that was all! And I am sure that his real capital after so many years of successful racketeering amounted to at least a million roubles. Where did all the money go? No one knows for sure, but again one can guess.

Instead of money, an interesting notebook was found in the Sailor's house. Matross had kept his accounts in it. The entries read: '1,000 roubles to Vadim, 1,000 roubles to me when all calms down . . .' '1,200 – when quiet . . .'; '1,250 roubles to each . . .'; '22,000 from Avetisyan . . .' and so on and so forth. Against the background of all these thousands, fifteen roubles and seventy-three copecks look like a bad joke . . .

The Sailor's connections were not limited to Dnepropetrovsk. He was somehow able to free convicts from other Ukrainian prisons, which meant that he had considerable influence in Kiev. He was also treading water with some top bureaucrats in Moscow. Living in Dnepropetrovsk, he could nevertheless appoint and dismiss managers at some of Moscow's prestigious shops.

There is a militia term, 'operational data', meaning information obtained by the militia through their own channels but not well-enough grounded to serve as evidence in court, and derived from confidential sources. Being unable to disclose some of this data, I can only urge you to believe that Matross had connections in the highest echelons of power, and many of his high-ranking patrons are still at their posts. This becomes self-evident if you remember the persecution of Adamov, and the tragic fate of other honest militiamen who were active in combating Matross. Some of them were sacked, others had to transfer from Dnepropetrovsk to other cities, or were demoted.

And how else can you account for the fact that the first two 'Amur Wars' issues of *Krokodil* were not put on sale in Dnepropetrovsk at all? On the black market there they were going for thirty roubles apiece (remember the State price is thirty copecks), and our editorial office was getting worried cables from Dnepropetrovsk readers. So we had to inform the CPSU Central Committee of the strange (to put it mildly) attitude to our magazine on the part of the Dnepropetrovsk authorities. Only then did the third and fourth issues with the story appear on Dnepropetrovsk newsstands, although the first two still did not.

Who could issue an order not to sell the magazine? It was far beyond the powers of the militia. Such an instruction could originate only from the regional Party Committee.

The trial of Matross and Co. was also rather peculiar. For some time no judge would volunteer to preside over the case. Eventually there appeared a young 'dare-devil', a recent graduate of the Kharkov Law Institute, whose name was Leontiev. For a week before the hearing started he was guarded day and night by two armed militia men. The trial was closed to the public and the building where it took place was ringed by militia. The witnesses were searched and X-rayed before they were allowed into the courtroom and the whole case was conducted in an atmosphere of utter secrecy. *Cui bono?* Who was to benefit from this? You can make your own judgement.

Matross is serving his twelve year sentence not far from his native Amur, though according to the regulations he ought to have been sent somewhere in Siberia. There is evidence that he and his comrades are 'sitting pretty' (to 'sit' in Russian has a colloquial meaning of 'being in prison'). They do not labour as hard as other prisoners and they receive much better nourishment. After my novel was published they were deprived of their illegal privileges. But somehow this doesn't sound that reassuring.

III

At this point the reader may ask: why Dnepropetrovsk? Wasn't the same thing happening in other cities and towns? It probably was. But on a smaller scale. Among other cities that come to mind are Leningrad, Moscow, and Krivoi Rog, the town in the Dnepropetrovsk region where the Guys from Amur were thrown out by local bullies. This large mining city could boast of its own 'Guys' – members of a gang comprising militia officers and headed by Captain Kosyuk, the chief of the district militia duty force. During the day these uniformed gangsters were in charge of law and public order; at night-time they removed their masks and themselves became robbers and burglars. They attacked people in the streets, they robbed banks. The gang was armed not only with pistols and rifles but with machine-guns too.

Still the Dnepropetrovsk regions was special. Being Brezhnev's 'patrimony' and the place from which he traditionally recruited his closest supporters, it was above criticism from the press. It was very important for Brezhnev's henchmen to maintain the image of Dnepropetrovsk as an exemplary city in the eyes of 'our beloved Leonid Ilyich', who was notorious for taking things at their face value. I remember writing a piece about the shortage of some important goods like electric bulbs and socks in Dnepropetrovsk shops at that time. I was trying to be funny, and joked that when you have no electric light you can easily do without your socks: no one will notice. The article never saw the light of day. No editor in his right mind would venture to criticise the native city of 'our great leader'.

The same was true of the militia and government inspectorates from Kiev and Moscow. In order not to spoil the image, they were simply not sent to Dnepropetrovsk. Until the Matross investigation, the Soviet Ministry of the Interior had not sent a single inspection team there for fourteen years!

Some time after the nucleus of the Sailor's gang was liquidated, the city militia headquarters started receiving numerous telephone calls from the United States, Australia and other Western countries. The former 'victims' of the Guys from Amur were calling – dealers, tsekhoviks and others who had emigrated to the West for only one reason, to save themselves from constant extortion. 'Is it true that the Sailor's gang is done for?' they would ask. 'Has Soviet power really come back to Dnepropetrovsk? Maybe we should return?'

The emigrant callers were right about one thing: under Brezhnev there was actually no Soviet power in Dnepropetrovsk. There was the Sailor's power, the mafia's power, instead. Indeed the Guys from Amur used to have their own 'prosecution' and 'court'. They had their own 'procurator of Amur' – a gangster nicknamed Glaz (the Eye). Together with Matross he selected potential targets for the racketeers and pronounced 'verdicts'. A criminal's GLAZnost' . . .

'Milchenko was an extraordinary character,' I was told by Major Serebrennikov, the head of the special investigation team. 'He knew the Criminal Code well enough to establish his own code of conduct. He was a good psychologist too, and knew the rules of arbitration, pretending to be a champion of justice. In fact his unlimited authority was based on two cornerstones – money and fear. A person like that was bound to find himself at the very top of the criminal hierarchy. But of course he wouldn't have been able to climb that high if he hadn't been supported in his rise to power.'

What was the upshot of the 'Amur Wars'? Major Serebrennikov got a government award and was promoted to lieutenant colonel. I received an honorary diploma from the USSR Union of Journalists and a watch from the Minister of the Interior. This watch is ticking on my left wrist as I write, and reminds me that life goes on. The immediate results of the publication were less positive. As usual I was flooded with readers' letters, some of which contained nothing but threats and curses. It was only natural: a number of Amur Guys were arrested as a direct result of the story. I still felt at times a dull ache in my shoulder – the reminder of a Dnepropetrovsk encounter . . . There were also a couple of telephone calls of the type that say: 'Do you know whose toes you're treading on? Look out!'

I had several strange visitors at my office. One of them, a woman, had been asking for an appointment for over a month. I was very busy at that time and couldn't see her. She kept insisting that she knew something very important about the Guys from Amur. She came from Dnepro-petrovsk, as was evident even by phone, because of her distinct southern Ukrainian accent. In the end we fixed a meeting on a day when I had to see lots of visitors. I was just finishing with the granddaughter of the famous

Russian poet Sergei Yesenin. She was worried about the fate of her grandfather's archives, which had fallen into the hands of a crook. Suddenly there was a knock at the door and a woman with wide-open burning eyes peeped into the office. 'Are you Vitaliev?' she asked with that familiar accent. 'Yes,' I said, 'and you must be the woman from Dnepropetrovsk. You'll have to wait for a while. In fact you're an hour earlier than we arranged'. But the woman didn't move. She kept standing there in the doorway, silently staring at me. Her eyes were bulging from their sockets. I felt uneasy. 'Excuse me please,' I said to Yesenin's granddaughter, then stood up and took a step towards the door. As soon as I did that the woman suddenly turned and ran along the corridor to the staircase. Without looking back she started running down the stairs.

Our building comprises the offices of all the magazines published by *Pravda*, and is guarded by militia. But now I was so curious that some time after the woman's escape I went down to the guard and asked if he'd seen a plump, pop-eyed woman running downstairs. 'No, I didn't,' he said. It's still a mystery who this woman was. Probably she was just a crank. In fact, lots of maniacs visit our office. I remember a woman dressed in an overcoat and fur hat, even though it was summer. I asked her what her profession was. 'I work as a dog,' she answered. I thought I had misheard her. 'What do you do for a living?' I repeated. 'I bark,' she replied, and burst into a fit of loud, angry barking . . .

As to the woman, the one who escaped, probably she just wanted to see what I looked like. One of my militia friends suggested that she came to photograph me covertly. Who knows . . .

Anyway a few days after this strange visit I was coming back from a friend's house at about midnight. On my way I had to pass a construction site. The place was completely deserted, as Moscow always is at this hour. When I reached the half-finished framework of a big building there was a rustling noise above. Before I knew what was happening, something heavy whistled through the air above my head. I jumped aside, and a huge red brick, possibly five kilograms in weight, crashed down near my feet and broke into pieces. One of the fragments brushed my right hand. I ran around the corner of the building and looked out. There was no one in sight. But the broken brick was still there, and its crusty fragments, scattered around, looked in the darkness like frozen stains of blood.

Whoever conjured up this plan, it was devilishly clever: accidents are frequent at our construction sites, and bricks do come down occasionally onto a passer-by's head. Only this time it was supposed to be my head, which made a certain difference. For me at least. Or was it just a coincidence? I don't think so.

Soon a subpoena came to my office. Appearing in court is also part of a Soviet journalist's daily routine. Especially for a feuilletonist. The heroes of our stories often claim that they have been defamed. I have been in court as a defendant in libel claims many times, and (fingers crossed) I've never lost a case. This time the girl Natasha, friend of the Sailor's son Igor, was suing me for libel. From the beginning it was evident that her case was hopeless. She was a drug-addict, had a long criminal record and was an active member of the Little Sailor's gang. I had irrefutable proof of all these facts.

No one in his or her right mind would start a court hearing on their own initiative in a situation like that, especially against a popular magazine. My doubts grew stronger when I saw this slim, blonde girl with exquisite features at the courtroom. She brought an advocate from Dnepropetrovsk (the trial was held in Moscow). No, it couldn't be her own initiative, since a trial like this, especially if covered by *Krokodil*, which was a possibility, could only further harm her reputation. Besides, in case of failure, she would have to pay all court expenses (we had all twelve volumes of the Little Sailors' trial record sent from Dnepropetrovsk), plus her and her advocate's return train tickets. Being a fruit-seller at a wage of 80 roubles a month, Natasha could hardly afford it, unless backed by someone.

My suspicions proved right when, on quickly losing the case to me and my lawyer, Natasha burst out crying and blurted through her tears: 'What did I tell them? I should have come here with some of the Guys!'

I must confess that this tearful remark of hers sent shivers down my spine. I didn't expect, of course, that the Guys from Amur would come to Moscow and machine-gun me in the courtroom, but still there was something ominous behind this absurd trial. More likely, it was just a mafia ranging shot, using poor Natasha for ammunition. Thank God it was not the building brick again! At least they now knew that I had a good lawyer and the whole editorial office behind me. I was not on my own – that was the main message I sent to *them* by easily winning the case.

But the most striking development came a whole year after the novel was published. Before I expand on it, let us recall A. S. Vokal, the head of the Dnepropetrovsk tsekhoviks. He was arrested at the same time as Matross, and tried. During the hearing it was proved that the total sum embezzled by him amounted to two million roubles. I am sure the figure was far from complete, but still it was enough for the industrious tsekhovik to be sentenced to death, and so he was.

I think that the execution of a criminal is generally unacceptable. Every crime is a product of society and every criminal in the long run is just a bearer of some social mistake or injustice. The easiest thing, of course, is to wipe out the bearer. But his death won't mean that the society's problem is corrected. Its burden will simply be shifted onto someone else's shoulders. Besides, a modern powerful State, to my mind, must not under any circumstances become a murderer itself. The practice of many countries shows, by the way, that there is a reverse correlation between the number of death sentences and the crime-rate. Now, when the Soviet press is debating the problem of capital punishment, I go along with the supporters of its abolition. My main reason is that we have shed too much innocent blood in the past, so it is high time that we should stop. Why 'innocent' – you may ask – since we are only speaking about criminals? But tell me, are we fully guaranteed against court mistakes? Not yet.

Some years ago, there was a chain of violent murders of women in Belorussia. An unknown killer-rapist assaulted thirty-six young females. Seventeen people were arrested and tried on suspicion that they were the murderers. One was sentenced to death and shot, another attempted suicide in his cell, a third went blind in prison. And a year or so later, the real culprit was found. A certain Mikhasevich – a State farm engineer, an active Party member and good family man – not only confessed to all the killings, but showed the places where he had hidden the corpses, leaving not a shadow of doubt that *he* was the only murderer[8] . . . You can imagine the methods with which the investigators had obtained all the previous 'confessions'. And the court went along with them . . . So while there is the slightest possibility of a court's or a prosecutor's mistake (let's call it so, though abuse would be a better word), the death sentence must not exist. The execution of a single innocent person cannot be justified.

Neither Dolgov nor Vokal should have been put to death, I'm sure. But Dolgov was and Vokal wasn't. Seventeen advocates hired by him had made the court reconsider its decision: the death penalty was replaced by fifteen years in prison – the maximum term by Soviet laws. So far, so good. I did not in the least wish Vokal to be executed. Fifteen years seemed like a good opportunity for him to think over his dirty tricks against our country. But this matter was neither the last word, nor the last sentence.

A couple of years passed. Vokal was diligently studying English in his cell, and confided to his wardens that he would soon be set free and emigrate to the West. 'There's no hurry, pal,' the wardens would grin, 'You've still got a dozen years to go, or rather to "sit".' But they proved to be wrong. Two years after the second sentence the court, prompted by the gang of well paid advocates, commuted the fifteen years to five.

But this wasn't all. Here comes the development I wanted to tell you about. At the end of 1988, I received a mocking telegram from Dnepropetrovsk: 'We have bought out Vokal. He is free. Now we will start buying out the other guys and you'll soon have to return your awards.' The cable was signed 'Fridman'. Refusing to believe it, I hastily dialled the Dnepropetrovsk militia and they confirmed that Vokal had just been set free. 'But it's impossible because it can never be possible!' I cried out the famous quotation from Chekhov. 'Yes, it is possible,' they told me. 'And though there is no direct evidence, by hearsay we suspect that huge sums of money have been involved here, and big connections too. But we cannot prove it.' I telephoned the Kiev court by whose decision Vokal was released, but all I could get out of them was that the case had been reviewed. 'Then why don't you prosecute the people who sentenced Vokal to death?' I demanded furiously. 'Who is the criminal – he, or you? Or both?' No reply.

Each democracy, as you know, has two facets. We are building a democratic society now. Isn't the appearance of a Soviet mafia and large-scale racketeering just the reverse side of our young democracy? There couldn't possibly have been a mafia under Stalin. Totalitarian rulers consider major crime their own prerogative. Still, I don't believe that organised crime is unavoidable in a democratic society, if it is a really democratic one. We are still a long way from full democracy, but when we achieve it, I hope there will be no mafia in our country.

As to the present: with the progress of perestroika, the mafia's organisation is being shaken, but it doesn't seem to be collapsing. In the face of its threatened annihilation, it pulls its battered ranks together. The mafiosi's main aim now is to show that they are not scared of glasnost' and democratisation, that they don't care. They do, of course, but use every opportunity to demonstrate the opposite.

In January 1987, *Literaturnaya Gazeta* published an article 'How They Buried Us'.[9] It was the story of the plushest funeral thrown by the Rostov-na-Donu trade mafia for their former chief Budnitsky, who died in prison serving his fifteen-year term. Budnitsky's body was flown to Rostov from Karasnoyarsk where he died. No one knows (again!) how this illegal transportation was arranged. More than 150 people came to mourn the former head of the city's trade department. The procession moved through the very centre of Rostov, escorted by the militia! Whom were the militiamen guarding? The Godfather, the focus of corruption. They were guarding the body of the crook who in his lifetime had created a whole efficient system of bribery, fraud and profiteering.

All the city's élite were there. Many were Party members. At the cemetery they pronounced heart-felt speeches on what a fine person the deceased had been. Budnitsky's grave was in the Avenue of Fame, where the most respected citizens of the city are buried. Could one imagine a bigger insult to perestroika? The mafia was showing us that it still had great power. It was like spitting in the public's face. They were really trying to bury *us*, but in the end they failed: Budnitsky's body was exhumed and buried in a more modest place, and many high-ranking participants in the procession lost their jobs and Party membership.

A very similar but even more impertinent case took place in Moscow in 1988, when one of the heads of the Georgian mafia was buried in the most 'prestigious' Moscow cemetery, Vagankovskoye, next to the grave of the prominent poet, actor and singer Vladimir Vysotsky.

Here I must explain that shortages for the common people of our country do not always end with the end of their lives. It is very hard to get a place in certain 'overcrowded' cemeteries whose personnel is notorious for corruption and bribe-taking. There are the more prestigious cemeteries like Vagankovskoye and Novodevichie in the centre of Moscow, and the less prestigious ones which are usually in the outskirts. For many years, it was a tradition for the élite to be buried separately from those whom they ruled during their lifetime. If you go to Novodevichie cemetery, which until recently was closed to visitors (and was probably the only 'closed' cemetery in the world), you will see almost exclusively the graves of high-ranking bureaucrats and their close relatives, and occasionally those of famous artists. Khrushchev, who was denied a place in the Kremlin wall, is buried there. Brezhnev's mother lies there. Vagankovskoye is a little more 'democratic' – there, there are mainly the graves of famous actors, men of letters, film directors and so on. To get a place is practically impossible for a common person. Only the Moscow City Council can authorise it.

There is a joke about a wealthy crook who was eager to be buried in Novodevichie or Vagankovskoye cemetery after his death. He asked another influential swindler to help him. One day the latter telephoned him and said: 'OK, it was difficult, but I did it. You will be buried in Vagankovskoye.' 'Thanks a lot,' said the first crook, 'I'll pay all your expenses of course.' 'Yes, but there is one small condition.' 'What condition?' 'You've got to be buried tomorrow.'

This was where a mafioso from Tbilisi, who had served eight terms in prison during his lifetime, decided to have his last resting place. 'I want to lie next to Vysotsky,' he wrote in his will. Vysotsky's grave is a place of mass pilgrimage all year round. So the Godfather decided to share posthumously the poet's fame.

It is worth noting that by an unwritten law, no one can be buried in a given city (especially in Moscow) unless they are permanently registered there. The dead mafioso had been registered in Georgia, so he had no 'right' to a grave in the capital. But all laws – written and unwritten alike – were flouted by his mourning mafia comrades. God knows how (I have to repeat these words often when speaking about our home-grown mafia) they got all the necessary permissions.

A crowd of more than 300 sorrowfully honking cars blocked the streets leading to the cemetery on the day of the funeral. Mafiosi from all over the country had come to pay their last tribute and were demonstrating their loyalty to the old mafia ties in the very centre of Moscow. People who witnessed the procession said they had never seen anything like it in their lives. Some of the mourners were openly carrying fire-arms; they were sporting luxury clothes, driving the latest Western cars, holding their clenched fists out of the windows. *They* were burying *us* again.

The body of the Georgian mafioso stayed in its plot for several months, which seemed like an eternity. All this time, people kept asking how this sacrilege could occur at the height of perestroika. Many newspapers published furious articles of condemnation, but the authorities remained aloof. Only after several months of public protestations was the body removed from the grave and taken back to Tbilisi. But the mafiosi had had their feast day.

In the aftermath, as usual, several petty officials were 'reprimanded' and the cemetery director was sacked, though I don't think he regretted his removal much. I simply cannot imagine the size of the bribe he must have got from the mafiosi, but it was probably enough to last till his great-great-grandson's lifetime.

Such open demonstrations of unity and influence can perhaps be explained as symptoms of the mafia losing its strength, since when it is really strong it prefers to remain in hiding. Or am I just trying to console myself?

At least nowadays the press is full of stories about rackets and racketeers. This 'trade' has really been boosted by the development of the cooperatives. The number of cooperative cafés and restaurants, work-shops and public toilets is growing every day. If properly guided, I'm sure that the cooperatives can save the country from economic stagnation. Their members, for the most part, are honest and hard-working people. They do earn much more than an average worker (let alone engineer) at a State-owned enterprise, but they toil much harder too.

Cooperators are much envied and looked down on by bureaucrats trying harder to hinder the cooperative movement, which to my mind is one of the major parts of Gorbachev's reforms. Unfortunately they have become easy prey for racketeers who usually represent the lowest echelon of the mafia. Cooperative cafés and restaurants are especially popular with them. The height of their activities was observed at the beginning of 1989.

On the 5 January 1989, *Literaturnaya Gazeta* reported in an article headlined 'Enigmatic Fire' that unknown racketeers had set fire to two cooperative cafés – 'Ochag' (The Hearth) in the Moscow region and 'Traktir' (The Inn) in downtown Moscow. The Hearth was burnt down completely, the Inn was badly damaged by fire.[10] These two cases were not even recorded by the militia, who seemed to be scared of the racketeers, as the paper concluded.

The 'Lastochka' (Swallow) cooperative, specialising in baking fancy bread, was also attacked by racketeers. They demanded 50,000 roubles and threatened to kill the cooperative chairman's wife and child if he disagreed. The threat worked. The chairman borrowed 30,000 roubles and paid the racketeers without mentioning the matter to the militia. The intimidation continued. Every window in the cooperative was smashed, along with furniture and equipment. The racketeers demanded more money. It was only then that the Lastochka members approached the militia, who caught one of the gangsters, but released him after only three days' detention when he claimed that the cooperators were simply reluctant to pay back money they owed him.[11]

At the end of January 1989, *Ogonyok* magazine carried an interview with an anonymous cooperator who said: 'The racketeers control almost all of the cooperative restaurants, cafés and shops, and if it goes on like this they'll soon take the whole cooperative movement under their belt – I'm not exaggerating.'[12]

Cooperators have started taking counter-measures. They are hiring bodyguards, and they have merged into the USSR Cooperative Union, but the last word must be said by the militia, whose position is aggravated by the absence of a law against racketeers. First, organised crime must be officially recognised as a social phenomenon existing in our country, and the press is valiantly struggling for this. There is a parallel in the case of prostitution, which executive bureaucrats also refused to recognise at first, until numerous articles aroused public opinion so thoroughly that it could no longer be ignored. A prostitution law was eventually passed. Whether it has proved effective or not is another question, but the very existence of such a law means official recognition, which is crucial in fighting any social vice. Again, glasnost' is the main thing. It is the only way for society to curb the hold of rackets and the mafia. It gives us hope that eventually the mafiosi will have a hard time in our country.

The first convincing example has been set already. I am referring to the trial in Autumn 1988 of Brezhnev's son-in-law, the former first deputy Minister of the Interior, Yuri Churbanov. I was present in the Supreme Court of the USSR when he was tried there together with his high-ranking accomplices from Uzbekistan. I stared intently at this handsome man, sitting on a wooden bench for criminals with his face covered by his hands. What incredible power he used to hold in these same hands! But he was exposed and prosecuted despite all the connections he had, and I'm sure still has. This is a symbol of the changes in our country. There is still a lot of work to be done, but the process of purification has started. I am sure that in the long run we will clear our land of crooks, racketeers and mafiosi.

This probably sounds idealistic, but such idealism to my mind is indispensable for the success of perestroika.*

---

*In July 1989 when the script of this book was already delivered to the publishers, I learnt about the brutal murder of my young colleague, a journalist from *Sovetskaya Torgovlya* (Soviet trade/daily) Vladimir Glotov. An Afghan war veteran, he attempted to expose some of the mafia's machinations in Central Asia and was sadistically killed in the court-yard of his Moscow house. He survived Afghanistan to be murdered by mafia mongrels in the heart of 'peaceful' Moscow. One of the mafia's aims here was probably to intimidate us journalists. But we are not easily scared. I've just finished the big story on organised crime in Leningrad. Rest in peace Volodya. We shall continue your fight.

Letter Box

Milchenko and most of the Guys from Amur must be isolated from our society forever. They won't be corrected at labour camps, since the whole of their psychology is perverted. Coming out of prison, they will feed off the working people again . . . Why were some of the Amur Guys' patrons not punished? These high-ranking people are much more dangerous than the gangsters themselves. Being still in power, they use their influence and immunity to undermine our society from within. They encourage crime . . . Amur Guys and the like must be deported to capitalist countries, where they will quickly find jobs to their liking . . . We are thankful to Comrade Vitaliev for his honest publication 'Amur Wars'. This novel makes us even more sure that perestroika is progressing in the right direction.

S–v, and a group of comrades, Mogilev.

Dear editorial office! This letter is a sign of my special respect and gratitude to Comrade Vitaliev. I am writing it under the profound impression of his novel 'Amur Wars'. I have always been an avid reader of the press, but this novel was like a bolt out of the blue – there hasn't been anything so grandiose, both in an artistic and documentary sense, in recent times. The novel makes you look at many things differently, it has made me believe that perestroika, democratisation and glasnost' are for real. Thank you very much. You give hope to honest people.

Ch–kh, Moldavia.

I have just finished reading 'Amur Wars' – a bitter, sad novel. I am full of anger and protest against our home-bred mafia. Like its Western counterparts, it seems to have an iron grip. The most unpleasant thing is that some Communists happen to be among its members. As for me, I have never met a real Communist in my life. This doesn't mean, of course, that they don't exist, but probably the very word 'Communist' has lost some of its initial noble meaning. I do hope very much that attempts at social purification taking place in our society will bring the renewal of our life, more democracy and glasnost', which is still in a rudimentary state. Both you and I have a lot of work ahead of us. This work must not be forced, but voluntary and constructive. I stand for creative socialism. I am for the kind of socialism that trusts people to read Nietzsche and

141

Rozanov* and allows them to go to Finland or West Germany of their own accord.

M–v, 26. Leningrad region.

Dear Editor, 'Amur Wars' is the biggest exposure of corruption in the Soviet press. In this connection, I am very worried for the fate of V. Vitaliev. The time of glasnost' will end, and there may be a lot of trouble waiting for him in the future. The corrupt Communists won't forgive him. During the stagnation era, such Communists received gold stars as Soviet heroes, built monuments to themselves and led the country to a crisis. Now they are enjoying personal pensions and laughing at our perestroika. Stalin was better than they: he was not so corrupt . . . I have decided to subscribe to *Krokodil* for the next year. Thank you.

Ch–v, Dnepropetrovsk.

The novel is very artistic, it is full of humour and reads very well, like a classic whodunnit. But its main merit is that it is written in the spirit of socialist realism. That's what all our perestroika literature should be like – fighting, courageous, revolutionary . . . I'd like to see the novel in the form of a separate book.

R–va, Kazan.

I used to meet guys similar to the Sailor's gangsters in other parts of the country. They are all the same in one way: their crimes were blessed by top-ranking leaders. The result is that the gangsters are in the dock for criminals and the officials who supported them are in peaceful retirement with their pockets full of money. These officials are nothing but the criminals' direct accomplices.

K–tsin, Moscow.

Soviet readers are waiting for the continuation of 'Amur Wars', in which the system of exploitation of our people by the leaders originating from the Dnepropetrovsk region would be exposed. All leaders who come from Dnepropetrovsk must be sent to correction camps, and the hundreds of millions of roubles looted from the people must be confiscated. Don't be afraid of the mafia, my friends. The people will always back you.

Sh–sky, Gomel region, Belorussia.

*V.V. Rozanov (1856–1919) a Russian writer and philosopher whose works were banned until recently.

I'd like to speak about the excesses in our psychiatric services started under Brezhnev. Due to the lack of control, Milchenko, the Sailor, as you stated in your novel, managed to receive a fake certificate of mental handicap. I have to say that this is still quite typical not only for Dnepropetrovsk, but for Latvia as well. The old inhuman Regulation on committing people to psychiatric hospitals contributes to the abuse. These disgraceful procedures hampering perestroika must be abolished once and for all.

B – lov, school military tutor, Liepaya, Latvia.

To my mind, the main reason for all the events described in 'Amur Wars' was that Dnepropetrovsk region was a 'closed zone'. Local Party and Komsomol leaders are to blame most of all. Who are the Guys from Amur if we think of them properly? Ordinary Soviet people educated by school and Komsomol. If the latter had worked at least satisfactorily, they wouldn't have let them turn into gangsters. The Guys from Amur were energetic, vigorous and far from stupid. They could have made good Ministers and rulers if put into different circumstances. As to Matross himself, he could have become a Premier. Then probably we wouldn't have had so many shortages and such high prices for clothes and furniture and our living standards would have been better.

S – ko, Kharkov.

I am glad to have lived to see the time when it is possible to speak and write about things previously banned. Mafia can only exist under the wing of protective militiamen. This was the case in Leningrad, where Feoktistov's gang operated for many years. 'I had a hand in the militia,' he confessed in the courtroom. It's very difficult now for a militiaman to remain honest, and I'd like to thank heartily those valiant investigators who helped to have the Guys from Amur arrested and tried.

S–kaya, Leningrad.

(*Telegram*) Help me, dear Comrade Vitaliev! My only daughter Lyuda was murdered. She was stabbed in the heart. She lived in Amur and the investigators from the local Procurator's office didn't want to do anything to find the criminal. 'Take your daughter's body and then we'll see' – that's what they said. My daughter was a graduate of Dnepropetrovsk University and worked at a hospital. No one would investigate the murder and I had to start looking for the criminal myself. I found him. He proved to be the professor of Marxism and Leninism at the mining institute, and he confessed. But the court was lenient with him, and I want him to be sentenced to death. Now I'm in hospital myself, being treated for a heart-attack. Please help me to find someone who could look into my daughter's murder objectively. We don't have honest investigators in our city. You were quite right in your novel: mafia is ruling it. The murderer must be punished!

S–va, Dnepropetrovsk.

(*This letter was written in printed characters.*)

Dear Comrade Vitaliev, thanks for your courage. You've done a lot. But . . . Abkhazia [an autonomous republic on the Black Sea coast] is the land of all-powerful mafiosi. Racketeering has been flourishing here for many years. A lawyer was hanged two years ago near the entrance to the university. His trouser pockets were torn out and stuffed into his mouth. It meant that he took the bribe but did nothing. His wife's skull was broken. Thieves and tsekhoviks execute each other. But the biggest mafia is employed in allocating flats. They make thousands of roubles in bribes. We want an objective inspection team to be sent from Moscow to check all this . . . We haven't signed our names since we don't want to be run over by a car, which is an easy thing for our mafia to arrange.

Sukhumi.

I am an ex-convict. The last time I was released was in 1982. Used to drink a lot, but gave up. Now I'm working as a miner and am not afraid of anyone. Just live like all normal people . . . The novel 'Amur Wars' struck me. Socialism and mafia are incompatible. We are sick and tired of the trash about our bright future. What kind of future can we hope for when so much scum is living among us? Imprisonment is nothing for them. The Sailor is serving his stretch very comfortably. Some time he will come out, and being still a strong healthy man, will start his tricks all over again. The mafia is like a plague, like a malignant tumour. If we don't look into its roots, we will never destroy it.

V–kan, Udmurtia.

You cannot imagine what a big thing you have done by having unmasked the hypocritical bastards who have wormed themselves into our ruling apparatus. Thank you for that. But I can assure you, wars similar to the Amur ones are taking place in many cities in our country, on a smaller scale maybe . . . And there are lots of Stuzhuks everywhere in the militia. Take our town's militia chief, for example. I wrote to him about the crimes of my factory director, who steals automobile spare parts. And what do you think? I was dismissed from my job! So the militia is defending the rulers and covering their abuses.

Z–lin, Kaliningrad region.

We have been reading 'Amur Wars' and think that Vitaliev is just the man for whom we would vote with both hands in the elections to the Supreme Soviet of the USSR. He seems to have an in-bred sense of social justice ... Lots of bribe-takers, embezzlers and thieves still occupy executive positions. Their speeches haven't changed a bit: they go on calling for us to pull together. Where is the revolution to sweep them away?

Respectfully, S–sky, war invalid, Krasnodar region.

Reams have been written recently about the so-called stagnation time. Why don't we call a spade a spade? 'Stagnation' is just a euphemism, the real terms being low living-standards, 'inflation', 'waste of natural resources' and so on. Lies and disinformation became State policy. All the rulers were interconnected with 'mutual guarantees'. Our valiant militia have been unable to expose mafia ties. I came to these conclusions while reading 'Amur Wars'. They are no secret for an average, sober-minded Soviet citizen. And the blame rests on one person – 'our respected, beloved, faithful Leninist, champion of peace, etc etc, L. I. Brezhnev. Or maybe I am wrong?

Ch–nikh, 18, a worker, Tuapse.

7

Doublethink: Mechanism of Privilege

George Orwell is my favourite writer and journalist of all time. His books helped me to survive the most difficult years of stagnation. I admired his lucid, precise language, enjoyed following his line of thought and was fascinated by his logic – especially in his brilliant essays.

What made Orwell's books especially dear to me was his hatred of any form of totalitarianism. Because of it he was ignored outright by the corrupt literary bosses of the Brezhnev era, who were part and parcel of the totalitarian State. Orwell's name sounded like a curse and was mentioned only negatively, in critical articles alongside Solzhenitsyn and other so-called 'anti-Soviet' writers rejected on the principle 'I haven't read their works, but still . . .'

I will never forget a scandal which followed after American publishers tried to put *Nineteen Eighty-Four* on display at the Moscow International Book Fair in 1979. I was working at the fair as an interpreter and heard some petty Soviet officials demanding the book's removal. 'We don't want to see this piece of libel,' they clamoured. 'Display whatever you like, but take this dirty book away!' In the end, the Americans had to cooperate.

What was so dangerous about the book? There is not a single mention of Russia in it. Orwell himself warned more than once that *Nineteen Eighty-Four* wasn't just a lampoon on socialism, that the book equally concerns both the East and the West.

The Stalinist bureaucrats were probably unnerved by the striking similarity of Orwell's 'negative Utopia', of his imaginary totalitarian State, to the way *they* perceived their own country.

Let's take Orwell's neologism 'doublethink' – the ability of one person to hold two contradicting beliefs at the same time. It was *their* principle, it was *their* lifestyle. Completely detached from the people, enjoying every kind of luxury and privilege, the high-ranking functionaries and bureaucrats of the Stalin and Brezhnev eras made themselves believe they were building the world's first State governed by the working masses. That was pure 'doublethink'.

But my favourite Orwellian quotation comes from *Animal Farm*: 'All animals are equal but some animals are more equal than others.' Here Orwell's sardonic satire reaches its peak. The above-quoted commandment of the Farm, ruled by pigs, can serve as a motto for any corrupt leader.

Ten years ago, I was dead sure Orwell's books would never be published in this country. But I was mistaken. *Animal Farm* was published in 1988 by the Riga magazine *Rodnik*, and in January 1989 by the Frunze monthly *Literaturny Kirgizstan*. The publication of *Nineteen Eighty-Four* is now under way in *Novi Mir* magazine, and a volume of Orwell's selected novels and essays is being prepared by Progress publishers.

Does this mean that we have got rid of 'doublethink'? No, not yet. But at least we have started.

When did 'doublethink' appear? When did some 'animals' become more equal than others? How did it happen that the State, founded on the principles of fraternity and equality, at some stage became inhuman and socially unjust?

Lenin was famous for his honesty, asceticism and simple lifestyle. To make sure, one can visit his modest study in the Kremlin. In the first years of Soviet power, there was a big drive for democracy. Leaders of the Lenin school lived side by side with rank-and-file people. Grandpa Misha once showed me in Kharkov, the old capital of the Ukraine, the former headquarters of the Ukrainian Executive Committee, a forerunner of the present-day Council of Ministers of the Republic. It was no more than a shabby single-storeyed house with just a few rooms. If you compare it with the pompously decorated multi-storeyed bulk of the present day Ukrainian Council of Ministers in Kiev, to which the capital of the Republic moved in 1934, the difference will be striking. This building, like many other similar huge office blocks, was built under Stalin. They were designed to dominate the cityscape, to bear down upon a miserable underling of an ordinary person. These Stalin buildings are colloquially called wedding cakes, so ornate are they, with all their stone stars, spires and columns.

Architecture is the reflection of an epoch. The democratic drive soon started to subside when Stalin came to power. It came to a complete halt at the end of the Forties, when the paranoid dictator was lavishing dachas, cars and privileges upon his most faithful supporters, those of them who miraculously survived his own purges. The whole concept of Soviet power was distorted. Instead of the power of the people, it was transformed into the power of Stalin, a huge pyramid with just one man on top. To be close to the 'great leader and teacher of nations' meant safety – at least for a while. That is why Stalin's henchmen clung so desperately to this pyramid of power; they praised Stalin to the heavens, they savoured his every word, in fact they deified him. These collaborators readily accepted the crumbs from the dictator's table in the form of different privileges, pushing them further and further away from the people, making them a separate class. 'All animals are equal but some animals are more equal than others.' It was then that the first VIP rooms appeared at train and bus stations, and that special shops and hospitals for the élite started to emerge.

Old habits die hard. They did not die with the death of the dictator. Khrushchev made some attempts at democratisation, but he was a product of Stalin's rule, he himself was brought up on privileges and could not (or would not) resist them. His role in denouncing Stalin is indisputable, and we should be ever grateful to him for this. But he didn't stop the gross social injustice which was running rampant in the country. He didn't abolish government dachas, special shops and polyclinics. In fact he supported the system of privileges. Or to be more exact, he just took it for granted.

It was under Khrushchev that the grand regional Party Committee building with stars and columns was erected in Kharkov. Everyone, even children, knew that there was a militia-guarded luxury canteen serving sumptuous meals there. For us ordinary people it was the time of incessant queueing for white bread and butter. Everybody realised that Obkom (the regional Party Committee) was one world, and our everyday life quite another. No one protested: the memory of Stalin's terror was still too fresh.

Under Brezhnev, the distinctions within society reached their height. Like mushrooms after a rain in July, there appeared innumerable summer cottages and hunting lodges, special health resorts and bookshops for the élite. Such terms as 'closed shop' (meaning a shop for the privileged), 'closed polyclinics', even 'closed exhibition', came into use and entered into the great Russian language. Every regional, city or district Party Committee (let alone their republican and all-Union counterparts) considered it essential to have its own 'special' hotels, restaurants, guest-houses, dachas and what have you. Visits among apparatchiks turned into rowdy drinking sessions at out-of-town cottages with saunas, women and the like.

A big patch of forest land in the picturesque outskirts of Kharkov was separated from the rest of the world by a fence, barbed wire and round-the-clock militia patrols. It was the Obkom dacha estate, and it stood close to the highway by which my father used to travel to work. Sometimes he was stuck in the office until late, and took the last bus home. Often I heard him telling my mother of drunken shrieks and wails reaching him from the Obkom dacha as the bus passed by.

The old Bolsheviks' hospital in one of Kharkov's parks where my grandfather died was renamed Obkom hospital. No more old Bolsheviks were accepted there.

The elderly apparatchiks generously extended their privileges to the young Komsomol leaders, who became notorious for their open career-ism. 'The rosy-cheeked Komsomol boss' from the banned poem by Yevtushenko was an archetype of that time. Once I myself met a delegation of Komsomols returning from their congress in Moscow. They were literally loaded with crates of exquisite food, imported clothes and attaché cases (also in short supply at the time). One of the group explained that they had acquired the stuff at the special shop at the Kremlin Palace as part of the privilege of having been elected to the Congress. A delegate to the 25th Party Congress in 1976 told me on a train that a food coupon for twenty-five roubles a day was issued to every participant in this stately gathering. (An average person spends no more than three to five roubles a day on food.) They also had special shops with imported goods where they could buy things at big discounts. No wonder everyone at that Congress was constantly raising his hand in favour. No abstentions.*

By the end of the Seventies, the ruling bureaucrats had grown so detached from the 'population', as they derogatorily called us, that they formed a special caste of Soviet noblemen, having nothing in common with their 'serfs'. George Orwell's prophecy of the late Forties became reality in the late Seventies. When I started my job as an interpreter, I was able to look inside this unreal, bloated world. The impressions I received at the Durmen government dacha near Tashkent will never be wiped from my memory. But it was only during my first years as a journalist that I was able to grasp the full extent of moral decay pervading State, Party and Komsomol élite all over the country under Brezhnev.

One of my first missions as a *Krokodil* special correspondent was to the city of Kirov in December 1981. There I was received by the Chairman of the city's Council of People's Deputies Executive Committee. With him I made a tour of the big modern building which housed both the Council

*It is significant that at the first Party Congress under Gorbachev – the 27th, in 1986 – there were no special shops for the delegates. It looks like a minor change, but it is quite an eloquent one!

and the city Party Committee. There was only one canteen there (guarded by militia of course), but on four different 'levels'. The lowest one was for typists and petty clerks working at the building. It served much better food than at ordinary city canteens and the prices were lower, but there was a self-service system there.

The 'level two' canteen adjoined the first one and served the same food, but its dining area was separated by a wooden partition to create some privacy for the customers, who were mainly lesser executives. They were served by neatly dressed waitresses and didn't have to shuttle between their tables and the counter.

'Level three' was a cosy separate dining room where the tables were covered with white starched cloths. The cutlery there was all silver and the choice of meals much better: lots of fancy appetisers, elaborate dressings, cakes, pies and so on. There was even a big samovar puffing on a table in a corner. And the prices were lower than in the first two rooms. The diners here were heads and deputy heads of departments. They enjoyed complete privacy and were served by slim, busty waitresses in white aprons and low-cut dresses.

At the top of this dining hierarchy, there was a small wooden-panelled room with carpets, piano and TV set. In the centre of it stood a massive round table with delicacies: caviare, salmon, smoked sausages, oranges, bananas and the like – just for appetisers. I don't suppose these delicacies have been seen in ordinary Kirov shops since the Revolution. But this was not all. There was a small button on the table. When my executive guide pressed this executive button, a rosy-cheeked woman named Nadia appeared with a tray of steaming main courses. She was wearing a traditional hand-made Russian dress with lace and embroidery, and was smiling the broad, stupid smile of a plain country girl. The meal was *absolutely free* here. This room was for the exclusive use of the First Secretary of the city's Party Committee and his deputies, and of my voluntary guide and his deputies. The latter confided in me that he preferred having his meals in utter solitude in yet another special room – for himself only. I did not see this fifth-level room, and frankly I cannot even imagine what it might look like – this Lucullan holy of holies.

'What if a clerk or an instructor wanted to dine in a room of a higher level?' I asked the Chairman. 'It's impossible,' he smiled. 'Such things simply don't happen.'

The most striking fact about this was that the Chairman was quite a pleasant, witty fellow. He didn't see anything strange about the four (or five) levels of one canteen. He thought it was all right for him and his colleagues, elected to represent ordinary people's interests, to make use of all these most outrageous privileges. *He took them for granted.* Yet the city at this very time was living on food coupons. Shop counters were empty. No milk, no sausages, no nothing, just cheap red wine. And I thought I knew why. The city leaders simply didn't care. They were well fed – nothing else mattered.

Kirov was in no way an exception. Similar canteens, cafés and buffets were functioning in Obkoms and Gorkoms (city Party Committees) all over the country. I even observed one peculiar correlation – the barer a city's shops, the more plentiful the food in the 'closed' canteens.

I remember a basement dining room in the Obkom building in Vologda. All day long, it served exquisite meals plus canned Finnish beer, Georgian wines, export vodka. As soon as you left the building, you found yourself in a completely different world: snow-capped wooden huts, starving dogs roaming the streets, and a dark, silent crowd of poorly dressed people queueing overnight at the closed doors of the Vologodskoye Butter shop. Vologodskoye was a famous type of country-made butter which was difficult to get even in Moscow. These people were queueing for ordinary butter, any kind of butter. They stood in a piercing wind, clutching paper butter coupons in their frost-bitten hands.

Now you must understand even better why we needed perestroika so desperately.

Working with the local militia in Kishinev, the capital of Moldavia, the wine-growing Soviet republic, I got a unique chance to visit the famous wine cellars in Novie Maleshty. It was by courtesy of the militiamen, since no outsider was allowed there. The cellars were like an underground city. Forty-two kilometres long, they had their own streets, lanes and crossroads. 'Champagne Avenue', 'Port Wine Street', the dimly-lit plates stated. The 'streets' were so wide that lorries drove to and fro along them. On both sides, instead of houses, stood huge wine barrels.

We were escorted by a wine-maker who worked at the cellars. He had a professional wine-glass corn on the bridge of his nose. At one point he took us up to a solid wall, groped along its absolutely flat surface, then made a pressing movement. The wall slid open like a theatre curtain. We went numb. Behind the wall was revealed a spacious, brightly lit underground hall with chandeliers, parquet floor and a tiled fireplace. In the centre of the hall there was an ornate fountain with goldfish in it. Elaborate wooden sculptures in an avant-garde style were scattered here and there, each one illuminated from underneath by a special spotlight. It was like walking into a fairy-tale palace. Only this one was real.

There were several other rooms there. In one of them stood a long

151

wooden table with exquisite Arabic chairs. The room was decorated in blue – blue walls, blue upholstery.

'What is this? A museum?' I asked our escort when I regained the power of speech.

'No, this is the place where the highest leaders of the republic receive their guests and throw banquets,' he explained.

I recollected this tour soon after perestroika began, when the First Secretary of the Moldavian Party, Bodiul, was removed from his post for gross abuse of power, and some of the 'highest leaders' of the republic – Deputy Prime Minister Vishku among them – were tried. They must have been paying for those banquets at the underground palace. Even now, I sometimes see that palace in my dreams. Does it still exist, I wonder?

But the rulers' privileges were not limited to luxurious eating and drinking. Each Obkom and Gorkom had its special drugstores, bookstalls and barber's shops. In Zhitomir, in the Ukraine, I had an opportunity to buy some very good books at the Obkom book store, on sale after the top Party bosses had taken whatever they wanted. I was glad their tastes differed from mine.

There was a popular anecdote at that time. Brezhnev's old mother comes to see her son at his luxurious dacha near Moscow. He shows her around the building, boasting of his collection of guns, hand-made furniture, carpets, tapestry, a dozen Western cars in the garage. The old lady is genuinely fascinated. At some point she says: 'Oh, Leonid, you live so well . . . But aren't you afraid that the Communists will come back and take everything away from you?'

The joke was true to fact. At the beginning of the Eighties, most of our rulers, headed by 'our beloved Leonid Ilyich', practically stopped being Communists at all. They were much worse than capitalists. Capitalists make their money in the open and usually have to work hard until they make a fortune. Our corrupt leaders masqueraded as the champions of justice, catering solely for the interests of the people. Hypocrisy, to my mind, is the worst feature of the human character, the mother of all vices . . .

One of my readers told me a spine-chilling story. Some top bureaucrats from a Ukrainian city were keen on hunting. But there was no real game in the vicinity – just ducks and hares. So they telephoned the local circus and demanded some tame bears to hunt. The bears were driven into the forest, where the valiant hunters were already waiting with their rifles loaded. The poor animals were let out of the cage, but being tame, they didn't want to escape, they just stayed by the circus van. And the hunters started shooting them on the spot. When all the bears were dead, these drunk and laughing louts photographed one another with the 'trophies', and feasted upon bear's liver. Can anyone imagine more depraved behaviour?

Another striking instance of the bureaucrats' hypocrisy was in 1986, immediately after the explosion at the Chernobyl atomic power station. When the radiation quickly started to spread to nearby Kiev, the local top-ranking officials launched a hasty evacuation of their children from the city. This was done in secret, lest any 'outsider' should find out. And the common inhabitants of Kiev were officially assured by these very bureaucrats that there was no danger whatsoever.

Certainly, the 'population' knew about their leaders' lifestyles. And hardly anyone believed their words. The most dangerous kind of devaluation occurred – the devaluation of trust. So Gorbachev was right in saying that the country was on the verge of an abyss. Both an economic and moral abyss, I would add.

To quote Professor Vladimir Tikhonov in the *Moscow News* weekly: 'For six decades we lived with a total ban on self-expression and self-assertion. Why? To prevent possible crimes by a dozen social monsters? And what was the result? Society had to reconcile itself to the ideology of bans. Meanwhile, social monsters multiplied hand over fist – including the ones who were issuing the bans.'[1]

As soon as Gorbachev came to power, he started cleaning the Augean stables inherited from his predecessors. The first thing to be done was to restore the shattered building of social justice. And his team set to work. The goal was clear.

Little by little, reception houses, government dachas and cottages, hunting lodges and small hotels were converted into holiday homes for orphaned children, war and labour veterans, boys who fought in Afghanistan. The special shops for government appointees were eliminated. With a sigh of relief, Muscovites bade farewell to the notorious 'raspredelitel', the special shop in Granovskovo Street from which the 'servants of the people' used to emerge holding heavy bundles thoroughly wrapped in thick brown paper against prying eyes. Glancing stealthily around, they made their way to the black Volgas waiting at the kerb. They looked like thieves, and they *were* thieves – they had stolen their positions, their cars, their careers. They had stolen the Soviet power.

'Peace to the hovels, war to the palaces!' – that was one of the main slogans of our revolution. It sounds very fitting for the present when the palaces (underground too, I hope) of new noblemen, of the privileged minority, are given to children and veterans. Just as in 1917!

The revolution is under way. But it is a peaceful revolution. That is probably why it is not progressing as quickly as we would wish, and why there is still a lot of work to do. And here the press plays a very important role. Stories about problems of social justice are like an artillery barrage: they expose the 'enemy's' weak points, which makes it easier for the main forces to launch an attack. The main forces are that 'population' whose interests were neglected for so many years. Public opinion seems to be reappearing in our country. And the government listens to it.

For two years, the press and the public demanded the removal of the name of Zhdanov, one of Stalin's closest yes-men, from the map of our country. There were dozens and dozens of cities, towns, streets and institutions named after this evil man who had made himself infamous by his ruthless attacks on our best poets, writers and actors. The press carried numerous readers' letters petitioning to erase this shameful name from the maps. Public rallies were held. Eventually, in January 1989, the CPSU Central Committee, the Presidium of the Supreme Soviet and the Council of Ministers of the USSR jointly decided to rename everything which bore Zhdanov's name. Social justice triumphed.

Another case involved the subscription campaign for 1989. On the first day of August 1988, when it started, it suddenly became clear that it was impossible to subscribe to most of the pro-perestroika periodicals. The official reason was that the Ministry of Communications had limits on paper, but that was a phoney excuse: our country has the largest paper resources in the world. Somehow, everyone felt that there was something else behind this: bureaucrats hostile to perestroika and angry with the press for its democratisation campaign had simply decided to curb glasnost' by blocking public access to the most progressive magazines and newspapers. A flood of furious letters poured down on the editorial and government offices. 'We won't let them fool us!' the readers stated. There were demonstrations under the slogans 'We want *Moscow News*!', 'We want *Ogonyok*!' And the bureaucrats had to give way. The limits were withdrawn.

Thus we are proving to ourselves that we are no longer a silent mass, that our opinion cannot be neglected.

I would like to tell you about my recent publications on the subject of social justice. And if earlier in this chapter I spoke mainly of the past, of things gone by, now I will switch to the present time, and to those phenomena which have not yet been eradicated.

Potemkin Villages

Most Russian-English dictionaries do not contain any such word as 'pokazukha'. There is no direct English equivalent, probably the closest being 'window-dressing'. It means 'boasting about non-existent achievements'. The message is not easy for a Western reader to understand: if achievements do not exist, what's the point of boasting? But the fact is that 'pokazukha' was one of the major elements of the system of stagnation and social injustice.

The traditions of 'pokazukha' in Russia go back to the eighteenth century when Prince Grigory Potemkin (1739–91) constructed fake cardboard villages on the banks of the Volga to impress Catherine the Great. The decorations were painted in bright colours and were designed to mislead the short-sighted empress when she sailed down the Volga to inspect her dominions. Behind the cardboard walls there was famine and poverty, but from the river it all looked nice and prosperous. Ever since then, the phrase 'Potemkin villages' has been used to denote pulling the wool over the eyes of the rulers to misinform them about the real order of things. The word 'pokazukha' appeared much later, under the Soviet regime, but it is synonymous with 'Potemkin villages'.

'Pokazukha' is hard to combat. Even Gorbachev was subjected to it in the first month of his rule when he decided to pay a visit to an ordinary flat of an ordinary Soviet citizen. He was taken to a plush apartment with excellent furniture and lots of books and was genuinely impressed by the seeming prosperity of his hosts. But as he was drinking his tea, he looked at the bottom of his cup and saw the stamp of the CPSU Central Committee canteen. He was so angry that he left the flat immediately and never tried to repeat an impromptu visit like that again.[2]

In fact, a friend of mine was living in that very house in the Proletarsky district. He saw how, the day before the visit, the new furniture was delivered to the flat by a lorry, and the next day, after Gorbachev left, the same lorry took the furniture away.

While I was writing this book, I received information about another such performance from my native Kharkov, where the all-Union Agricultural Seminar was held early in February 1989. Several Politburo members took part and in an attempt to pull the wool over their eyes the Kharkov authorities opened 'Potemkin' shops for the occasion. Ordinary people were not allowed in, and all sorts of goods were on sale. In reality, Kharkov lacked all major foodstuffs – potatoes among them – but at the time of the Seminar the city streets were washed down with hot water. And this happened in the fourth year of perestroika![3]

By arranging lavish economic exhibitions where high-quality goods and machines were displayed, our élite has tried to kill three birds with one stone: to pacify the 'population', to alleviate their own remorse (if any) for doing so little to improve the average standard of living, and to dupe foreigners into believing that we will live well. These exhibitions were the sole opportunity ordinary people had to cast a glance into the illusory world of plenty in which the rulers were actually living. Under Stalin, the so-called exhibitions of economic achievements appeared in every republic and every region. The face-lifting was extremely costly, but no expense was spared. Under Khrushchev, the regional exhibitions were closed, but the republican and all-Union ones remained and grew.

Every developed country must have a national exhibition if it can afford it – there is no question about that. But the achievements on display must be real, not imaginary, otherwise instead of elevating national pride, they create disbelief and irritation. What is the use of parading exquisite foodstuffs and stylish clothes when the shops are practically empty?

When I made up my mind to deal with 'pokazukha' at economic exhibitions, it was still a 'no-go' area. For many years all criticism on this subject was silenced. Of course I could try to write about the USSR Exhibition of Economic Achievements, the archetype of 'pokazukha' (in fact I did it later for *Ogonyok*[4]), but to begin with it was better to go somewhere in the provinces. So in November 1987 I went to Frunze, the capital of Kirghizia, a Central Asian Soviet Republic with one of the lowest living standards in the country.

The republican exhibition of economic achievements occupied an area of 120 hectares on the outskirts of Frunze. I was alone there – no other visitors. That is probably why, when I entered the pavilions, their staff were dumbfounded and watched me suspiciously, as if I were some kind of madman.

'Hey, what are you doing in here?' The dozing woman curator in the Agriculture Pavilion woke up and approached me threateningly.

'Just browsing around. Can't I do that?'

'No, you can't. It's a closed exhibition.'

The curator's words contained a ready-made paradox – the dream of every feuilletonist. A 'closed exhibition' is just like a four-cornered triangle . . .

All the three spacious halls of the Agriculture Pavilion were stuffed with food. If you close your eyes tightly and say the word 'plenty' out loud a dozen times, trying simultaneously to imagine its material equivalent, you will still be far from the real picture I saw there. Piles and piles of smoked, boiled and dried sausages (twenty-eight different sorts), sweets, cakes and puddings in beautiful boxes, dairy products I had never seen before – kumiss (mare's milk) among them; prunes the size of apples, apples the size of pumpkins, pumpkins the size of the globes displayed in planetariums. And above this horn of plenty, up-climbing diagrams and posters calling to accelerate the production of foodstuffs.

Troubled by this lone visitor, the director of the pavilion appeared. She explained that the exhibition was intended only for the participants in the Plenum of the Kirghizia Party Central Committee, which was to open in a couple of days.

'But before that, some of the foodstuffs may perish,' I interjected meekly.

'We'll replace them,' the director retorted cheerfully.

'Are these products on sale in Frunze food shops?' I enquired.

The director looked at me with a stern scrutiny, the way parents look at their child when he is being naughty.

'Walk around the shops and see for yourself.'

And I saw.

At the exhibition: see above.

In the shops: wrinkled liver sausage (50 copecks per kilo), canned sprats in tomato sauce, sticky sickly-sweet candies of the Anishchenko type – and that was all.

'Have you got "Grapes in Chocolate" or "Apricots in Chocolate"?' I would ask sales women, remembering the exhibits in the Agriculture Pavilion.

They would look at me with piercing psychiatrists' glances and offer no reply.

At the exhibition (in the Standards and Quality Pavilion): cheap and beautiful footwear, bright and fashionable clothes for children, lacy underwear, T-shirts with funny drawings.

In the shops (Frunze central department store): rubber high-boots of Gulliver sizes, light beach shoes (in the middle of winter), brown boots, clumsy and heavy as convicts' chains (30 roubles a pair); queues for women's underwear and men's socks; near the entrance, a huge crowd storming the street stall selling jerseys of Armenian make.

'Are jerseys hard to get in Frunze?' I asked a man vainly trying to penetrate the crowd.

'Everything is hard to get here,' he replied, screwing himself into the mob.

At the exhibition (in the main pavilion): meat products and other delicacies hidden under glass domes. On the domes, printed labels with the inscription 'Don't touch'. I once saw similar plates at the Hermitage Museum in Leningrad. They were hanging from noble wrists of antique statues. But here it would have been more appropriate to write 'Don't eat' instead. Above these sarcophagi of deficit hung a big coloured photograph, depicting the inside of a fridge bursting with gorgeous food. I wondered where this photograph had been taken.

In the shops: see above.

I'm sure the members of the Kirghizia Communist Party Central Committee were pleased with what they saw at the exhibition and went back to their offices thinking everything was OK in the republic. But wouldn't it have been better for them to walk just once around the city shops?

I managed to find out that the annual cost of the exhibition to the State was 1,031,000 roubles. Aren't these illusions too costly?

'Distorting Mirror' – that's what I called my feuilleton in *Krokodil*.[5] The drawing which accompanied the story depicted the famous sculpture of the worker and peasant woman decorating the entrance gates of the all-Union Exhibition, with only one difference: instead of the sheaf of wheat, they were holding a piece of sausage over their heads. Several years ago it would have been considered sheer sacrilege. The publication of the story and the cartoon gives hope that in the near future we will stop throwing dust into each other's eyes . . .

Recently I was asked by *Ogonyok* magazine to write an article on the all-Union Exhibition of Economic Achievements in Moscow. I went there, and what I saw was very much like Frunze. There was another 'closed' exhibition of foodstuffs in one of the pavilions. 'No cameras are allowed here,' the guard warned me when my press card got me admitted to the pavilion. It seemed like a wise precaution, since photographs of the delicious exhibits would only have caused the readers' mouths to water. When I approached the stand of my native Ukraine, the workers were in the process of constructing a glass dome (again!) over the exhibits. 'Why the glass?' I asked. 'So the products are not eaten,' they answered, very eloquently.

The curator of the Turkmenian stand explained that every week, the people from the local Agroprom (Ministry of Agriculture) came from Ashkhabad (3,000 kilometres from Moscow) on missions and brought bags full of food to replace the perished exhibits. 'I have to oil the smoked sausages from time to time, to make them look nice,' she confessed in a conspiratorial voice.

The sausage did look great! Gleaming like brand-new stylish shoes.

But it was nothing but gloss. Not only the sausages, but the whole exhibition. Wouldn't it be better to stock at least a few dozen shops with all this food? Somehow this thought didn't seem to occur to anyone.

Unable to quell my growing appetite any longer, I rushed out into the street for something to eat. No use. The food stalls at the main exhibition of our country were either closed or empty. So whom were they trying to fool? Themselves? And for how long will a sausage be considered an achievement instead of what it really is – an ordinary thing to eat?

For a long time, 'pokazukha' was all-pervasive. It permeated the mass media, and especially television. Once in a village near Moscow, I became witness to a tragi-comic episode.

My attention was attracted by a crowd packed around the village greengrocer's. I came nearer and saw that it was closed. The mob was gaping at the shop windows, and there really was something to gape at: an unheard-of variety of small cucumbers, fat radishes, appetising mushrooms and the like. This Epicurean display was surrounded by tins and cans of pickles and marinades. The window couldn't just be looked at – it had to be admired, like Fujiyama by the Japanese.

'Attention,' came a voice. 'Let the TV crew pass!' I looked around and saw two men with cameras on their shoulders, their lenses aimed at the shop window. The crowd divided and let them pass. The cameramen were accompanied by a tall, slender woman in a fur coat, who approached the shop door and pulled the handle. It opened magically and she gracefully entered the shop. The men were filming her every movement and followed her inside.

With the radiant smile of a film-star, the woman took several tomatoes, a packet of mushrooms and some onions from the counter and was ready to leave. The crowd outside instantly organised itself into a queue. But suddenly a man in an Astrakhan hat appeared in the street. (In our country, Astrakhan hats are especially popular with middle-level bureaucrats.)

'Comrades,' he said, 'the TV film is being shot in our village – it's a great honour for us. On behalf of our State farm administration, I request you to stop staring and go home. Whatever you see in the shop is just a . . . a . . . window dressing and won't be on sale.'

In a couple of days' time, I saw this shop on my TV screen. 'So you see how well our villagers live,' the announcer remarked . . .

Secrets of the VIP Hall

Among the privileges for the élite introduced by Stalin, were the so-called 'deputies' halls' at airports and railway stations. It is interesting that they have proved resistant to changes and are still in existence. In April 1988 I decided to explore just three VIP halls at the Leningradsky, Yaroslavsky and Kazansky railway terminals in Moscow. They stand side by side on Komsomolsky Square, smack in the centre of the city. Each station building has a big clock on its façade, which enabled our great satirists of the late Twenties and Thirties, Ilf and Petrov, to joke in their novel *Twelve Chairs* that the Square was ideal for meetings, because since all three clocks used to show a different time, there were always several minutes to spare . . .

The three VIP halls had much in common – carpets, sofas, soft armchairs, TV sets, cosy kitchens. There are of course certain minor differences: in Yaroslavsky's VIP hall I saw six telephones, in Kazansky, ten. Leningradsky VIP hall boasts a fireplace. But there is one detail common to all three – the portrait of Lenin looking sadly from the wall.

Why is Lenin so sad? To answer this question let's enter an 'ordinary' waiting room – say in Yaroslavsky Station. It's a large gloomy hall with crumbling stucco on the walls. No carpets, no armchairs. On stiff wooden benches, resembling the ones for criminals in court, sit hundreds of hunched-up people. There are not enough places for everyone, so the would-be passengers with bags, suitcases and small children are sleeping crouched on window-sills, on empty buffet counters and simply on the floor. The children are screaming and demanding food, as if in a refugee camp. There is nothing much to offer: station buffets are notorious for their poor quality meals. A stench of toilets, combined with strong body smells, creates a distinctive aroma. It is very stuffy, and I wonder how anyone could stand it for more than a few minutes. But people – mainly transit travellers – sometimes have to spend several days here.

In Kazansky Station it is even worse, since reconstruction is under way. People have to stay out of doors and to sit and lie on newspapers spread on the bare ground.

'The deputies' rooms must be isolated from the rest of the station premises,' says the Instruction from the Ministry of Railways. This instruction was issued in 1987, in the third year of perestroika. And isolated they are. The door of Leningradsky's VIP hall was locked. I pressed the button and the bell rang. A woman appeared and said she couldn't let me in without permission from the station-master. When I finally got permission I was mercifully allowed into the large hall with carpeted floors and walls. It was empty.

In Kazansky Station I was allowed into the VIP room only after the station-master got permission from – the KGB! 'Do you think my visit carries a threat to State security?' I asked. 'That is the instruction,' she shrugged.

This VIP room was separated from the rest of the world not only by closed doors but also by a metal turnstile. 'What do you need this partition for?' I asked the woman on duty. 'So all sorts of people won't lean against our doors and damage them,' she explained.

'All sorts of people' did not try to lean against the privileged doors. They were peacefully sleeping nearby on the ground. As I entered the hall some of those who were not asleep, lifted their heads and eyed me with open hostility, even hatred: it was nothing but *class* hatred, directed not towards me but towards privileged bureaucrats of all kinds.

The VIP rooms are chronically empty whereas the ordinary ones are packed like sardines all the year round.

'How many VIP visitors do you have each day?' I would ask at every station.

'A lot,' duty women in Leningradsky and Kazansky replied. 'Fifteen or even twenty daily.'

'One or two,' said their counterpart from Yaroslavsky Station.

'Why don't you let in invalids and children?'

'We have no right to.' And the Yaroslavsky woman recounted a moving story of how once in winter she took pity on some freezing children, let them in and gave them tea. For that she got a good scolding from her boss, the station-master. Since then she hasn't given in to her emotions.

In Yaroslavsky's VIP hall I was given a clue to the secret of its impregnability. I got hold of the full text of the above-mentioned Instruction of the Railways Ministry. It was supposed to be 'for staff use only', but the kind-hearted duty woman, who once took pity on the children, sympathised with me too and showed me the document.

You must have noticed that I am calling the halls in question 'VIP halls' not 'deputies' halls', as they are named officially. I started doing this after I read the instructions. Initially the rooms were intended only for deputies to the Supreme Soviet of the USSR and of Union Republics. But in the course of time the range of the privileged ones was extended. By the Instruction, the deputies' hall can now be used by: party functionaries of different ranks, government apparatchiks, ministers and their deputies, procurators, Komsomol leaders, chairmen, Red Cross societies, secretaries of the artistic unions and so on. A unique list of the Soviet élite.

But the most striking thing about the Instruction is the addendum giving access to VIP rooms to high ranking railway officials and leaders of the railway workers trade unions. A vivid example of mutual protection. Or rather of a vicious circle. Now it is clear why our railways operate so badly, why trains are often late and stations are dirty. Simply because those in charge look at the world through the heavy curtained windows of VIP halls! That's how the mechanism of privilege works. That's how it blocks the way to progress and perestroika.

At this point you may ask, what is so bad about VIP rooms? Many Western countries have them too. Yes, it is true, but, first, Western countries are capitalist; they don't proclaim equality to be the main principle of their society as we do. And, second, there can be no comparison between the conditions in 'ordinary' waiting rooms in the West and in our country. When going to Britain, I passed through half of Europe by train and could see for myself how clean, quiet and comfortable Western stations are. Besides, Westerners do not have such long distances to travel. If we had similar empty and comfortable station buildings there would be no need for VIP rooms even for the élite themselves. So it is more a question of social divisions.

Let's take the problem of getting a ticket. In our stations, even if you are an invalid you have to wait in long exhausting queues for hours on end. But the clients of the VIP rooms, shamefully enough called 'deputies' halls', get a ticket without a problem. To supply tickets for them is one of the duties of the woman in charge of the room. She goes to the ticket window, buys their ticket and brings it to the client. Her other duty is to inform the train attendants and the engine-driver that a client of the VIP room is going on their train. The message of this is: be careful, you're not carrying just an ordinary guy, but a big shot who can put you in trouble if anything goes wrong. Is there such a procedure in the West, I wonder?

Remember the inverse correlation which I suggested between the quality of Obkom canteens and the choice in a city's shops? The same applies to VIP rooms. At Kazansky Station, with the best deputies' hall, the ordinary premises are the worst – simply abominable, and including a smallish waiting-room for war invalids where there is no buffet and the toilet doesn't work. Why not swop the signs on these rooms? The deputies and leaders should know how 'their' people live. Is there a better way to do this than to mix with the 'population' in a station waiting-room, to queue for a ticket, to sit on a wooden bench or even to lie on the floor beside those who elected them, and on whom their power rests? Isn't it shameful for a socialist country to have such social distinctions? It is very shameful.

162

Hopefully this shame will affect those who use the privileged facilities in a State where, by the Constitution, there should be no VIPs.

What gives me some hope is that none of those who have used the VIP room at Kazansky Station have written their name legibly enough in the guest book where clients are supposed to evaluate the service they have received. Perhaps they were just in a hurry. But I hope they were ashamed. This is a case where shame can become purifying.

I recall interviewing one of the station-masters. 'From a political point of view, I'm in favour of VIP rooms, from a purely human one – I am against,' he said. How could I explain to him that in the time of glasnost' and democratisation political and human points of view *must* coincide? Policies are worthless if they don't have a human being at their centre.

Shame or no shame, luxury rest rooms must be either closed for good or given to veterans or children. This would be fair enough. Then perhaps Lenin wouldn't look down so sadly from his portrait on the wall.

No Roubles, No Windows

Apart from our 'home-bred' élite, there is one more privileged class in the Soviet Union at present – foreigners (though their privileges are certainly 'home-bred'). Foreigners are still considered a special kind of people, and to some extent this can be explained by the Iron Curtain lowered by Stalin to close our country from the rest of the world. Or maybe the roots lie deeper in Russian history. A foreigner in the Soviet Union provokes in most people rather a complex blend of suspicion, apprehension and admiration. The right name for this is probably xenophobia.

Hear how my friend Martin Walker, the former *Guardian* correspondent in Moscow, describes what it means to be a foreigner in this country:

By Russian standards we live well ... We have a special hospital assigned for our use, where the facilities are rather better and the supply of drugs more reliable than in the standard Russian Health Service. We can ... obtain tickets to the Bolshoi ballet, the theatre, the circus and other entertainments in short supply. We can usually get a room in a reasonable hotel, by reserving in advance and paying in hard currency ... When we fly on Aeroflot we are assigned to a separate departure lounge [*sic!*] from the Russian passengers, who are frequently bumped off the plane to make room for us. We are therefore less popular with the locals than we might be. Privilege is a clever mechanism to keep people apart.[6]

I have taken this quotation from Martin's excellent book, *The Waking Giant*. It gives the reader the direct impressions of someone who has been 'on the other side of the fence'. But having worked for several years as an interpreter, I couldn't help noticing much the same. When I was about to board an internal plane with my foreign guests, we were always taken from the Intourist lounge by special bus, separately from the Soviet passengers who had been waiting for us to arrive near the gangway. When we came, the stewardess would shout: 'Make way for foreigners!' And the people, who were sometimes freezing and had crying children in their arms, readily obeyed: we got into the plane first so as to occupy the best seats. The non-smoking rule aboard the plane concerned the Soviet passengers only. Foreigners were allowed to smoke. On a plane to Tashkent I remember a Russian stealthily producing a cigarette when we stopped climbing. He was rudely halted by the stewardess, whereas the foreigners beside him were openly enjoying their cigars. 'Why do you allow them to smoke, then?' the guy asked. 'Because they're foreigners,' the stewardess snapped back.

Some of my 'delegates' were taken aback by this self-humiliating 'hospitality' and refused the privileges. But it is one thing to be on a short visit. To live in the country for several years is another pair of shoes, as our saying goes. Most of the foreigners stationed in Moscow have to make use of the hard currency Beriozka shops that constitute one of the main parts of their privileged position. There are about a dozen Beriozka shops in Moscow, selling not only books and delicacies but Japanese and Dutch stereos, clothes from Western countries, Russian artifacts and souvenirs. Of course it is very humiliating for us to have stores in our own country where our money is not valid, where in fact Soviet people are not allowed at all.

In Russian 'Beriozka' means 'birch tree', which is a symbol of Russian nature. I don't think the name is appropriate for a shop which neither serves the Russians, nor accepts Russian (Soviet) money. Why not rename it say, 'Eucalyptus' since, unlike roubles, it does accept Australian dollars!

Why are Beriozka shops so hated by our people? Because they breed the same inequality and social injustice as the aforementioned 'closed' shops for the élite. But the 'closed' shops are being closed lately, while the Beriozkas remain.

Are they so indispensable for foreigners? To quote Martin Walker again: 'We [foreigners] can use the Russian shops, depend on our roubles and learn the art of Russian queueing.'[7] So you can, can't you?

My feuilleton 'No Roubles, no Windows' was and still is the only publication in the Soviet press describing and condemning hard-currency Beriozkas.[8] To visit them I had to obtain written permission from Rosinvaluttorg – a special agency under the Ministry of Trade supervising Beriozkas. The first shop I went to was in Kropotkinskaya St – a stone's throw from the Kremlin. It specialised in selling Soviet-printed books. For hard currency, of course.

Despite the fact that statistically we publish annually more books than any other country in the world, our society is still very book-hungry. This is due to the fact that books are printed according to a plan drafted by someone at the top, who is governed not by the principle of public demand, but by vague ideological considerations. Consequently the ordinary bookshops are stuffed with reading matter no one buys or reads, and books which are really good are very hard to get. Especially fiction.

My tour of the book Beriozka was like a dream. The shelves were sagging under the weight of books by my most coveted authors: Bulgakov, Akhmatova, Tsvetayeva, Paustovsky. On a top, yet unconquered, shelf three volumes by Mikhail Zoshchenko (a brilliant satirist, persecuted by Stalin) were winking at me with their glossy covers. No matter how hard I ever tried, I couldn't buy anything at this bookshop, even though half of my yesterday's *Krokodil* salary rested in my pocket. Roubles here were null and void. I could only gape at the books, I couldn't buy them. Besides I hadn't the status of Academician Sakharov who, the legend goes, once entered a Beriozka and, having chosen a lot of things, got away with paying in roubles. When the shop manager tried to object, Sakharov showed him the inscription on a rouble note saying that: 'the banknotes of the USSR State Bank must be accepted by all institutions, enterprises and persons all over the country's territory'. Probably the manager just didn't want to get into an argument with Sakharov himself. Or maybe it is just a myth.

A dim ray of light is fighting its way through the heavily curtained windows of the bookshop. My every movement is vigilantly watched by nine young saleswomen in case I should filch something from a shelf. Under their steady glances I feel ill at ease. Am I really not socially healthy enough to be a customer here? My only handicap is having not dollars or pounds but roubles in my pocket.

'Why don't you let Soviet people inside?' I asked the bookshop manager. 'Let them at least gape at the books if not buy them.'

'The idea of such a thing!' she snorted. 'Let the Soviets in and we'll have dirt, theft and speculation.'

She spoke of 'the Soviets' in a disparaging manner, as if she was not one herself. 'Aren't there speculators among foreigners?' I pressed. 'Yes, there are,' she agreed, 'but they are *foreigners*!'

Many of the Beriozka staff tend to look down on their compatriots. The trade for roubles they contemptuously call 'retail' and the word 'Soviet' they hiss through clenched teeth. Such social perversion inevitably breeds crime. Each year several dozen Beriozka employees find themselves behind bars for stealing, profiteering and changing goods. The last term means buying something (say, an amber necklace) in an ordinary shop for roubles and selling it in the Beriozka for hard currency. Thus accumulating lots of foreign money, some of the salespeople can take the goods from the Beriozkas where they work, though buying anything there is strictly prohibited for a Soviet citizen.

The food Beriozka in Krasnopresnenskaya embankment looks very much like the book one from the outside, only the curtains on the windows are heavier. Clairvoyant or not, you won't be able to discern a thing through them. Indeed, it would have been better for me not to see all these hoards of high-quality foodstuffs shielded by the curtain from any inquisitive *Soviet* glance.

It was interesting for me to look at the boxes containing all sorts of Soviet-made sweets. Most of them I was seeing for the first time in my life. Tiny price-tags with the word 'Beriozka' were stuck on the boxes to cover the names of the factories that produced them: Bolshevik, Red October, Red Front. Beautiful names, aren't they? Help yourself, please! S'il vous plaît! Bitte! But what about 'Pozhaluista' ('please' in Russian)? Out of the question!

The Ministry of Trade Instruction regulating Beriozkas specifies that 'goods sold for hard currency must be of high quality'. Funny, but there is no such instruction relating to rouble shops. For the 'Soviets' any quality will do, as well as its complete absence . . .

There was a shameful case in 1987, when packets of a Belgian powdered food for children called Taridin suddenly appeared in ordinary Moscow shops. They came from Beriozkas. Why? It was simply because Rosinvaluttorg, and the Beriozkas' supplier, had bought too much Taridin in Belgium. Maybe a demographic explosion among Moscow-based foreigners was expected, who knows? But the packets of Taridin remained unsold in the Beriozkas until after their expiry date. Seeing this, Rosinvaluttorg, rather than suffer losses, decided to throw Taridin out . . . into the ordinary shops to be sold for roubles. Soviet babies were strong – they would probably cope even with the perished product, it may have been thought. No comment . . .

'It's just fleecing money out of foreigners,' remarked an Australian museum curator with whom I worked as an interpreter, when she entered one of Moscow's Beriozkas. She didn't mean the choice, she meant the prices. A Western tape-recorder, for instance, costs here several times more than in the country of its production. Can you imagine a foreigner – a Dutchman, say – who would be crazy enough to come to Moscow and buy a Phillips recorder for a price much higher than in his native Hague or Eindhoven? Or a West German lady who would rummage through the Moscow shops in search of Burda fashion magazine published in the Soviet Union in Russian and sold at Beriozkas for hard currency? Our customs people would probably assure you that there had never been a case of a Westerner trying to smuggle out Western-made electronic goods, bought in Moscow. Then to whom do the Beriozkas sell them? Well to Soviet citizens. Not all of them, only a special sort who find ways to circumvent the Instruction. Who are they? Prostitutes, profiteers and some members of the artistic élite who travel abroad and illegally manage to keep certain amounts of hard currency.

As to some 'People's Artists of the USSR', in buying goods at Beriozkas they are not simply breaking the law. With them it's much worse. By feeding upon privileged goods inaccessible to ordinary people, they risk ceasing to be real people's artists. When they enter Beriozkas, they leave the country's highest artistic title outside, tying it to a nearby tree like a dog. When they emerge from the commercial paradise, loaded with goods, they are at peril of not finding the 'dog' in its place.

To get to Wonderland, Lewis Carroll's Alice had to crawl through a rabbit hole. To sneak into the fancy-land of the Beriozka one must negotiate an impassive doorman. When touring Moscow's hard currency shops, I was in no hurry to show my official authorisation from Rosinvaluttorg and had some funny clashes with Cerberus-like doormen. A typical dialogue would look like this:

Doorman (blocking my way): 'Soviets are not allowed here. This shop is for foreigners.'
Vitaliev (trying to pass the doorman on the right): 'I just want to have a look.'
Doorman (stepping to the left to block my way): 'Soviets are not allowed to look either.'
Vitaliev (trying to pass the doorman on the left): 'And how do you know I am a Soviet? What if I am Henry Ford the fourteenth? Learnt Russian and came here on a friendly visit to buy the whole shop together with the doorman?'

Doorman (stepping to the right to block my way and critically scrutinising my Moscow-made suit): 'No! You're a Soviet!'

And so on until I finally produced my authorisation . . .

On gaining some experience with the doormen I decided to change tactics. After all, I used to be an interpreter! Now approaching the doorman I tried to assume a smiling and self-assured – ie foreign – look. As soon as he opened his mouth to utter his sacramental 'This shop is only . . .', I blurted out a sentence from *Pygmalion*: 'The rain in Spain falls mainly on the plain . . .' Or a quotation from my beloved Longfellow: 'Pleasant it was when woods were green and winds were soft and low . . .' Or just some random English gibberish . . . The doorman's attitude changed immediately. 'Aah! *Then* you're welcome,' he would mutter, and what might have been a smile appeared on his ruddy face . . .

Funny as it may seem, it is very serious all the same. Beriozkas are extra-territorial shops unique in the world. Situated on Soviet soil, they neglect Soviet people and Soviet money. They even ignore some Soviet laws, one of which lays down that spirits all over the country must be sold from 2 pm to 8 pm. Beriozkas sell spirits from 9 am to 9 pm. And there are no queues.

'Beriozkas do not bring us profit,' a Rosinvaluttorg official confessed to me. What do they bring then? Trampled national pride. Violated civil rights. Perverted morals. Public humiliation. Dislike of foreigners. Social injustice.

It is high time to realise that national pride is also a currency – no less hard than dollars, pounds or yen. When on earth will we stop wasting it?

Welcome to the Soviet Union, my dear readers! But unwelcome to the Beriozkas!

The Fourth Department

The struggle for social justice conducted by the press is in full swing, and progress is evident. But sometimes bureaucrats are not easily stripped of their unearned privileges. The special hospitals for the élite seem to be one of the hardest nuts to crack.

The Ministry of Health of the USSR runs the so-called 'Fourth Department', responsible for treating high-ranking apparatchiks, with a network of special VIP hospitals, polyclinics, sanatoriums and so on. Its institutions are much better equipped than their ordinary counterparts and do not suffer from a lack of medicines.

When my father's health began to deteriorate, his doctor said he needed a rare Belgian-made medicine to combat arrhythmia. 'You are not going to find this drug at ordinary chemists',' he said. 'The only way to get it is through the Fourth Department, if you have connections there.'

At that time I was working as an interpreter at the Moscow Medical Information Institute, so I approached the director and asked for help. He agreed to write an official letter to the Fourth Department asking for the medicine to be sold to me from their 'closed' drugstore as an 'exception'. With this letter I went to Granvskogo St, where the Kremlin drugstore (as it was popularly known) was situated next to the above-mentioned 'raspredelitel' – special foodshop. There was no sign on the door, only a small plate inscribed 'Bureau of Passes'. The doorman inside was on the alert. I showed him the letter and he ordered me to go upstairs and drop it into a special post box, which I did. On my way back he gave me a telephone number and told me to call in ten days. When I called, a polite but firm man's voice answered that they had got my letter but unfortunately they couldn't help me with the drug. 'Why?' I asked. 'Because of certain conditions,' the man retorted and hung up. This was my only personal encounter with the powerful Fourth Department. Soon after that my father died and I didn't need any more rare medicines.

The experience was disheartening. I felt I was treated like an ant and not like a human being . . .

It is known that doctors who work at the Fourth Department are better paid than their colleagues in ordinary clinics. To get a job there you must have good connections. This has resulted in a paradox. The doctors working at the Fourth Department hospitals are now notorious for their lack of skills, since the main thing in getting a job there is not proficiency but pull. That is why some apparatchiks prefer going to ordinary polyclinics for an examination. Kharkov Obkom Clinic, also belonging to the Fourth Department, won a reputation as a mortuary, meaning that anyone who was hospitalised there was going to die despite good equipment and food. So as you see, the privileges here are rather illusory, but still they are privileges. Inequality in health care to my mind is the worst kind of inequality. Especially when it comes to children.

I recently visited the Crimean resort of Yevpatoriya, where I was shown the Fourth Department children's sanatorium, Brigantina. Children of high-ranking officials were staying there. Most were quite healthy, but they lived under excellent conditions: neat, cosy rooms for two, beautiful playing grounds, school, swimming-pool and so forth. I wouldn't have minded all this if it were not for the fact that at the neighbouring 'ordinary' sanatorium for children suffering from tuberculosis the conditions were abominable: dirt, shabby houses, plaster peeling off the walls, mice and cockroaches. But what struck me most was that in Brigantina the daily food budget per child was four roubles eighty-seven copecks, while at the neighbouring sanatorium it was just seventy-eight copecks. The privileged healthy children were eating salmon and caviare, the under-privileged children suffering from tuberculosis got bread and potatoes . . .

My wife is afraid of having a second child: her memories of the 'ordinary' maternity home are so frightful that she doesn't even want to think of going there again. When she got home she described how there had been just one pair of slippers for twenty women and only one toilet for the whole floor. The sheets on the bed were dirty and blood-stained and were changed once every ten days. No anaesthetic was given during the birth. But the main problem was with the staff, who were rude and didn't care. So now you can understand why foreign journalists and diplomats living in Moscow usually take their wives to their home countries to give birth, though they are assigned to much better maternity homes.

Thank God, I have never been to a Fourth Department hospital myself. But a story told by a colleague of mine serves as a good illustration. When he fell ill, his wife used connections and managed to have him hospitalised in one of the Fourth Department clinics. The conditions were excellent and the food was OK. Once his wife came to see him and brought some tomatoes from an ordinary shop. When the duty-nurse came into the ward and saw my colleague eating them, she was flabbergasted. 'What are you doing?!' she cried in terror. 'You're eating tomatoes for the population!!!'

My colleague also said there was a bathroom in every ward. In this connection I remember the Kharkov hospital where I was treated for my ulcer. There was only one toilet for a building which housed about two hundred patients. The doctors and nurses were generally good, but they had a nasty habit of lavaging patients' stomachs on a massive scale, when several dozen people received the procedure almost simultaneously. You can imagine what kind of corridor races started after that, and how violently the door of the only toilet was pounded . . . There was no shower at all, by the way, and very little hygiene. Almost all of my fellow-sufferers had infiltrates (skin lumps) caused by dirty syringes. Thank Heaven, AIDS did not exist at that time.

I cannot forget how once in 1974, when I was just twenty, I was visiting my first wife's parents who lived in a remote Ukrainian village, and was suddenly laid up with a very serious case of pneumonia. For two days I was running a temperature which was close to 42° centigrade (the fatal mark). When on the third day I started spitting blood, it was decided to send me to hospital. There existed only one for the whole district, and it was situated in the town of Apostolovo, the district centre, about 50 kilometres from the village. The shabby old jalopy of an ambulance picked me up during the night and took me along the bumpy crooked country road to Apostolovo. On the way I fainted, and when I came to myself in the morning I was lying in a big hospital ward with peeling stucco on the walls and dirty streaks all over the ceiling. There were at least forty patients there. Some, I felt, were dying, while others looked healthy, even robust, and were drinking vodka and playing dominoes. The toilet was in the courtyard. It was just a hole in the ground . . .

The man who was lying in the bed next to me (he died in a couple of days) was suffering from some kind of kidney trouble. Day and night – almost without a stop – he was urinating into a big glass vessel standing under his bed: he was too feeble to go to the toilet. Thin and yellow, he really looked more dead than alive. His last name was Sokolik (little falcon). Never in my life have I seen someone whose name could be less appropriate for his looks.

Sokolik's constant urinating unnerved the healthy inmates of the ward who used to hurl empty bottles – made from heavy glass – at the poor chap. All this was unbearable. After Sokolik died I felt that I was definitely going to go the same way if I stayed there much longer. I implored the doctors to let me go home, and they finally agreed on the condition that I would have regular penicillin injections for a month to follow. Coming out of this 'ordinary' country hospital was like coming out of hell.

In 1986 I published a story in *Krokodil* which was called 'Medical History'.[9] It was the result of my trip to Bataisk, a town not far from Rostov-na-Donu. Klementiev, a specialist at the local polyclinic, had murdered his sixteen-year-old sister-in-law. He had intended to murder his wife out of jealousy but, being drunk, in the dark he mistook her sister for her and stabbed the poor girl sixteen times with a home-made knife. After Klementiev was arrested, it came to light that he had not only been a chronic alcoholic since his student days, but was a double murderer as well: several years before he had killed his friend in a drunken brawl, but had not been brought to trial (it was categorised as an unpremeditated murder) and went on working as a doctor! I also discovered that the head physician of his polyclinic was very much in favour of boozing, and didn't think it abnormal when a doctor received his patients drunk. Further investigation revealed that there was one more criminal doctor in that health care establishment. Once, when drunk, he had stabbed his wife (not to death luckily) and then spent several years in prison. After his release he had resumed his job as a doctor. To crown it all, a third specialist out of the seventeen on the staff had also been a jailbird several times for some smaller peccadilloes.

'There is a shortage of doctors,' an official at the Health Ministry told me, trying to account for the situation.

But isn't it better to have a shortage of doctors than doctors who are criminals?

In January 1989 a striking case of negligence at an 'ordinary' children's hospital in Elista (Kalmykia) resulted in thirty-two small children and six women being infected with the AIDS virus. The tragedy was caused by syringes which had not been properly sterilised by the hospital staff (disposable hypodermic needles and syringes are still a problem at 'ordinary' hospitals, but the Fourth Department has no shortages). 'The employees there must have lost all sense of shame as humans and medical professionals,' said Vadim Pokrovosky, the leading Soviet AIDS expert.[10]

So, you see, the conditions under which our 'ordinary' medical service sometimes works. Considering this, the Fourth Department with its beautiful premises and excellent facilities looks even more outrageous. If it were abolished and its resources equally distributed among 'ordinary' clinics, this would immediately improve our Health Service as a whole, and make it more democratic.

Then, probably, we would have another child.

Passportless Person

Several days before I set about writing these lines, *Literaturnaya Gazeta* published for the first time in forty-odd years the full text of the Universal Declaration of Human Rights adopted by the UN General Assembly on 10 December 1948.[11] It was an unprecedented act on the part of the newspaper, since although having heard something about the existence of such a document, hardly anyone in this country knew exactly what it was about.

And now if we look at Article 13 of the Declaration, signed among others by the Soviet Union, we read that: 'Every individual has the right to move freely and to choose their place of living in every state.'

Unfortunately, this essential right is not yet fully realised in our country, and the main obstacle is the existing system of internal passports.

An internal passport, according to the Instruction of the Council of Ministers, is 'the main identification document of a Soviet citizen'. Without it one cannot move around the country. One must show the passport to get accommodation at a hotel, to be admitted to a hospital, rest-home or sanatorium, to get a plane ticket, etc. If you are going to stay somewhere for more than one and a half months, you are supposed to be registered there. 'Propiska' (registration) is the main stumbling block for freedom of movement. The point is that the largest cities and towns are so crowded and congested that for a newcomer it is practically impossible to be registered there unless he/she is married to a person with local registration in his/her passport.

I know the hidden meaning of propiska only too well. As I explained earlier, when I was about to marry my second wife, who had Moscow registration, I faced a dilemma. My passport was registered in Kharkov, and a Moscow marriage certificate would automatically give me the right to a Moscow propiska, but on one condition only: that no adult members of my would-be wife's family should object. My future mother-in-law did object. Her reason was that as soon as I acquired Moscow registration, I would also acquire the right to 'living space' in the capital, ie in her flat, and if my wife and I divorced, I would be entitled to go to court and appeal for the flat to be divided. Of course, I didn't have the slightest intention of doing so, but to her mind there was always the possibility.

So my dilemma was as follows: to be registered in Moscow I had to cancel my Kharkov registration first. But as soon as I did that I would lose the right to return to live in my native city if anything went wrong. I was aware of my future mother-in-law's reluctance to grant me Moscow registration: it was within her powers. This could create a situation in which I might find myself without any registration at all.

The night before our marriage neither Natasha nor I could sleep a wink. Shortly before dawn we came to a decision: to ask the marriage registration clerk not to put a marriage stamp in my passport. That would leave me the possibility of preserving my Kharkov registration if something went out of synch. In the morning I bought a box of expensive chocolates and we went to ZAGS (the Marriages, Births and Deaths Registration Office). I gave the sweets to the female clerk and asked her confidentially not to stamp my passport. It was a certain breach of the regulations on her part, but she grew sympathetic and agreed to go along with it. If she hadn't, we simply would not have been married on that day.

Not being sure of whether we'd be married, we were wearing just our everyday clothes – no suit, white dress or bridal veil, which was very

173

unusual for the occasion. But at least it was not typical, and hence something to be remembered, or so we consoled ourselves.

My second encounter with the absurd and inhuman passport system occurred after my father's death. My mother was left all alone in Kharkov and naturally she wanted to come and live with me in Moscow. Moscow registration rules are much stricter than elsewhere. In breach of the Constitution, Moscow City Council introduced its own regulations by which parents from elsewhere can obtain the right to live in the capital where their child lives only if (a) they are retired, or (b) they have no other adult children. So I had to wait until my mother was fifty-five (the official retirement age for women) to comply with the first condition. As to the second one, it was OK since I had neither brothers nor sisters nor even cousins.

The other problem was to find a flat for my mother to live in. She had to exchange her two-bedroomed apartment in Kharkov for some 'living space' in Moscow. The unofficial exchange rate was: two rooms elsewhere for one room in the capital. For one and a half years I looked for a suitable exchange. It was not an easy thing to do, since the overwhelming majority of people do not want to leave Moscow for good. In the long run I found an elderly lady whose son lived ... not in Kharkov but in Dnepropetrovsk. She wanted to join him. The next stage was to find someone in Dnepropetrovsk who had to go to Kharkov. Such a person was found with the help of a flat exchange bulletin. It took more than half a year to have all the papers stamped and certified – and at last the elaborate scheme worked: the old Moscow lady went to Dnepropetrovsk to rejoin her son, the guy from Dnepropetrovsk moved to our two-roomed apartment in Kharkov with his family, and my mother came to the old lady's one-roomed kitchenette.

All this sounds bizarre, but we had to comply: we had no alternative. In a way we were even lucky to bring off the whole project successfully. I know many families who are separated within their own country due to the absurd registration system.

It was not always like that. After the Revolution and throughout the Twenties, there were no internal passports and no registration in the Soviet Union. It was only in April 1933 that Stalin introduced the current passport system with residence permits.[12] Internal passports were issued to all urban dwellers. As to country residents, they were not supposed to have any documents at all, and were fully dependent on the mercy of the collective farm heads, who had the right to grant or withhold peasants' passports when the latter wanted to move or return to some other place. In fact, this was nothing but serfdom, and was part of Stalin's infernal plan for forced collectivisation. Passports were given to the collective farmers only under Khrushchev.

For many years I have been eager to write about this dreadful system, but before perestroika even to try was hopeless. Passports and registration were taboo for journalists. In the summer of 1988 I finally wrote an article 'A Passportless Person'.[13] The title had a strong connotation of Stalin's purges – to be more exact, of his crazy anti-semitic campaign of 1952, the so-called 'doctor's plot', when a group of Jewish doctors were blamed for a conspiracy to murder Zhdanov a few years earlier. For the dying Stalin, it was just a pretext to launch a massive anti-Jewish campaign which was to be consummated by the removal of all Jews to the Far East. It was then that the labels 'pygmies', 'cosmopolitans' and 'passportless vagabonds' were invented and used by the press as euphemisms for Jews.

Being one of the first articles to condemn the existing passport system, 'A Passportless Person' was hard to publish even in 1988. Neither *Krokodil* nor *Literaturnaya Gazeta* ventured to accept it. It was finally accepted and published by the weekly *Ogonyok*.

For many years before and after the war, *Ogonyok* was a mouthpiece of the ruling élite. Edited by the tame conservative poet Anatoly Sofronov, it was broadly neglected by readers. If someone did buy the magazine, it was solely for the sake of a crossword puzzle it carried in every issue. In 1986, the new *Ogonyok* editor-in-chief Vitali Korotich was appointed. I have mentioned our brief meeting in Kharkov in 1970, when as a tyro poet I was sent to some obscure gathering of Ukrainian writers. Korotich came from Kiev where as well as being a brilliant poet, he also edited the monthly *Vsesvit* (The World), the first magazine to publish Mario Puzo's *The Godfather* in the mid-Seventies. The new editor-in-chief quickly changed the face of *Ogonyok*. Within a year it had become the most courageous, progressive and pro-perestroika periodical in the country, and its circulation has more than tripled – from less than a million under Sofronov to 3,200,000 in 1989. And while this circulation is still much lower than, say, *Krokodil*'s (5,300,000 at present), *Ogonyok* is also much more difficult to buy. Both the magazine and its editor are thoroughly hated by all anti-perestroika forces – from the conservative press to the members of the openly anti-semitic Memory Society, who have even made some attempts to beat up Korotich, the superintendent of perestroika, as some would call him.

The coverage of social injustice has become one of *Ogonyok*'s many topics. It has consistently exposed corrupt leaders, judicial errors, biased law enforcement. The so-called 'small person' – an underpaid worker, a neglected collective farmer, even a tramp – has found in *Ogonyok* his main

175

protector. In an article about the growing suicide rate in the Soviet Union, the magazine stated: 'It has turned out that in our country, with its old optimistic and promising slogan "All for the sake of an individual", the least was actually done for this very individual. No achievement in science and engineering, agriculture and heavy industry, space exploration and ballet will help a person to understand himself and others, to teach himself how to live and to find ways out of his inner crises. We must return to the human being. Otherwise another night will set in and hundreds of people won't wish, won't be able, to live any longer.'[14] I would readily put my signature under these noble words . . .

So 'A Passportless Person' was published by *Ogonyok*. What was the article about? For the greater part, it was not merely critical of the existing passport system. It argued against the spirit of mutual distrust between the people and the authorities, with the passport system as one of its reflections.

To begin with, I informed my Soviet readers that in most countries there are no internal passports, only foreign ones. For many this was a revelation: even some of my friends were quite sure that passport systems similar to ours were ubiquitous and existed all over the globe. 'How can they do without internal passports?' they would ask. 'Doesn't this create social anarchy, and so a good cover for criminals?' 'No it doesn't,'I answered in the article. 'How on earth do they determine who is who then?' 'Simple enough. By checking a person's driving licence, insurance policy or any kind of identification paper. But more often they just tend to take someone's word for it.'

What if you are really dealing with a criminal or someone who is in hiding, perhaps so as not to pay maintenance for his children? Of course, a certain risk is involved when you take someone's words at their face value. But the number of criminals and fathers-in-hiding is so small compared with the number of honest people that it seems absurd to institute huge paperwork for their sake. To believe is merely cheaper than to have doubts. The expenses of catching a bunch of spies or bullies are not comparable to the cost of a well-oiled bureaucratic machine. Capitalists, with all their defects, are very good at calculating.

So what happens? Capitalists believe their people and we don't? But isn't that a paradox? Where if not under socialism should everything be based on mutual trust?

Alas, we are still far from that. We are distrusted all the time: at hotels where you have to produce your passport for the reception clerk to compare the photograph with the faded original, and see whether you are married or single (what business is it of his?). We are distrusted at libraries, where they make us fill in lengthy forms, supplying so much information about ourselves that we might be intending not just to leaf through a couple of books but to get a job with the Ministry of Defence. Once, filling in a reader's form at a small rest-home library, I wrote 'Scythian' in the column for nationality, and what do you think? No one noticed.

The very term 'nationality', in our sense of the word, may prove confusing for a Westerner. You may think that everyone who lives all his life in Russia, automatically becomes Russian by nationality. Nothing of the kind. You and your parents may not know a word of, say, Yiddish or Hebrew, and may never go near a synagogue, but will still be listed as a 'Jew' in your passport. The same applies to Armenians, Ukrainians and others. Mind: not your origins are meant but your 'nationality', which is something not simply beyond your powers but often beyond any understanding too. For instance, in the highlands of Dagestan (an autonomous Soviet republic in the Caucasus) there lives a small ethnic group of 'mountain Jews' or 'Tats'. In Dagestan I was told that it took a big bribe for a mountain Jew to be entered as a 'Tat', since having the word 'Jew' in your passport was until recently a severe handicap.

If you ask a citizen of the United States what he or she is by nationality, the most likely answer will be 'American'. But if you enquire about their origins, you'll hear 'Irish', 'Indian', 'Jew'. Of course, nationality is important, but it's too bad when it starts and finishes with the inscription in your passport. It must be somewhere deeper – in one's heart, in one's soul, in one's memory. This passport entry is superfluous, since it doesn't say anything about you as a human being. But it does enable some nationalistic bureaucrats to use it in their own interests by discriminating against you in one way or another. The nationality column should be excluded from our passports. There is already a precedent – the Soviet international passport issued to those who go abroad, in which they are written down as 'Soviet' irrespective of their 'nationality'.

To get such a passport, you must pay a hefty tax every time you travel. Besides you have to fill in a lot of forms with irrelevant, sometimes insulting questions. This is the quintessence of stubborn, primeval distrust. 'Have you been abroad before, where, when and with what purpose?' If you have been, is it good or bad? 'Have you got any relatives abroad?' You feel the urge to answer, Odessa-style: 'What business is it of yours?' 'Your wife's maiden name?' 'The names of your dead relatives?' Someone at the top must be sure that these names are indispensable in deciding whether or not you are 'worthy' of going abroad. And 'nationality', of course ... Such forms have become shorter now, but innocent people still keep filling them in with 'No', 'I haven't', 'I didn't', which every time sounds like a plea of not guilty. And what about the presumption of innocence? It is as if someone high and mighty is stamping his feet on the floor and frowning angrily . . .

By the way, I was very surprised to find similar forms in the British Consulate Office in Moscow when applying for a British visa. They were even longer, and contained such questions as: How much money are you going to take with you to the United Kingdom? Where are you going to get this money from? (a) from your bank account?, (b) from your friends? – and so on. Strange for the motherland of democracy, isn't it?

A friend of mine who was going to France told me that at the French Embassy the forms were even more impertinent and included the question: 'Are you going to beg while in France?'

So not everything is a vision of mutual trust in the West either.

But back to registration (propiska) – the essence of our passport system. Paragraph 34 of the above-mentioned Instruction states that: 'Citizens living without registration for more than three days are liable to fines.' Some freedom of movement!

Propiska is a purely Soviet term. Linguists call such untranslatable words 'Sovietisms'. Among them you will also find 'sputnik' (artificial earth satellite), 'avoska' (just-for-chance bag to be carried in the pocket in case one comes across some good products on sale), and 'dostat' (to obtain with difficulty).

But are we really so different from the rest of the world that we cannot do without the word 'propiska'?

Our propiska advocates assume that if it were not for registration all the people would rush to the big cities with their undergrounds, circuses and sausages (if any). The countryside would be empty and the cities flooded with newcomers. But recent public opinion polls prove quite the opposite: often it is only the fear of losing their precious registration that prevents urban dwellers from living and working in the countryside for several years and having a whiff of fresh air. They would also willingly go to the north or the far east to earn some money and to help in developing these remote regions. But propiska stands in their way.

The registration system, many tend to believe, was created by the housing shortage in the cities. This is not true. Propiska is not the cause but a mere reflection of the housing situation in our country. It has no influence on the lack of housing. To think otherwise is like attempting to change someone's appearance by retouching his photograph.

That's all about nationality and registration. What further information does a Soviet internal passport contain? Marriage certification. What is to be done about that? Won't the country suffer an epidemic of polygamy if we abolish the marriage stamp? Won't harems appear? Won't unmarried individuals of the opposite (or same) sex seek accommodation in one and the same hotel room? Yes, they will. But who is going to lose (or to profit) from this but themselves? And is it realistic to try and suppress the most powerful of human instincts by stamping (or not stamping) someone's passport? It is nothing short of naïve. Better to build more hotels.

As to harems and polygamy, do you think our present passport system protects the county against them? Just drop into the nearest militia precinct and they will tell you. As a matter of fact, the stamp in one's passport can be (a) forged, (b) erased without a trace. To catch brothel-keepers, polygamists and other underworld creatures, the militia may use fingerprints – which cannot be forged – direct evidence, hearsay and even the obscure science of odorology, enabling them to identify a criminal by the smell he or she gives off. All these are much more effective than a passport stamp.

So what is finally left of our famous internal passport? Nothing but a hammered-and-sickled red cover. Plus a multi-million (in cost and in staffing) bureaucratic machine. Plus the everyday humiliation for each of us, as if we are being watched constantly. Plus mutual distrust between those who hold power and those who are held under their power.

'A passportless person' and 'A person with a passport' – what is the difference between these two concepts? No difference whatsoever, if we think of a person as a human being, not just as a passport holder.

Ashes in Polyethylene

My next article in *Ogonyok* was entitled 'Ashes in Polyethylene'.[15] It dealt with a sad and terrible subject – the state of our cemeteries and crematoriums. As I wrote in the previous chapter, even our graveyards have been divided into privileged and ordinary. Social injustice, starting at birth, does not end with the end of life. It extends further – into death.

'Everything is quiet in the cemetery,' a popular song goes. In a privileged cemetery, I would add, a cemetery like Novodevichie and Vagankovskoye in Moscow. In the rest of them it's far from quiet.

To write about this is frightening, but it is even more frightening *not* to write about it.

There are two inevitable states for every human being – birth and death. Start and finish. Joy and sorrow.

179

We have learnt to measure the economic potential of a society with the help of figures, percentages, statistical data. But how can its moral potential be estimated? I think the attitude to the dead may serve as the surest criterion for determining the moral level of this or that society.

BECAUSE OF THE ABSENCE OF URNS
ASHES WILL BE GIVEN OUT
IN POLYETHYLENE BAGS

What's that? Someone's monstrous joke? No. This sign hung on the doors of Kharkov crematorium. To those who were curious, the crematorium clerks readily explained that the shortage of urns was due to the fact that the factory which used to supply them had converted to making lavatory pans . . .

In this dreadful place several years ago I was paying my last tribute to my father. Through the black, leaden veil of unbearable grief I saw a fussy, fast-moving young man – the crematorium worker. He was the master of ceremonies. At some point he started to read banal words of commiseration from the tattered sheet of paper he held in his hands. He kept forgetting the name of the deceased, and would stumble each time he had to mention it. 'What is he doing here, this alien, uncaring man?' I thought. On his right wrist there was a black and red satin band with a bonfire on it. A metal pin – again with a bonfire – was on his chest. This outrageous sacrilege was for some reason called 'ritual'.

When we came back some days later to collect the ashes, the crematorium people had no shame about extorting a bribe: they gave us the urn (urns weren't yet in short supply) only after we gave them the money, although the funeral service had already been paid for.

After that I went to the cemetery office to get permission to bury the urn. Behind the door with the sign 'Director' a fat, heavily made-up blonde with lots of rings on her fingers was sitting in state. Just above her table hung a red triangular pennant with the inscription:

TO THE VICTOR IN SOCIALIST EMULATION

Could anyone's spirit be more bureaucratised?

Last year my distant relative died on Donetsk, another Ukrainian city. He was a labour veteran and a war invalid. He died on the eve of the first of May, the national holiday: death doesn't recognise red-letter dates. This was awful. Not just because the grief fell on his family at a time of national gaiety. The real horror lay in the sheer impossibility of finding a coffin in

Donetsk at this time of festivities. The dead man's sons had to roam all over the Donetsk region in search of a coffin. They found it eventually, but this wasn't the end of their troubles. When the procession of mourners arrived at the cemetery, they saw a huge stone blocking the grave. It had appeared during the night and didn't seem to have fallen from the heavens. To remove the stone, the labourers demanded one hundred roubles. A cemetery is no place for bargaining, they reckoned, and they proved to be right. I'm sure that their portable stone was safely transferred to another empty grave on that very day. Dirty primitive blackmail! And there is no one to remove the stone that presses heavily upon our hearts and souls, upon our conscience.

My friend's father died last summer. On a scorching July day we came to the mortuary of the First Gradskaya Hospital in Moscow. In the lobby of this sad institution I saw a sign, printed in gold letters:

THE DEAD ARE GIVEN OUT ON THE PRODUCTION OF DEATH CERTIFICATE, PASSPORT AND RESIDENCE PERMIT

For some reason, I recalled the sign I saw in 1980 at the headquarters of the Moscow Olympics Organising Committee:

FANTA IS GIVEN OUT FROM 2 PM TILL 4 PM

What is going on? Have they forgotten that *living* people come to the mortuary? Don't they know that the dead don't need residence permits any longer? To me, only someone with a *dead spirit* could have written such a sign.

The hearse, painted bright yellow, with a strict 'NO SMOKING' sign inside (it was just an ordinary city bus in fact), took us to the crematorium of Nikolo-Archangelskoye cemetery on the outskirts of Moscow.

A long line of bright yellow hearse buses waited their turn at the gates, black smoke belching incessantly from the tall crematorium chimney visible from all over the vicinity ... Seeing this smoke some women fainted.

When 'our' turn came, we were led into a hall. 'No more than ten minutes for parting,' warned a woman clerk in a grey mouse-coloured dress. Many people wanted to say a few words at the funeral meeting, but all of a sudden an organ started playing somewhere above. The words of respect were drowned by the music.

When the music stopped, our time was up. The woman in the mouse-coloured dress materialised out of nowhere and demanded that we finish the ceremony. Hastily she nailed down the coffin and ordered us to disperse. She didn't even try to hide her hatred for us all. The detestation was stamped on her plain, puppet-like face. 'Wind it up! Stop talking!' she snapped.

We went outside, giving way to the next procession. Around the building, under the scorching rays of the July sun, hundreds of people were waiting. There was nowhere they could shelter from the sun, nowhere to sit. They could only have a drink from the black rubber hose stretching along the ground like a snake. The water was warm and rusty. The death march was being played somewhere nearby. More and more buses were driving through the gates.

Suddenly the hot air was pierced by the deafening sound of gunshots. In one of the crematorium halls a military officer was receiving last respects. A military guard of honour was saluting the deceased from outside. Hearing the shots the exhausted people outside jerked convulsively. Elementary conveniences for the *living* did not exist here. But on the fence – above all this concentration of grief – hung an advertisement publicising the 'convenience' (just this very word they used!) of placing an urn in a closed columbarium. And the black smoke dissolved in the blue sky . . .

I am not calling for the punishment of the indifferent crematorium and cemetery workers – though there have been many such calls. I am not calling for the reorganisation of our funeral services – these suggestions are not news either. I am not even going to condemn the bastards who profiteer on human grief – those who speculate on death have no feelings of shame, only of greed.

I just want to say . . . Or rather to scream:

INDIFFERENCE TO THE DEAD IS A DANGEROUS SOCIAL DISEASE. WITHOUT CURING IT WE WON'T BE ABLE TO BUILD A REALLY DEMOCRATIC SOCIETY. DEMOCRACY IS HUMANITY. AND HUMANITY IS ABOVE ALL RESPECT FOR THE DEAD. WE ARE ALL STANDING IN THAT MOURNFUL LINE WAITING FOR OUR TURN. DOWN WITH THE POLYETHYLENES OF INDIFFERENCE! RE- MOVE IDIOTIC BLASPHEMOUS PLATES AND SIGNS! TAKE STONES AWAY FROM GRAVEYARDS! HIDE THE SMOKING CREMATORIUM CHIMNEYS FOR NO ONE TO SEE!

PEOPLE, BE HUMAN!

IS THERE ANYBODY ALIVE?
OR HAVE WE ALL BEEN DEAD FOR A LONG WHILE?

After the article was published, a reader sent *Ogonyok* a price list from a Moscow crematorium. One entry read: 'Burning of a child's corpse – 67 copecks apiece.'

The struggle for the spiritual renewal of our society continues. Some people don't want to know the truth of how we really lived and live. It embarrasses them. Indeed, truth is often embarrassing, and not always an easy thing to tell. But it is the truth and we must know it all.

Step by step, the truth finds its way on to the pages of newspapers and magazines, to the TV screens. A Society is healthy only when it is not afraid to look at itself critically. It is not a simple thing to build a democratic and law-abiding State in a country which has just narrowly escaped an economic crisis. The aftermath of the long stagnation period is still felt. Only this time we are not going to silence our problems. 'The shops are empty. The country lives on food coupons. Many promises remain mere promises. This cannot be denied. But there is no need to,' wrote Yegor Yakovlev, the editor-in-chief of *Moscow News* weekly, in 1988.[16] And the last phrase, 'there is no need to', sounds encouraging.

Here is a letter published by *Pravda* – the main Party newspaper: 'We can no longer close our eyes to the fact that Party, Soviet, trade union and even Komsomol officials sometimes deepen existing social injustice by using special canteens, special shops and special hospitals . . . Let the bosses stand in queues with everybody else in ordinary shops. And then, perhaps, at last, all these depressing queues will come to an end.'[17]

Let's not close our eyes. Let's open them wide. Then we'll have a chance of improvement. A very good chance.

The liquidation of rulers' privileges recently became one of the main planks in the election programmes of the candidates to the Supreme Soviet. These elections, held on 26 March 1989, were the first for seventy years in which we had to choose from two or more nominees to one deputy's chair. As it said in the programme of Professor Savitsky: 'We must struggle for complete abolition of the privileges of the ruling officials. These privileges poison the moral climate of society. Special shops, special canteens, special polytechnics and all other "specials" are the antipodes of true socialism. Until they are abolished, open and hidden antagonism between "upper" and "lower" strata will continue to exist.'[18]

Recently in *Ogonyok* there was a revealing article about Yuri Chur-banov, the former Deputy Minister of the Interior and Brezhnev's son-in-law, recently sentenced to twelve years' imprisonment for bribe-taking. After spending some time in a preliminary detention cell before the trial, he asked one of the investigators: 'Is it true that there is neither meat nor sausage in Moscow shops now? Under Leonid Ilyich Brezhnev they were on sale. How would you account for that?' 'But in your time, there was no truth, and that is much worse,' the investigator answered.[19]

Letter Box

No Roubles, No Windows

Beriozka hard currency shops are disgraceful for everyone who earns their daily bread honestly and in roubles, that is for the most part of the Soviet people. When in Moscow with my husband, we passed one such shop near Kievsky railway station and decided to peep inside but were shooed away by a wild-looking uniformed doorman. Wouldn't it be better to open good department stores for our children instead of the Beriozkas? I've got a daughter, Alyonushka, who is just one year old and I cannot buy any good clothes for her, not even a pair of tights. The food shops are also as bare as a bone in our city: there is nothing but mineral water there. So roubles cannot buy anything. And the hard currency shops are bursting with high-quality goods ... My name is Tatiana, I am a laboratory assistant.

D–va, 23, Vladimir.

I read your article 'No Roubles, No Windows' and came to a bitter conclusion: no need to fight prostitution. On the contrary, we must encourage it, since prostitutes bring us hard currency. It is for them that the Beriozka shops in Moscow, Leningrad and other cities are open.

S–va, Morshansk.

I am a non-commissioned officer from Tomsk. I am a regular subscriber to your magazine and usually read it from beginning to end. When I read the feuilleton 'No Roubles, No Windows', I felt sorry for us Soviet citizens. Why do Beriozkas sell foreign clothes and electronics? That's not what foreign tourists want to buy in Russia. They are mainly interested in matrioshka dolls, Palekh boxes, Dymkovo toys and other Russian artefacts. I know that in Japan a pair of traditional Russian bast sandals costs no less than a Sony tape-recorder. But these things are not easily found in Beriozkas. This makes me think that these shops exist not so much for foreigners but rather for the sake of our prostitutes and hard-currency dealers. Or at least for those foreign tourists who speculate in Western goods, selling them on the black market for roubles to buy the same bast sandals and matrioshkas in ordinary shops. When on earth will the sweets made in the Red October and Bolshevik factories be accessible

185

not only to capitalists, but to Bolsheviks as well? To say nothing of salmon and sturgeon, which I have never seen in the twenty-five years of my life, just heard of.

Closing the Beriozkas will make our society healthier just as much as the fight against alcoholism will. The old Russian saying goes: 'We are rich in what we have' so let's be happy with what *we*, not *they*, have. Let foreign guests buy *our* goods, not *theirs*, bought for hard currency just to be resold at Beriozkas for much higher prices. I feel ashamed to peep into the small Beriozka paradise which is just fifteen minutes' walk from the Kremlin. What a real shame!

Respectfully, M–sky, Tomsk.

Do the shops like Beriozkas exist in Western countries, I wonder? I'm sure they don't. We must spare our citizens' national pride and self-esteem. Beriozka shops must be closed.

G–v, Vladimir.

You may think I am too sentimental, but reading that in some of our Soviet shops Soviet citizens are not allowed to be served sends shivers down my spine, and especially terrifying is that these words are spoken on behalf of the Russian Soviet Federative Socialist Republic in the notorious Instruction of its Trade Ministry quoted in your article. I was on the point of tears when I read this. 'We Soviets have our own pride and look down on the bourgeois' – this line from a formerly popular song is well forgotten. Now we have another slogan: 'Soviet means alien', as you justly put in your article. Someone at the top who encourages Beriozkas is not going to forgive you your courage. So, for the sake of your safety, don't write any more courageous articles.

M–nkom Leningrad.

When shall we stop being obsequious towards foreigners? When shall we learn to respect our own people's dignity? I am a war invalid, fought in Finland, Stalingrad, in Latvia. Recently I was flying from Leningrad to Moscow. There were some foreigners on the plane who were speaking English. When we landed in Moscow, the bus for foreigners was standing on the airfield. Soviet passengers were told to go on foot. It was quite a distance, especially for me walking with crutches. One of our passengers started protesting and then the airport woman official reluctantly agreed to let me into the bus. There were no vacant seats in it and I had to stand there on my crutches all the way. And the foreigners were comfortably sitting. It was an insult not only for me, but for our country as a great power. We have forgotten that we are a great people – not toadies. Pride is what we need!

K–pov, war invalid second grade, former teacher, Uralsk.

Secrets of the Vip Hall

Deputies' rooms exist not only at railway stations but at airports as well. Sometimes, these are not rooms but palaces full of carpets, crystal, expensive furniture. They have refreshment rooms stuffed with rare foodstuffs, and personal waitresses. In Yakutsk airport next to the deputies' hall, dozens of ordinary passengers sit hunched on the steps, on the floor and on windowsills, due to lack of space. I would agree to allowing war and labour veterans, pregnant women or just old people in the VIP rooms. But not healthy strong, self-centred deputies. Why separate them from the people? Let them stand in queues for the café and for luggage registration. Let them see all our problems. They should only be allowed to jump the ticket queue if they are flying to take part in a government meeting. In all other cases, they must be together with the people.

Sh–gin, Yakutia.

It's no good for the deputy elected by me to be hiding from his elector in a VIP room, thus underlining our inequality.

B–zov, Sverdlovsk

We will never move forward, never progress, until our ruling élite starts living one life with the people. Only then will real social justice emerge. I have just retired from the army and have no flat to live in. And I've got a wife, two children and an elderly mother-in-law to support. I used to have a flat in Moscow, but gave it to the state when I was drafted. Now they say I must wait for three or four years. What is it but a crime? We desperately need social justice.

T–n, army veteran, homeless lieutenant-colonel of the reserve, Moscow.

Our socialist State has been turned into an underground empire where some enjoy carefree, plentiful lives, and others have to work from dawn till dusk. I am forty-two, but I feel like an old wreck, having to support my son, a schoolboy, my daughter, a student, and myself on 200 roubles a month. Awful living conditions, unending queues. Russian people are

187

patient, that's what they count upon. Gorbachev has woken the country up from a slumber. Now the future is in our own hands: to be or not to be. We Russians are hard to harness, but quick to move. If we succeed with perestroika, our life would be beautiful, beautiful . . . Am I not right? Sincerely,

P–va, assembly worker, Ulyanovsk.

VIP rooms are trifles. In Omsk the authorities have a road of their own. No one can drive along this special highway without a special pass. It is used only by the chosen few and is called Government Road. It begins at Victory Park and leads to the airport. The highway was built in the time of stagnation, but it is still there to make it easier for those in power to reach the airport.

Sh–ko, Omsk.

Palaces must be given to the people, not the rulers – that was the main principle of our great Revolution. But what happens in reality? If you are a deputy or a city council official, you can quickly get a flat, you are assigned special food supplies and a VIP room and you don't care about the rest. If you are a real people's deputy – welcome to the ten year waiting list for a flat, be so kind as to sleep on a wooden bench at a station, and will you please take your place in the long queue to a half-empty shop counter! Then probably you'll start thinking how you could improve your country's life. Sitting on the cement station floor with a child in our hands, carrying a tin of sprats in tomato sauce from a shop, we can't help detesting those who lounge in the soft armchairs of an empty VIP hall, or carry home a bagful of delicacies from their office in a city council . . . I remember reading my little daughter a story about Lenin visiting a nursery school. When I read that Vladimir Ilyich took one girl in his hands and lifted her in the air, my daughter asked: 'And who was the girl's father?' I wondered why she asked that? And my daughter said that at the New Year morning party at her kindergarten one girl was presented with a big teddy bear and all the others with just a couple of sweets each. The kindergarten teacher explained that the first girl's father was a 'nachal'nik' [a big shot] and so she must get a better present.

B–va, Irkutsk region.

I heartily support the suggestion of V. Vitaliev to give the VIP rooms to war and labour veterans who really need and deserve them. As to the deputies and high-ranking officials, let them mix with ordinary people, not just address them from high platforms.

Zh–k, Krasnoyarsk region.

The party must find the strength to strip its members of all privileges except one – to lead the people in overcoming hardships. Then probably only one or two million people, instead of sixteen, will remain in its ranks, but they will be real communists. Stalin and Brezhnev have destroyed the genes of courage and pride in many Party members.

B–khov, Novosibirsk.

The top functionaries are so used to the privileges they have given themselves that they will never reject them of their own accord. Only by changing the whole ruling caste can we achieve improvement. The main weapon for this is glasnost'. The élite will spare no effort to keep their lives under closed covers. It's like fighting in combat. That's why the profession of a journalist is the most dangerous one in the time of perestroika. I wish you success in your difficult job.

A–ov, Krasnoyarsk.

Every big railway official has a sleeping carriage of his own. He uses it only a few times a year. These carriages are equipped no worse than VIP rooms.

P–ko, a railway worker, Chardzhou.

I cannot believe that the time will come when waiting for a train I would not have to lie on the ground or asphalt next to the deputies' room, but to have a real rest. I am seventy-eight. Bureaucrats are resting in the hall with carpets and polished furniture and I, who crawled on my belly from Moscow to Berlin and got six medals for it, have to sit on the asphalt. Where is social justice?

B–v, war veteran, Moscow region.

Three years of perestroika haven't taught anything to the Minister of Railways, Comrade Konarev. He signed the Instruction on deputies' halls contradicting the principle of social justice. To his logic, all people are equal, but bureaucrats are more equal than others. With them everything is like that: special hospitals, sanatoriums, reception houses, dachas and even special places in cemeteries. Vitaliev was right saying that everything begins with deputies' halls.

Kr–kov, Vladimir.

For my part, I appoint Vitaliev the chief inspector of railways. He is on the right track, and if he proceeds, he will find out why we have so many problems with our railway transport.

T–k, engine driver, Surgut.

I am sorry to admit it, but I have never taken your magazine seriously – humour, cartoons, that's all I used to look for. But in the last issue, Comrade Vitaliev spoke out loud about what those in power are trying to hide carefully, about the shameless privileges of those who call themselves servants of the people. Vitaliev writes that when he opened the doors to deputies' rooms he got contemptuous looks from ordinary passengers. I am afraid Comrade Vitaliev was mistaken: this was not contempt but hatred. Yes, yes, the real class hatred of authoritarian bureaucracy, of powerful rulers . . .

V–n, Sochi.

We must start with eliminating flower-beds in front of the city council buildings. It is bitter for me to watch how in my small town with hordes of unresolved problems, conceited gardeners cut the grass in front of the town council and the town Party committee buildings. Then the special machine comes to water the grass and the flower-beds. Meanwhile, hundreds of children have to swallow dust on their way to school or kindergarten.

K–rev, foreman, Bielorechensk.

I have just read the feuilleton 'Secrets of the VIP Hall' in *Krokodil*. What an honest and timely article! Have glasnost' and democracy really come in to our life? Yes, but they move slowly and painfully. If correspondent Vitaliev had to overcome obstacles in preparing his article, what is there to say about ourselves – humble people? If I ever dared to reproach a station-master for the disgraceful VIP room, he would not hesitate to report me to the militia. Am I not right?

Ar–v, Voronezh region.

Once with a friend we found ourselves quite by chance on the territory of the so-called Obkom dachas. We were amazed at the beautiful architectural design of these small palaces. Entering a small shop on the territory, we were even more surprised: there was everything but pigeon's milk there. We were about to buy something when we saw the sign 'Goods sold only on production of special permits'. How do you like that? And the saleswoman was genuinely perplexed: 'How did you get here, boys?' Since then, I have felt inferior . . .

L–sky, Novosibirsk.

Once, with my little son in my arms, I was trying to catch a taxi. It was raining and a piercing wind was blowing. When I finally succeeded and was about to get into the cab, I was stopped by a bossy-looking man who showed his deputy's card to the driver and, pushing me aside, climbed into the taxi. I know that he was acting according to the rules saying that deputies have the right to be served first everywhere . . . But what kind of rules are these? And what kind of a deputy was he?

K–va, Krasnodar.

I was buying two coach tickets to Kiev at the bus station in Priluki, a town in the Ukraine. The cashier gave me two back seats and I, having a child with me, asked her to give me front ones. She said that they had been reserved. But the bus was quite empty! I went to the station-master for an explanation and he said that in every Kiev-bound coach four seats are reserved for Kiev officials, another four for the Priluki Party committee, and four more for the local KGB. So it turns out that only back seats remain for ordinary people, and I am wondering: why should local functionaries, having State cars at their disposal, go daily by bus to Kiev? And why necessarily in the front seats? I think I understand why: to comply with the Party slogan calling communists to be always in the vanguard of the people!

Gr–n, Kiev.

Unfortunately, in your article, you didn't say a word about the thousands of special hospitals for bosses in the USSR. Let them have separate rooms, even floors, but in ordinary hospitals for standard people. Then the treatment of the sick will improve and their food will be better. A boss doesn't have to bribe an orderly to remove a bed-pan from under him. He doesn't see the cockroaches running to and fro in hospital fridges. The bosses and their family enjoy stores, shops, buffets with the coveted high-quality goods sold at State prices. They don't know what it means to queue for a kilo of rotten fruit or vegetables for hours on end. They don't know what it's like to ride on overcrowded public transport during the rush hours. They perceive the world around them only through papers, telephones and TV sets. If the process of their isolation from reality continues, our perestroika will fail in the same way as the infamous Brezhnev five-year plans.

L–nko, Poltava.

Passportless Person
(Letters to *Ogonyok*)

I had been waiting for an article on our passport policy for a long time. I support V. Vitaliev. Our passport system is nothing but serfdom in the late twentieth century. What kind of freedom can we enjoy with such a system? We all understand now that internal passports were a mistake. Then why don't we correct our mistakes? Because a slave is sitting very deep down inside each of us. While internal passports exist in our country, nationalism, registration fiddlers and such like will flourish. How long shall we allow ourselves to be humiliated?

B–sky, Moscow.

I disagree with the author of 'Passportless Person'. We have too many criminals and other law-breaking felons in our country. To say nothing of foreign spies and polygamists. We also have drones, tramps, prostitutes, drug-fiends, racketeers. A lot of criminals are in hiding. The others make 'guest appearances' in different cities and towns. Our militia cannot cope with them even with the passport system. And if we abolish it altogether, this will result in anarchy. Once, one's place of work had to be mentioned in a passport. Then this point was abolished, and now we cannot tell a drone from a worker. I think this entry must be restored.

S–n, Severodvinsk.

I am thirty-eight and a Chuvash by nationality. Until I got a passport I didn't pay any attention to that. No one did. But after getting it, I started feeling inferior. Even in the Army, I was looked down on as a Chuvash. After the Army, I lived in the Tatar Republic, where there are lots of Chuvashes. But they don't think of us as a nation. Half of the people in our district are Chuvashes, but there are no Chuvashes among the district leaders. Where is the justice? Now I can understand what lies behind the events in Karabakh ... My passport has always been the cause of my humiliation: at a hotel, at the marriage office, at the militia. But it is not my fault I am Chuvash. In fact I'm proud to be one. I am proud that my father and mother were Chuvash, and that my children are ... But internal passports should be abolished to spare us undeserved humiliation.

Respectfully, S–v, Tataria

'Passport (from the French "passeport") – a written identification of the bearer's person intended by a legislature to serve as an additional guarantee against the free movement of criminals and persons with restricted rights. However, the passport system does not justify itself, since criminal elements can easily obtain false passports. At the same time, bearing passports often proves embarrassing for loyal citizens. That is why, in most countries, they are issued only to those who go abroad.'

This quotation is taken from the Encyclopaedia edited by S. N. Yuzhakov and published in St Petersburg in 1909 (volume 14). I don't think it needs any comment.

V–sky, Leningrad.

8

Passport with Swastika

Young people were the ones who suffered most during the stagnation. They experienced not just food and clothes shortages, hypocrisy and lies, but great spiritual devastation too. 'Doublethink' is especially ruinous for the young, whose souls and minds are not tempered enough to comply with double standards. Primitive propaganda on the one hand, and dull, uninteresting everyday life on the other, have split the souls of those who were teenagers and schoolchildren under Brezhnev, bringing about emptiness and spiritual vacuum.

In *Living with Glasnost*, Andrew Wilson and Nina Bachatov, Western journalists, make these very shrewd observations:

> The generation brought up immediately after the war and under Khrushchev was highly politicised. It believed in Progress – technological, political and cultural – and knew what the war had meant, often from first-hand experience. Times were hard, with very few material goods in which to take an interest. But every small additional comfort was seen as proof of Progress. In every way, things were going to be better than they had been yesterday ... The generation brought up under Brezhnev was depoliticised, cynical and bent on material consumption. At the same time, there was an unprecedented stress on the study of 'social science' in school. It was obligatory to study the speeches of Brezhnev and his cronies, every one of which caused the student to withdraw further and further from politics. This was the high season of cynicism and pretence in the Komsomol, when young people joined wholesale in their last year at school for the naked purpose of improving their chances of a place in an institute.
>
> The longer Brezhnev stayed in power, the worse it became, since the gerontocracy blocked every means of young people's progress and every relationship became based on deceit and corruption.[1]

With my own generation, brought up in between Khrushchev's thaw and stagnation, it was a little bit different. We were still believers and much less cynical (me especially, as the boy who grew up in a family of old Bolsheviks). We didn't take everything for granted, and always tried to provide an explanation. When I was a fresher, I had a girlfriend who studied at the medical institute. At some point they had to pronounce the solemn oath of a medical student. I remember how puzzled she grew after the ceremony. The first item of the oath was: 'I swear to study diligently the history of the Party and social sciences', the second: 'I swear to take an active part in the institute's social life', and only the third was about 'a conscientious study of medical sciences'. 'Do they mean to tell us that social sciences are more important for a future doctor than medicine?' she wondered.

The denigration of eternal values was running rampant on the threshold of the Eighties. Knowledge, proficiency and honesty hardly meant anything to the ruling bureaucrats. Obsequiousness, cynicism and unquestioning obedience came in their stead.

This was the time when the young people about whom I'm going to write in this chapter were maturing and learning their first lessons in life. To know this is of paramount importance in understanding (or at least trying to understand) the dreadful phenomenon of Soviet neo-fascism.

Our country at present is swarming with youth groups of different kinds. We regard them as 'informal' in comparison with the Komsomol, Young Pioneers, Young Friends of Nature, and so on, which became very formal indeed under stagnation.

There also used to be Young Firemen Brigades. When I was in the seventh form (aged fourteen) it was announced that such a brigade would be organised in our school. We boys were very happy. At the first meeting of the would-be firemen, a young man who introduced himself as our leader promised us pie in the sky: a brand-new red fire engine, uniforms, lots of training and competition. We were in seventh heaven with joy and kept imagining ourselves in the gleaming and honking red engine with firemen's helmets on our heads. At the next meeting, the young man collected a membership fee – 50 copecks from each boy – and vanished into thin air. We didn't hear any more of him.

This is rather a minor example, but it left a scar on my teenage soul. I can only imagine how many scars like that the schoolchildren of the Brezhnev era acquired.

Today's informal groups do not collect fees from their members. They do not have adult leaders or supervisors. They are just trying to be dogma-free, though their image of freedom is often bizarre and perverted.

195

Among the most popular youth groups I can name the 'rockeri' – young motorcyclists whose single aim is to harass militiamen and pedestrians; 'liuberi' – a youth gang from the Moscow suburb of Liubertsy, with a cult of body-building; hard rock metallists sporting chains and bracelets; punks and some others.

What I am going to dwell upon is much more serious than mere street bullying, in which all of the above-mentioned groups indulge from time to time. The flocks of young neo-fascists who appeared in our country in the early Eighties are of a completely different sort. The very fact of their existence is a challenge to our State, which lost 20,000,000 lives in the war against fascism. This is not just the reverse side of democracy, as you may consider similar phenomena in the West. For our country, fascism is the last stage of moral and human degradation. 'Fascist' here is a term of abuse worse and more insulting than four-letter words.

But young fascists do exist.

Where did they come from? And why? These were the questions I put to myself before starting to probe into this terrible phenomenon. This investigation proved the most striking and revealing in my journalistic career. And the most dangerous too. It was stimulated by a few lines in a *Moscow News* article on local laws published in the first issue of 1988. They said that the Leningrad city Soviet had recently reached a new decision on breaches of public order. Specifically, the violation, entailing a warning or fine, was defined there as 'wearing symbols, attributes and other items or imprints which contradict the norms of morality and ethics'. In the article, the head of the legal department of the Leningrad City Executive Committee explained to the *Moscow News* correspondent that 'the measure was directed mainly against those who wear badges with fascist symbols'.[2]

I was petrified by what I read: in Leningrad, which suffered a terrible blockade and became a symbol of the struggle against fascism, there are now thugs who wear swastikas! It was hard to believe, though rumours had been circulating among journalists that some kind of Nazi rallies had been held in Moscow and Leningrad on the day of Hitler's birth. But gossip is one thing, a newspaper article another.

I decided to go to Leningrad – where, by the way, some of my distant relatives died during the blockade. I didn't know then that Leningrad fascists wore not only badges and swastikas but Nazi uniforms and arms.

On coming back from Leningrad at the end of January 1988, I had a nervous breakdown and couldn't write for a long time. The subject matter, everything I came to know there, were too much to bear. I thought that the pressure of horrific facts would diminish after a while, but with the course of time the burden only grew heavier; at some moments I even felt tempted to dismiss the whole thing as a bad dream.

I concluded that I didn't like Leningrad as much as I used to. In my heart of hearts I realised that the city of Pushkin and Peter the Great was not to blame. But still, it was like walking out on a woman you once loved.

Document No 1

Order No. 7322/2   Confidential

On this occasion of the Great Jubilee – the birthday of the vice-president of the national-socialist movement in the city of Leningrad – I hereby order:

to promote cadet Wolf Gold to the rank of non-commissioned officer;

to put non-commissioned officer Wolf Gold in charge of the party security department (gestapo).

The security department's fields of activity must be:

1. Psychologically grounded recruiting of persons able to be useful to our party.

2. Checking the person's past and their political biographies.

3. Compiling secret files on every party member and every recruited agent, no matter which department he belongs to.

I hereby order this department to be treated as a politically important one.

Vice-president of the national-socialist workers' party
SS Standartenführer V. Fon Gruntal
(signature)
(stamp)

Certified by
Vice-president of the national-socialist party movement in Leningrad
SD Captain 2nd Grade
Anri Hoken, En.
(signature)
(stamp)

What is this? Where does it come from? From the achives of the Third Reich? But why is it in Russian then? Who is Wolf Gold? And why Leningrad?

From my talk with a girl, a former young Nazi:

'How long were you with the organisation?'

'For about two years. Then I decided to quit.'

'How did they react to your quitting?'

'They persecuted me for a long time. Threatened. Eventually they left me alone.'

'What were you doing in the organisation?'

'All kinds of things . . . Invented German names for ourselves. I, for instance, was Elsa Braun [hence Wolf Gold, etc].'

'What else?'

'Made Nazi uniforms. Wore them at night time. Walked in the streets shouting "Heil Hitler!" and made passers-by shout too.'

'What if they refused?'

'Made them kneel, hit them.'

'Do you know how many people died in Leningrad during the blockade?'

'Don't know exactly, several thousand, perhaps.'

In 1939, 3,119,000 people lived in Leningrad. In the course of the blockade, more than a million people died of hunger and bombing. The pre-war population number was not re-established in Leningrad until the early Seventies.[3]

I tell you now that never before in my journalistic career (not even in Dnepropetrovsk) were the facts so hard to get. Most of the Leningrad officials whom I approached pretended ignorance: 'What? Nazis? Not the faintest idea!'

I had to act cautiously, sometimes even by deception. But still it was extremely difficult to circumvent bureaucratic obstinacy and fear of disclosure.

Some officials made partial admissions: 'Yes, there have been some cases . . . Yes, they made uniforms and wore swastikas. But don't generalise! Don't jump to conclusions! They are just children who are being naughty.'

At the city's court, they tried to get rid of me quickly: hear no evil, see no evil, speak no evil – this was the official stand there. But I was lucky. On that very day, a conference of all the Leningrad judges was held at the city court building. I asked permission to address the audience. 'In the spirit of glasnost', the court officials had to agree.

'Have you had any cases involving Nazis recently?' I asked the judges in the conference room.

Silence. Guarded looks from the officials.

I decided to change tactics.

'Those who have presided over Nazi cases, raise your hands, please!'

After a pause, one hand, like a heavy wounded bird, rose slowly above the audience. Then a second. A third. A fifth. A ninth.

These hands were not just answering my question. They were voting in favour of glasnost', against lies and over-cautiousness.

Document No 2

To the chief of the
national-socialist workers'
party

Application

I ask you to allow me to retire from the rank of rotenführer for reasons of a personal character. I ask not to be stripped of the rank in case I return to the organisation at some time.

(Signature)
(Spread-eagle stamp)

I saw lots of similar 'documents' in Leningrad. Some stamped 'confidential', others not. I also saw armbands with swastikas, Wehrmacht officers' insignia and SS soldiers' belt-buckles with the inscription in German 'SS man! Your honour is in your loyalty!' Some of these were skilfully hand-made by young fascists, the rest had been excavated by them on the outskirts of Leningrad, where heavy battles occurred in 1941–2. Artillery shells fell in the city streets.

From the flight plans of fascist bomber pilots: 'Target number 9 – Hermitage Museum. Target number 89 – Erisman hospital. Target number 192 – Pioneer Palace. Target number 295 – "Guest Yard" department store. Target number 708 – Institute of Childhood and Maternity.'[4]

Holding a lovingly polished SS belt-buckle, I felt uncontrollable fury boiling inside me. A random sentence from a book on the Second World War came to my mind: 'SS men took the screaming child by the legs and struck his head against a tree trunk.'

Document No 3

From the statement of the accused Kravchenko, aged 16, a worker:

'On 22 April, I discovered that the portrait of Hitler I kept in my house had vanished. I realised it had been taken by my younger brother. I went to the school were he was studying and asked him about the portrait. My brother explained that he took Hitler's portrait to his class, the teacher saw it and tore it into pieces. For that, I kicked my brother in the stomach and when he fell down, I hit his head against the wall. Meanwhile, I kept calling him names.

'Since 1980, I have been attracted to fascist ideology. I was fascinated by the swastika and by Hitler's personality. I have read about 30 books on Hitler. I think he was a positive figure. Hitler's portrait I cut out of a magazine and was treasuring it. I think Hitler was a remarkable man, comparable to Stalin and Suvorov [eighteenth-century Russian general].'

The evidence of R., the accused Kravchenko's mother:

'At the age of ten, my son went out of control, started reading a lot about Hitler, tried to learn German, but failed. I have spoken to him about his strange passion but to no avail. He used to beat up his younger brothers at home, that's why I didn't risk leaving them in his company.'[5]

No comment is necessary. But one small detail is essential: psychiatric expertise maintained that Kravchenko was mentally healthy and acted quite consciously.

Children's games? Hardly – though both the Komsomol and Party bodies in Leningrad stick to this version.

On 11 July 1986, *Leningradskaya Pravda* newspaper carried an article on young fascists entitled 'Standartenführer from Malaya Okhta' (Malaya Okhta is one of Leningrad's city districts). To be on the safe side, the article was cautiously subtitled 'The results of miscalculations in educating teenagers.'

Miscalculations? Or complete failure? For some reason, these 'children' do not play at being Chapaev.* Nor even Napoleon. It's not the red stars that attract them, but swastikas . . .

Here is the arithmetics of only one of the 900 blockade days – 20 February 1942:

From Leningrad mortuaries registers:
Frunzensky mortuary – 987 corpses
Sverdlovsky mortuary – 749 corpses

---

*Vasily Ivanovich Chapaev (1887–1919), a legendary Red Army hero of the Civil War of 1918–21.

Vasileostrovsky district mortuary – 870 corpses
Botkin Hospital mortuary – 230 corpses
The Baltic Fleet mortuary – 450 corpses
Robespierre Embankment mortuary – 1,075 corpses
Kuibishev District mortuary – 680 corpses
and so on. *All in all, 10,043 corpses were buried ON THAT ONE DAY at Piskaryovskoye cemetery.*[6]

The article in *Leningradskaya Pravda* calls the pro-Nazi position of a section of Leningrad's youth 'superficial and transient attraction to fascist symbols'.

If it were only symbols . . .

September 2 was the first academic day at the Leningrad technical school of nautical instrument-making. Since the early morning, flocks of festively dressed youngsters had been gathering near its entrance. For many of them, it was to be their first day of studies at a real 'adult' educational institution – not just a secondary school. The occasion was serious enough and the boys were naturally feeling a little nervous.

In the neighbouring gateway, stood two young men: Matveyev, a worker, aged seventeen and Didenko, a student, aged eighteen.

'Come here,' Didenko beckoned to one of the waiting freshers.

'A Komsomol, aren't you?' Matveyev asked the unsuspecting lad, who readily answered in the affirmative.

Matveyev gripped the Komsomol badge on the lad's chest and pulled. The badge came off with a tearing sound, ripping the boy's coat.

'We are old fascists!' Didenko cried to the petrified youth and hit him across the face. The boy collapsed to the ground, and Didenko and Matveyev started kicking him violently. 'If you wear the badge again, we'll kill you!' they threatened the bleeding student.

Half an hour later, they caught another fresher, tore off his Komsomol badge and started to beat him ruthlessly. After every blow they would ask: 'Are you still a Komsomol?' The boy could have answered 'No', and stopped the beating, but his broken lips kept repeating 'Yes', 'Yes', 'Yes', infuriating the fascists even more. Dima Terentiev is the name of the brave young man.

The timing of the attack was sadistically calculated by Matveyev and Didenko: the first day of studies, when the freshers were about to get symbolic keys from the technical school, for the new adult life on whose threshold they stood. When the first of the attacked boys came home later that day, he said to his parents: 'I don't want to study at that school any longer.' Terrifying words.

201

And isn't it striking that on the day of the attack the 'old fascist' Didenko was himself a Komsomol member!

During the blockade, people tried to quell fits of hunger by eating pets and birds. They made soups and jellies from joiner's glue. They ate any medicaments they could get hold of. Many Leningraders went to the incinerated Badayev foodstores to pick clods of frozen earth from the places where sugar used to be stored. The burnt sugar left after the fire had been collected long ago. But Badayev earth was considered a luxury foodstuff. The people ate the clods, washing them down with hot water, or put them into their glasses instead of sugar . . . In January and February 1942, the mortality reached its highest peak – 199,187 Leningraders died of hunger during these two months alone. Whole families, whole apartment blocks were dead.[7]

When in Leningrad, I often remember my distant relative who lived there, or rather the family stories about a man I never met. He was born in Petrograd (the pre-revolutionary name for Leningrad) at the end of the nineteenth century and was a nobleman by origin. His family was close to the Tsar himself, but welcomed the Revolution. Grandpa Nikolai (that's how he was referred to in our family) voluntarily renounced his big fortune and luxury house and went to work as an accountant. He was accommodated – together with his wife and son – in one tiny room of a huge Leningrad 'communal flat' where about twenty families shared one kitchen and one bathroom. The room had only one advantage: it faced the Fontanka river, and that made it look like a ship's cabin. At least it seemed so to me. As a schoolboy I went there a couple of times with my mother to visit my relatives. Grandpa Nikolai had long since died. He survived the blockade. Survived, despite the fact that his only son was killed at the front in his very first combat. Survived despite the hunger and all inhuman sufferings.

But hunger affected his sanity, and when the blockade was lifted, he couldn't eat enough. He ate and ate and ate. This intellectual, this graduate of Petrograd university, collected anything edible in the streets and in dustbins, hid it and then ate it in solitude. Before long he died. That is what the fascist blockade did to people.

Nowadays, whenever I am in Leningrad, I invariably go to the Fontanka embankment just to cast a glance at the window of the cabin-room. My relations who used to live there are all dead now, and the room is inhabited by some other people. But I am fond of looking at its window, calling back my childhood in my memory. As a boy, I used to lie flat on the windowsill looking at the river and imagine myself a captain of a big ship crossing rough seas somewhere in the tropics.

This time, I also went up to the old house on the embankment, looked at the familiar window – and froze numb: just underneath it, daubed on the weathered panelling of the house, I saw a coal-drawn swastika. Reflected in the Fontanka's rippling waters, it was moving its crooked claws and seemed alive.

Many of the modern Leningrad fascists (what an ironic phrase) study at technical or vocational (PTU) schools in the city. From black PTU tunics they make SS uniforms, achieving a striking likeness. I saw group photographs of the young Nazis (unfortunately I couldn't take them with me), sporting uniforms with iron crosses and high-peaked SS caps, and holding pistols – real, not toy ones – in their hands. Crass, drunken faces. Blank, glimmering eyes. A boy in an SS officer's uniform was nibbling at the peak of his Nazi cap in a paroxysm of alcoholic ecstasy. In some photographs there were young girls – also drunk and uniformed. A disgusting sight. It is hard to believe that these are not Hitlerjugend cut-throats but my young compatriots from Leningrad, the hero city.*

As you have already seen, young fascists do not just swagger around, they also take action. On Hitler's birthday in 1987, eight PTU students were 'enjoying' themselves in Kronstadt, a town not far from Leningrad. They were painting swastikas on the fronts of the houses in Kommunisticheskaya (Communist) Street and writing 'Heil Hitler!' there. It was not by chance they had chosen this street: so you strive for Communism, they meant to say – have a swastika instead!

Four schoolboys and PTU students hung a homemade red and black flag with a swastika on one of the houses in Lenskaya Street in Leningrad. They ran it up the flagpole that holds the Soviet flag on public holidays. This was just spitting in the country's eye.

But the head of the Leningrad PTU department refuses to accept the reality. Talking to me, he called the Nazi actions of the PTU students 'negative phenomena due to insufficient educative work'. Enough of that! Getting bad marks or skipping lectures – these are 'negative phenomena'. In the case described, one must use stronger language. Otherwise it looks as if they can slap us across the face and we will just turn the other cheek. When shall we learn to call a spade a spade?

*Hero city is an official title awarded by the government to those cities whose people showed especial heroism in resisting the Germans. There are ten hero cities in the USSR at present.

From the forecast of the Wehrmacht's deputy Quarter-Master, the director of the Munich Food Institute, Professor Zigelmeyer: 'We mustn't risk German soldiers' lives. The Leningraders will die by themselves, only we mustn't let any of them cross the front line. The more Leningraders stay in the city, the sooner they will die, and we will enter Leningrad freely without losing a single German soldier.[8]

Late at night, there came a peremptory knock at the door of a room in the women student's hostel in Trefolyova Street. A staggering, drunken lout was standing in the doorway. This was Popinachenko, aged seventeen, a student at the Leningrad technical school of construction and architecture.

'How are you?' he belched at the three students who lived in the room.

'Go away!' the young women answered.

'Do you know who I am?' Popinachenko burst into the room and bared his right wrist with a swastika tattooed on it. 'I'm a Nazi.'

'Sod off!' one of the women demanded. 'Nazis killed my grandpa.'

'Newspaper crap! What you read in the press is just a pack of lies about fascists. In fact, they were kind and treated Russians well. Communists – they are the real beasts. You are defending Communists and I will kill for that!'

Having locked out two of the women, Popinachenko who was by the way the son of a Communist lieutenant-colonel in the Soviet Army, started torturing the remaining one. He struck her on the head for several minutes, started to strangle her, then let go, took an aerosol container of hair lotion from the bedside table and sprayed the caustic liquid into his victim's eyes. Suddenly his gaze was drawn to the poster hanging on the wall. It depicted a young woman carrying a baby, with a dove of peace hovering above them and the word 'Peace'.

Popinachenko staggered to the wall. 'Children are future Communists. They must be destroyed,' he muttered, then struck a match and set fire to the poster.

At this moment, the two women outside broke the door lock and rushed into the room to help their friend. One of them saw the burning poster and hurried to put out the fire.

'Leave it alone, you bitch!' Popinachenko screamed, and threw an empty lemonade bottle at the woman. The bottle hit her on the head, but she kept on putting out the fire with her bare hands.

The sadist rushed at the woman, knocked her down, and thrust a burning cigarette stub into her face. She gave a shriek. Her burnt skin could be smelt in the room. But she didn't let go of the poster, clutching it in her hands. She did succeed in putting out the fire.

'Let it burn! I'll kill you!' Popinachenko was beside himself. And again – torture, insults, beatings. The girl's face was covered in burns, her skin was shreds, but battered as she was, she didn't obey the fascist's orders.

Thank you, Marina Degtyaryova! We are all proud of you.

What has happened to us? Are we living in the desert or in tundra where you won't see a single living person in miles and miles of space? Why did no one help?

These are not easy questions to answer. We could ask further: why did the school teachers in whose presence Kravchenko was beating up his younger brother fail to intervene, and just make 'disapproving remarks', as the militia statement put it? Can you imagine that – a thug tortures a child, and the teachers stand aside expressing their 'disapproval'! The technical school students who witnessed Didenko and Matveyev's violent action against their comrades just passed by like cowards and only the most 'courageous' of them dared to mutter something like 'Drop it, boys.' Why?

Are we really so mean-spirited that nothing apart from our own safety worries us? As long as they don't touch me – it's no concern of mine. Shall we continue looking indifferently at our children being tortured by Nazi brutes?

Forgive us, Dima Terentiev and Marina Degtyaryova. Forgive us if you can.

From the blockade diary of Tanya Savicheva, a Leningrad schoolgirl, aged twelve. 'Zhenya died on Dec. 28, 1941, at 12.30 pm; Granny died on Jan. 25, 1942, at 3 pm; Lyoka died on March 17, 1942, at 5 am; uncle Lyosha on May 10th, 1942, at 4 pm; mummy on May 13, 1942, at 7.30 am; uncle Vasya died on April 13, 1942 at 2 am; the Savichevs died; everyone died; only Tanya remained.' [9]
Tanya Savicheva died of exhaustion in July 1944.

There is only one thing more terrible than indifference, and that is hushing up the plain facts.

If you read the court sentence on Popinachenko (he was finally sentenced to six years' imprisonment), the fascist will look like an ordinary hooligan: there is not a word there about the swastika and his Nazi statements. Some cautious hand excised all 'embarrassing' facts – the ones of primary importance. Hooliganism is a major crime in itself – it goes without saying. But performed against the background of fascist propaganda it becomes much graver. Outrageous – that is the word.

So who thought it necessary to take away the very essence of the crime from the sentence? Obviously, those round-eyed safety-first men, thinking that glasnost' must have limits. Those who are ready to sacrifice truth and conscience for the sake of their own piece of mind. Such cowardice is almost as dangerous as Nazism itself.

Document No 5

Confidential
Instruction No 7321   August 25, 1986

I hereby urgently order all sectors to launch the campaign to provide sources of arms supplies.
Vice-president of the national-socialist movement party
SD captain second grade
Anri Hoken' En. (Signature)
(Stamp)

What are these arms supplies? The fruit of a childish imagination, fanned by Robert Louis Stevenson or Fenimore Cooper? I wish it were so. I saw some of the arms confiscated from Leningrad fascists: daggers, dirks, bayonets, pistols and even machine-guns in working order. Where do they get them? From the ground. From the long-suffering ground of the Leningrad suburbs where heavy battles took place in 1941–2. To this day you can dig up rusty bayonets, helmets with bullet holes in them, and rusting pistols and machine-guns. Young fascists search for them, clean and restore them before testing. For the time being, thank God, they fire mainly at inanimate targets. But for how long?*

How many fascists are there in Leningrad altogether? It is hard to give an exact figure, but the documents produced by the well-run 'chancellery' prove that it is more than just a few.

The cover of a fascist personnel file is made of red leatherette. Under the black spread-eagle perched on an encircled swastika is the Gothic inscription 'Deho'. The young fascist clerks probably wanted to write 'Delo', which in Russian means 'file', but being unfamiliar with Latin characters, they made a slip. Bad knowledge of letters, as you see, didn't prevent them from mastering Gothic script. When I saw the cover for the first time, I remembered the words of Goebbels, honest in their cynicism:

---

*On 20 April 1989 two home-made bombs were planted in the Moscow underground. By some miracle, they didn't explode. I have not a shadow of doubt that this was done by neo-fascists who probably wanted thus to mark the 'memorable' date – Hitler's centenary – in their own way.

'When I hear the word "culture" I reach for my pistol.' Present-day Leningrad Nazis comply with this utterance.

The other 'document' I came across in the same 'archives'(I cannot reveal the names of those who helped me to rummage through them) was a Nazi 'passport' (unfortunately I failed to take a copy). Its cover, similar to that of the file, has the inscription 'Passport' – this time in Russian – under the swastika. Inside, there is a photograph of a young Nazi holder and the following text: 'The bearer of this has the right to enjoy privileges, *to bear arms* [my italics] and to take part in the military and political conferences of the party.'

I have seen dozens of such 'passports', in which they officially allow each other to carry arms. Doesn't it seem strange that at the same time the authorities *officially* consider them just naughty children? Mischievous kids, with real pistols in their pockets – isn't that a paradox? And I cannot guarantee that someone will not fall victim to this paradox in the near future if the official attitude to young Nazis is not changed drastically.

From a secret directive from the German navy HQ, 'On The Future of the City of Petersburg', issued on 29 September 1941: 'Our Führer has decided to wipe the city off the face of the earth. After the defeat of Soviet Russia we won't be interested in preserving this big settlement.[10]

Now it is high time to ask a major question consisting of just one word: WHY?

To provide an adequate answer, we have to go back to the late Seventies and early Eighties, the height of the stagnation epoch. Just as Dnepropetrovsk under Brezhnev was a no-go area, closed to any kind of criticism, no matter how small, so Leningrad was immune as 'the cradle of the Revolution'. This cliché was a kind of safe-conduct for Leningrad, which, as you will see, preserves some features of a 'closed zone' to this day. By the unwritten rules of stagnation, in Leningrad neither corruption nor serious crimes could exist.

From the early Seventies, Leningrad was largely in the hands not only of corrupt Party officials but of gangsters too. The gang of robbers and racketeers led by Feoktistov (nicknamed Feka), though much smaller in number than the Sailor's, was very influential, well-armed and mobile: all its members had their own cars. Feka was quite well known in Leningrad, having monopolised prostitution, speculation and drug-peddling. He was friendly with the authorities too, and after he was eventually arrested, some of his high-ranking militia friends committed suicide – just as in Dnepropetrovsk.

207

Among other kings of the city's underworld one could name the hard-currency dealer Dahya, the swindler Simon, and the racketeer Vasiliev. The latter, a former boxer, led a gang of sportsmen – wrestlers, weight-lifters and karate fighters. With them he squeezed protection money out of wealthy dealers. At some point he took the whole of Leningrad in his grip. Vasiliev's men spared neither rich drug peddlers nor petty profiteers.

Together with such criminal sharks, Leningrad was swarming with petty underworld 'tiddlers'. Against the background of its classical architectural silhouettes, columns, palaces and monuments, prostitution, drug-addiction, speculation and hard currency dealings were flourishing. They were common knowledge.

Romanov was the Leningrad Party chief, and one of Brezhnev's minions. His rule was suffocating. Actors, scientists and writers were desperate to flee from Leningrad. Among them was Joseph Brodsky, the great Russian poet and the future (1987) Nobel Prize winner, who under Romanov was stigmatised as a drone and was even tried and imprisoned for no reason whatsoever. Anti-semitism was thriving in the city.

At the same time Romanov and his cronies were leading luxurious lives. Leningraders knew of the lavish banquets they used to throw for themselves and their faithful. The wedding party for Romanov's daughter was held in the Tavrichesky Palace Museum. For that the priceless crockery from the Hermitage Museum's collection was demanded. The museum workers resisted, but in vain, and drunken guests broke many plates and dishes which had come from the collections (Hermitage employees themselves told me about this). This ignominious occasion was the talk of all the city. But it didn't in the least embarrass the leaders themselves. What did embarrass them was the real situation, and they did their best to conceal the truth from the people.

'The sleep of reason creates monsters,' Goya said, and we can say that the sleep of glasnost' does likewise. The 'closed zones' like Dnepro-petrovsk and Leningrad (and elsewhere) where glasnost' was asleep did create social monsters. In Dnepropetrovsk it was an unbridled mafia. In Leningrad, the rudiments of fascism.

The school years of the young fascists in present-day Leningrad came in stagnation time. On the one hand they saw the symbols of the great Revolution: the Winter Palace occupied by rebellious masses in October 1917, the cruiser *Aurora*, whose broadside was a signal for the uprising, the Smolny Convent from which Lenin directed the revolutionary soldiers. On the other hand, innumerable social vices leapt to the eye.

It was then that a kind of spiritual vacuum was created in their as yet unformed minds – a vacuum that anything might fill. With some youths it was deafening rock music or night-time motor-cycle riding. With the others – the least able and mature – it resulted in Nazi 'games'. In both cases it was a spontaneous protest against lies and deceit, against the perverted values of the stagnation epoch – a protest which was in its turn perverted. Unable to accept the ideological postulates forced upon them at school as too contradictory to reality, the young people were more than often drawn to opposite social extremes, such as fascism. Their scant and one-sided knowledge of history offered them no choice. They wanted to stand against what was going on in the country, and could find no better means than to side with the country's sworn enemy – Nazism. They were not bright enough to understand the inhuman nature of fascist views. Living in the atmosphere of stagnation, they simply didn't know what it meant to be humane. The system was ruthless to them so they decided to be ruthless to the system, but in fact became the opponents not so much of the system as of their own people.

In my view, Leningrad can boast of the biggest variety of informal youth groups in the country. If you have a stroll along Nevsky Prospect, the city's main street, at night, you are likely to run into some of them. You will probably see the 'rollings' (dressed in the fashion of the Fifties), the 'nostalgists' (alias 'anarchists') sporting sailors' vests and Revolution-style peakless caps, the 'metallists' jingling like purses full of coins, and dinosaur-headed punks. They are all the living heritage of the stagnation years, a kind of lost generation brought up on doctored history and false ideals.

The frenzied Führer once threatened to grow an Aryan youth that would shatter the world. Stagnation produced young people who were shattered by a reality to which they couldn't adjust, and hence were thrown from one extreme to another.

The officials of present-day Leningrad do not seem to have learnt much from the sad lessons of the Brezhnev era, otherwise they wouldn't have turned a blind eye to the existence of Nazis in the city. Of course, it is much more comfortable to treat fascist thugs as naughty children. Comfortable and quiet: no one to blame for ideological 'mistakes'. As to glasnost', to hell with it.

One cannot but agree here with D. S. Likhachev, an academician and a prominent Leningrad public figure, who stated in *Literaturnaya Gazeta*: 'In Moscow the atmosphere is more favourable, more dynamic. More is allowed there. In our city [Leningrad] there is still the excessive caution that started in the post-war years.'[11]

This provincial overcautiousness does not only manifest itself in overlooking fascists. Here are some more examples of it, not directly connected with the subject, but very revealing as to the general atmosphere in the city which contributed to the appearance of the young extremists.

In 1988 the Admiralty Hotel building was demolished in Leningrad on the instructions of the City Council. It was destroyed secretly, during the night, since during the day lots of young people were demonstrating near the hotel to protest against its demolition. The reason was that Sergei Yesenin, the famous Russian romantic poet, the idol of Soviet youth, hanged himself there in 1925, and it was dear to the public as the poet's last abode. The City Council's spokesman appeared before the rally and solemnly promised not to destroy the historic building. The young people were ready to restore it free of charge and made this desire public. On that very night the hotel was blown up. Now there is a yawning gap in the downtown square where once it stood. What is going to fill this gap? Just emptiness and disappointment? Or something else?

On 14 February 1988, a big fire started in the Leningrad Library of the USSR Academy of Sciences. More than half a million priceless books and manuscripts were burnt, and about 150,000 more were waterlogged while putting out the fire. The library management, frightened by the impending responsibility, decided to conceal the full extent of the catastrophe. The employees were prohibited from rescuing the books. The bulldozer was sent for and the piles of wet, half-burnt books, many *incunabula* among them, were thrown on the ground and bulldozed to the dump. After that the Chief Librarian hurried to state in the local press that just three thousand roubles' worth of books had been burnt. He was supported by the city authorities, who also tried to minimise the real scope of the calamity and made public promises that the library would shortly reopen for readers.[12]

The true dimensions of the disaster became known to the Leningrad public only from the Moscow-based newspapers *Knizhnoye Obozreniye* (Book Review) and *Moscow News*. The people were outraged. 'The city fathers of the Leningrad City Executive Committee, *ordinarily inaccessible*, [my italics] were suddenly taking calls around the clock,' wrote *Moscow News*.[13]

But it was too late. Most of the books which could have been saved by timely intervention were lost for good. Likhachev called the library fire and its aftermath 'a Chernobyl of our culture'[14] and 'a national disaster'.[15]

So the Leningrad authorities and the local press remained in their pre-perestroika positions, sacrificing glasnost' for the sake of their own peace of mind.

Reluctance to see the obvious is a grave blunder. It was these 'unseeing' people who preferred to ignore Hitler's military preparations near our border in 1941. It was they who deliberately closed their eyes to Stalin's purges, they who lauded and awarded prizes to Brezhnev and they who looked the other way and were evasive when I confronted them with the question of whether Nazis existed in Leningrad.

At a concert of the Alisa rock group in the Leningrad Yubileiny Concert Hall its soloist Konstantin Kinchev sang the words 'Heil Hitler'. The words were heard by all present and were frantically applauded by some of the young audience. In the Leningrad militia headquarters I listened to the tape of the concert where these obscene words could be heard very distinctly. On 17 November, 1987, the Leningrad Komsomol newspaper *Smena* carried an article by a young journalist, Victor Kokosov, 'Alisa with the Hitler Fringe', where he described the general atmosphere of the concert as close to psychotic and gave the views of many spectators who had also heard the terrible words pronounced from the stage.

The city authorities, though, were reluctant to recognise this case of public sacrilege and launched a campaign – against the journalist. He was accused of slander and sacked from his job. His flat was besieged by young hooligans, Alisa fans, who harassed his sick parents and attempted to beat up the journalist. The cassette with the tape in question disappeared into thin air and the *Smena* newspaper, under pressure from the city fathers, had to publish an apology to Kinchev . . . Suddenly all the local press and TV, as if by command, became very prejudiced against Kokosov; people who had been previously friendly to him began to avoid him. The journalist became an outcast in his own city and addressed me for help. It was difficult to act without the tape as the main evidence, but we managed to provide some other proof. Kokosov was taken on by the other Leningrad newspaper and Alisa was banned from performing in big cities. But the story is not yet finished. The saddest result of it is that the young reporter who had written the truth was labelled a slanderer only because the authorities felt it would embarrass them to admit that they had let the whole thing happen. So Viktor Kokosov's belief in justice is shattered, but he didn't surrender and this does him credit.

The Leningrad leaders acted likewise after my story 'Führers from Fontanka' was published in *Krokodil*.[16] It dealt with the above-mentioned facts concerning the Leningrad fascists.

At first the Leningrad Obkom officials tried to deny my story through the highest possible body, the Central Committee of the CPSU, where they complained that the publication was not true to reality. But I had facts and documents in my file and proved that I had been right. The second attempt was made in the official reply they sent to *Krokodil*. It was signed by the head of the propaganda department of the Leningrad Regional Party Committee (Obkom), G. Barinova. In it she tried to relegate the facts in my article to the distant past, saying that I was exaggerating them. After I had proved to the CPSU Central Committee that all the facts had been true, she couldn't dismiss them altogether but stated that they had taken place many years before. 'There are no fascist-oriented youngsters in Leningrad at present,' she wrote. It was a pack of lies. But we published the official reply in *Krokodil*, with a short commentary to the effect that the facts had been fresh and not old.[17]

Life itself proved us right. Among the thousands of letters I received after the publication were a number written by present-day Leningrad fascists (see this chapter's letter-box). No denial of the facts was possible. But the worst outcome of such a hypocritical stand by the Leningrad authorities was the growth of the Nazi movement in the city.

In June and July 1988, rallies of the chauvinist Memory Society were conducted in one of the city's parks. Openly anti-semitic slogans were pronounced by the demonstrators, who this time were not youngsters but adult people. And again the local officials preferred to look the other way until a big row, stirred up by the Moscow press, made them recognise the incidents and ban further Memory Society meetings.

On 22 December 1988, *Leningradskaya Pravda* had to confess openly to the existence of Nazis in a story entitled 'Uncertain Ways of Vedism'. It reported that an organisation of military men led by the possesser of a PhD called Bezverkh was working in Leningrad, with fascist ideology as its guiding principle. The organisation aimed to liquidate Jews, gypsies and other 'inferior' nations. It was built along the lines of the German storm-troopers.

At the beginning of 1989 I got a letter from a group of Leningrad war veterans saying that fascists had desecrated and destroyed the monument to the dead marines who defended Leningrad during the war. I hurried there only to make sure it was all true. The monument which had been erected with war veterans' money had been vandalised, the statue of an unknown marine was pierced with bullet holes, and the marble tablets with the names of those who perished were smashed to smithereens. The heavy ship's anchors decorating the place had been taken away and left at some distance from the Monument. Each of them weighed several tons, so no bunch of hooligans could have lifted them without the help of some mechanical device. There were chalked swastikas and inscriptions:

'Marines, we won't leave you alone even after your death!' 'Long live Hitler!' and so on, all over the place.

'There are no overstatements whatsoever in Vitaliev's article,' the veterans wrote in their letter. 'The fascist escapades taking place in Leningrad at present are not just the acts of an individual. These are clearly expressed, politically oriented, anti-State manifestations. This is a great problem for Leningrad and the region. It must be neither concealed nor hushed up.'[18]

Leningrad Party officials needed 'fresh facts', and they got them all right. But wouldn't it have been better if they had recognised the truth earlier and tried to prevent acts of vandalism?

Sadly enough, it turned out that by playing possum, by silencing the obvious facts, the Leningrad leaders involuntarily sided with the extremists. For them it was like 'living inside the whale', to quote the brilliant essay by George Orwell:

> There you are, in the dark, cushioned space that exactly fits you, with yards of blubber between yourself and reality, able to keep up an attitude of the completest indifference, no matter what happens. A storm that would sink all the battleships in the world would hardly reach you as an echo. Even the whale's own movements would probably be imperceptible to you . . . Short of being dead, it is the final, insurpassable stage of irresponsibility.[19]

When the manuscript of this book was finished, information came from Leningrad TV, that a gang that raped and killed girls and women was operating in Leningrad. On the backs of their victims the criminals cut swastikas with knives or nails. Won't Leningrad's rulers even now come out of the whale?*

Never in my journalistic career have I received so many interesting letters as after 'Führers from Fontanka'. Never have I received so many threats and so many assurances of support. The readers stated it was not only in Leningrad that fascists existed. There were reports of pro-Nazi incidents

---

*Shortly after the book was finished there came news of G. Barinova, the omnipotent head of the Leningrad Obkom's propaganda department, having been removed from her post as a result of the publication of the above-mentioned veterans' letter in *Krokodil*. The lady who for many years had been the ideological bugaboo for all Leningrad intellectuals, gracefully retired into the position of . . . the director of the Leningrad branch of the Central Lenin Museum. Of course, it's a demotion, but an 'honorary' one. As you see, high ranking apparatchiks are mutually protected to the extent that they are hard to scuttle.

from more than thirty other cities and towns. I will quote some of the readers' letters at the end of this chapter, but here I cannot help quoting one of them, since it explains a lot.

The letter came from Riga. The author recounted the experience of a friend of his who was a war veteran:

> Coming back home one night I saw two uniformed figures in front of me. At first I thought they were railway men or airmen. But when they came closer I realised I was mistaken. Two young SS men were standing before me: uniforms, insignia – everything was there.
> 'Are you a Communist?' one of them asked.
> 'Yes, I am,' I answered.
> 'Then we'll beat you up now,' the other said.
> 'Well, do as you wish.'
> 'No, we won't,' the first one concluded after a pause. 'Communists lie, and this one isn't afraid to tell the truth. Let's go . . .'

What does this terrifying testimony prove? Not that the Communist ideology is wrong in itself, but that what was presented to our people under the guise of Communist ideology for many years has suffered a major defeat. I am not trying to approve of the words and deeds of the young uniformed thugs. I am just striving to understand their motives. They grew up with too many lies: too many hypocrisies surrounded them in everyday life. They thought it was all due to Communists, but it wasn't; it was due to those who pretended to be Communists, but in the bottom of their hearts were nothing but social parasites, parvenus and the new rich. The ideology, alas, was in their hands too. And now we must have enough courage to recognise that we have been wrong, to persuade young people that our ideology has been distorted. Distorted beyond recognition.

'By God, what have we done to our country?!' exclaimed Valeria Masyagina, an economist from the Gorky region, in *Literaturnaya Gazeta*. 'Just to think of the fact that we all lived throughout these years when the terrible stagnation mechanism was being assembled! Why did we keep silent?'[20]

Yes, we kept silent for a long time. And now, when there is an opportunity to speak up at last, we must repent. Repentance is purifying. And we have already started this process. At least the above-quoted letter from Riga about a veteran confronted by young Nazis was published.[21] Some years ago, it would have been absolutely impossible.

We must learn to tell our people the truth – no matter how terrible this truth may be. And first of all, we must honestly reassess our recent past.

Certainly it is necessary to differentiate between misled youngsters and those who consciously preach anti-human ideals of racism, national hatred and fascism. Now they too have the opportunity to speak up.

In spring 1988, the offices of many Moscow periodicals received typed leaflets from the Memory (Pamyat) Society calling for the death of Jews, Armenians and gypsies. 'We are blond and beautiful Slavs,' the leaflet ran. 'We won't tolerate any filthy, stinking Jews amongst us!'

Strange as it may seem, the Memory Society was also a product of perestroika. At first it declared the preservation of monuments and the protection of Russian culture its main goals. But very quickly it became evident that its sole concern was rabid anti-semitism in the best traditions of the Black Hundreds (a Russian anti-Jewish militant organisation of the beginning of the century). I have run into Memory thugs in Moscow streets more than once. They were all sporting black T-shirts with bells painted on them. They didn't even try to conceal their resemblance to the Black Hundreds who organised Jewish pogroms in pre-Revolutionary Russia. Their political platforms are very much the same.

The Memory Society ardently defends Stalin, saying that he was not so much to blame for the purges as his Jewish henchman Kaganovich. Its members oppose the most progressive pro-perestroika publications. On 9 January 1989, they tried to break-up the meeting at which Korotich, the editor-in-chief of *Ogonyok*, was to be elected a candidate to the Supreme Soviet. Memory hoodlums came to the meeting with anti-semitic, anti-perestroika posters and tried to provoke fights with Korotich's supporters.[22]

On 23 January, Memory had its sabbath at Moscow's Krylya Sovetov palace of sports. They were joined by right-wing journalists from *Moskva* and *Molodaya Gvardia* magazines. For the first time since Stalin, the slogan 'No to homeless cosmopolitans!' (meaning Jews) was brandished at this meeting.[23]

Can we dismiss Memory's existence as just an excess of pluralism? I don't think so. Pluralism accepts everything but subversion against pluralism. That's what Memory is doing. 'Divide and rule!' – this is their main watchword. Glasnost' against glasnost'? . . .

Fascism in Germany had its own historical roots: economic crisis and the feeling of national inferiority caused by defeat in the First World War. What about our home-bred fascists? Was their appearance historically inevitable? An attempt to answer this question was made by Anatoly Makarov in *Sovietskaya Kultura* newspaper:

The pro-fascist mentality normally appears at the critical moments of

215

social development – history testifies to this. Our stagnation years were a time of real spiritual crisis, which together with economic malfunctions and long-term blunders in international politics was equal to a military defeat . . . Looking at the participants in extremist rallies, at the hysterical champions of racial purity and patriarchal habits, I recognise life-embittered citizens, veterans of unending queues, dwellers in grim blocks of flats, disenchanted romantics, abandoned wives, unrecognised poets, unconsummated leaders, under-estimated craftsmen. Maybe exaggerated national pride serves them as a kind of heart-warming compensation?[24]

Can a country where 20 million people died in the fight with fascism less than fifty years ago tolerate this very fascism now? I'm sure it cannot. But paradoxically, we have no law against fascism. The introduction of a law must be preceded by official recognition of a phenomenon, and here history repeats itself. As in the cases of racketeering and prostitution, some of those in power are still unwilling to recognise the existence of neo-Nazism in our State. 'Yes, we love Hitler, but we are not anti-Soviet,' one young Nazi cynically confided in me. And though there is an obvious contradiction in these blasphemous words, they are legal from the view point of existing legislation.

Law is law, but again the main weapon against fascism is a healthy democratic society with well-formed public opinion. The neo-Nazis and extremists in our country are still too few and feeble to pose a serious threat to the State. But if not confronted, they could become a real danger.

'History cannot be played back,' Gorbachev said at the unveiling ceremony of the monument to Ernst Thälmann* in Moscow. 'But it is essential for us to learn lessons from it. Hitler's march to power would never have taken place if the Communists, the social democrats and all the democratic forces of the Weimar Republic had opposed him jointly.'[25]

We must never forget the lessons of history.

Each time I go to Leningrad, I invariably visit the Piskaryovskoye Memorial cemetery, where 500,000 Leningraders – victims of the fascist blockade – rest in peace. Standing there silently with my hat off, and listening to the incessant rustle of the trees, I recall the lines by a Leningrad poet Sergei Davidov:

*Ernst Thälmann (1886 – 1944) was a prominent German anti-fascist and Communist killed by the Nazis in Buchenwald concentration camp.

216

Leningrader, body and soul,
I am ill with the year of 1941;
Piskaryovskoye cemetery lives in me.
Half of the city lies here
Unaware of the falling rain.
My memory stretches out to them
Like a path
Through the forest of life.
More than anyone,
More than anyone in the world,
I know,
My city hated fascism.
Our mothers,
Our children,
More than anyone,
Have turned into these mounds.
More than anyone in the world,
We hate fascism.
We! We! We![26]

Letter Box

Hello, editor! My leave is coming to an end and I am going to Moscow. It's curtains for your laureate Vitaliev! He will be met in a doorway. Heil! (Three swastikas.)

Lavrov, Kislovodsk.

The Leningrad Nazis are not alone. We Nazis from Bratsk fully support them. We also worship Adolf Hitler, make uniforms and flags, and collect arms. The Führer's centenary is coming and you will hear about us soon! Heil Hitler!

Members of 'Union 88' group.
(Swastika.) Bratsk.

Rejoice in your graves and jump for joy, you Hitlers, Goebbelses, Görings, Himmlers! Rub your hands, SS mongrels, in your hidden villas in Paraguay. You have good reason for that: the grandsons of the killed soldiers desecrate the monuments to the perished and scream 'Heil!' over their graves . . . We are fighting in Afghanistan now. When we come back and meet these bastards, we won't waste our time educating them, we assure you. We shall act differently, as our conscience – our supreme judge – tells us. As to the fascist Lavrov [his above-quoted letter was published in *Krokodil*], who is coming back from his leave and going to meet your correspondent in the doorway, let him advise his brothers-in-arms to bid farewell to each other. We guarantee the complete extinction of his kind. And if some philistines reproach us for being ruthless, we'll answer that with their silent accord the most terrible crimes happen. We know better, since we are familiar with death, as you can judge from the photographs we enclose. [On the photographs, Soviet soldiers in Afghanistan are depicted crying over their fallen comrade.] And please, don't ignore the Nazi threats – they may be real: these bastards are capable of anything. But we'll protect you!

25 Signatures, Afghanistan.

Müller, chief of the Berlin Gestapo, used to say: 'If after many years since our defeat, a single young man cries "Heil!", it would mean our efforts were not in vain' . . . Have these words really come true?!

K–n, Perm.

I recollect the winter of 1942–43. Our guerrilla unit with a load of food supplies was making its way through forests and swamps to hungry, besieged Leningrad. More than twenty young fellows lost their lives during the journey, our commander, a young Leningrader, among them. It's difficult to describe how we were met in the frozen, hungry city. Exhausted, hardly moving women knelt before us and prayed. And now maybe the grandson of one of these women is marching around with a swastika on his sleeve! . . . I cannot forget a young sixteen-year-old girl hanged by 'kind' fascists by her legs between two burnt birch-trees. Her tongue was protruding from her mouth and her young undeveloped adolescent breasts were visible. She was executed only because her elder brother had gone to join the partisans. We wept bitterly at this terrible sight and swore to take revenge on fascists to the last drop of our blood.

K–tiev, war veteran, Semipalatinsk.

Hello, Vitaliev! You are a dirty scoundrel and we'll kill you. You call for a law forbidding Nazism. And we declare that a law against Communist propaganda is necessary. Death to Communists! . . . As to the sixteen-year-old slut hanged between two birch trees [the previous letter was also published], we think she should have been not hanged, but burnt in a crematorium, alive. You Communists will hear from us soon. All the members of our group are workers', not noblemen's, children.

A–v, 'Rossiya' group. (Swastika.)

Sieg heil!

The guy of about thirty standing next to me at the shop counter asked what my name was. I answered and asked what his was. 'Adolf!' the guy cried and threw his shirt open. On his chest 'Adolf Hitler' was tattooed in a semicircle. I couldn't utter a single word and only murmured 'Scum'. And then he hit me on the chin. I am a Soviet army invalid, my right hand is missing. I had a just-in-case bag with shopping in it in my left hand and I brought it down on his head. The guy fell over like a nine-pin and crawled from the shop on his belly . . .

V–sky, Samarkand region.

In April of 1988, in Lukhovitsy [a town in the Moscow region], I ran into Nazis for the first time in my life. Three burly youngsters were torturing an old man at the bus stop. The old man was crying and saying he had fought for them during the war. I didn't realise on the spot what was happening and when I did, I shouted: 'Stop it, at once!' All the three guys, each about seventeen years old, turned to look at me. One of them said: 'I am an old fascist! Go to hell!' Without further hesitation I spat into my sailor's fist and punched him in the face. They all rushed at me, but luckily another man, a teacher as it turned out later, came to help. Together, we gave them a good thrashing, which wasn't easy: the guys were all strong and tall . . . The souvenir of this encounter is the broken glass in my watch . . .

A–lov, sailor-helmsman, Kolomna.

The blame for our neo-fascism lies with the new class of Soviet Rashidov-style noblemen, formed in the years of stagnation. They were parasites on the working class. The fascists were bred by social injustice in our everyday life. Being teenagers, they were its most sensitive barometers.

A–va, Taganrog.

Our ideology has been indifferent to ordinary people and hasn't been human-orientated. And where humane ideology doesn't work well, there inevitably appear misanthropic tendencies – fascism among them.

L–ko, Kamensk-Uralsky.

For too many years, we have been counting the alcoholics, prostitutes, drug-addicts and neo-fascists in the West and haven't wanted to recognise the fact of their existence in our country. And here is the result!

T–va, Balkhash.

I am a member of a Nazi organisation. Why? In the beginning it was just for the sake of interest. But then I got fascinated with the history of Nazism and became a propagandist. I am a fascist because I am surrounded by cynicism, lies and double standards, where 'uncles' from the TV screen say one thing, and in life everything is different. I came to hate all this, to hate Communists with their fairy tales of a bright future. Komsomols make me sick. I want to kill them! Why am I so ruthless? Because our ments [derogatory term for a militiaman], salespeople, doctors are ruthless too. There is an atmosphere of universal hatred in our country. Real unity is in our organisation, where you can always feel the shoulder of your genosse [German for 'comrade']. I am ready to do anything for him . . . Our tactics are not as cruel as those of the German fascists. We are not going to decimate whole nations; only Jews: as a result of their behaviour, these conceited brutes leave us no other choice but to kill them. We will conquer the world not with arms but with ideology. Any criminal proceedings against us would only stir up our movement. Soon we will flood the streets and the squares and our torches will merge into one fire of struggle. Our mottos are: 'Kill a Communist (a Jew) – only then do you deserve to live!', 'You must not tolerate a Communist, a Jew, an alcoholic, a thief, a drug-fiend, a harlot, a homosexual and similar scum!' These mottos we carry in our hearts! Heil Hitler!

(Swastika.) Hauptmann Der Propagandabteilung, G. Walther Hartmann, Alma-Ata.

PS Let Vitaliev think hard before he ventures to criticise Nazis for a third time!

(I did 'think hard', and after 'Führers from Fontanka' and 'Passport With Swastika' prepared a third article, 'Vandalism'. It dealt with the monument to the perished marines destroyed by Leningrad Nazis and was published in Krokodil No 5, 1989.)

The article 'Führers from Fontanka' has provoked anger and indignation in all of us holidaying aboard m/s *Voroshilov*. We demand: 1. To include an article forbidding Nazi propaganda and symbols on the territory of the USSR in our constitution .2. To introduce changes into the criminal code to the effect of treating fascist elements not as ordinary bullies but as those involved in anti-State activities. 3. To introduce capital punishment for fascist propaganda.

306 signatures.

Vitaliev was the first to speak about fascism in our country in the open. If the Nazi guys start persecuting him, he may rely on me. I will do my best to defend him. I fought in Afghanistan and for me war is no abstract concept. My brothers-in-arms will be in the first ranks of the struggle against fascism. And many will follow us.

Ch–sky, Tyumen region.

Fascism as well as Communism may be of many kinds. If Hitler's and Mussolini's fascism is repugnant and inhuman, why must our young guys' fascism be the same? Similarly, Lenin's Communism was exemplary but Stalin's or Brezhnev's – rotten and stagnating. If Communism can have different faces, why do you deny them for fascism? You, Comrade Vitaliev, hail Communism because you feed on it. But tell me frankly, what has Communism given to people? Just sufferings and crazy ideas. There must be many parties in our country, not just one. Every man is born to be free. Give us different parties and organisations, and everything will improve. Why do different bourgeois and even fascist

221

parties coexist in the West? Because there is real democracy there. Totalitarianism is the enemy of democracy. Truth is born in debates and discussions. Give us freedom of choice and the people will decide for themselves who to follow.

P–v, Moscow.

I was going to work on a bus and saw a little boy who was absent-mindedly drawing a swastika with his finger in the condensation on the window. 'What are you doing?' I asked. 'Don't you know that fascists said, wherever there was a swastika, it was their home?' The boy stopped drawing. But none of the passengers supported me or ordered him to wipe it off . . . I got off at my stop and the bus with the swastika on its window went away. If was full of indifferent people . . . 'Don't be afraid of your enemies – the most terrible thing they can do to you is to kill you. Don't be afraid of your friends – the worst thing they can do to you is to betray you. But do be afraid of the indifferent, since on their silent approval both treacheries and murders occur.' [This is a quotation from Bruno Yasensky, a well-known Soviet writer of the pre-war era.]

G–va, 22, Moscow.

Fascists must be shot publicly – that's what I think.

P–n, a pupil in the 6th form of a secondary school, aged 12, Tomsk region.

(*The following letter was written in the Ukrainian language.*)

The Nazi party exists in the Ukraine as well. We play no games as our younger colleagues do. Their convictions appeared as a result of a great gap between the words of those at the top and real life. The youth has been deceived for many years. That's why they beat up Communists who have compromised themselves. Our party has its own programme and its own name – national communist party. We also think of Adolf Hitler as our teacher, though he didn't escape certain mistakes. Our dream is Communism, but the real, nationalistic one. This mission has been given to us by God. Our society is in decline because we have moved too far from the teachings of great Lenin. His theory lacked only one thing – nationalism – and we'll improve this. Christ, help us!

(Swastika) Heil! The great Ukraine.

Greetings from the north! Vitaliev is a fine fellow: he wasn't scared by these fascist scoundrels. Communists should be like that. Now there are not many real Communists left. But we will never tolerate any 'führers' in Vorkuta. We'll simply kill them, if they appear, and would advise Leningraders to act likewise. Vitaliev is a real man.

Respectfully, A–v, Vorkuta.

Those who try to cover up fascists, to make them look like simple hooligans, are nothing but their accomplices. The very word 'fascism' is associated with grief, suffering and blood all over the world. Fathers of Leningrad, have you forgotten the gloomy days of the blockade? What are you doing? Fascism and Communism will never coexist peacefully. There are still countries where Communists are shot without trial, where Communist parties are banned. So why do we have to tolerate fascism in our land? Leningraders, recall the motto of the Spanish brigades: 'No pasarán!' – fascism shall not pass!

N–m, Orenburg region.

I am only eleven years old and I want to ask you why in so many houses and in many doorways of our town swastikas are drawn? What will this lead to? Are these also 'children's games'?

Svetlana M–ko, Severodonetsk.

Young fascists should not be simply isolated from society, but killed, together with their parents. To kill and only to kill!

I–v, Rostov region.

Modern Nazis must be sent to concentration camps similar to those built by fascists during the war. They are not going to do any good for our society anyhow.

Many signatures, all pensioners, Holmsk, Sakhalin region.

We are fascists from Kaluga, and unanimously support our allies from other Russian cities and towns. We also revere the Führer's genius, make Nazi flags, record German military marches and get together on Adolf Hitler's birthday. We are not yet well united, but we exist. We want to see our city free from Jews and Communists. This day is imminent. We believe in fascist ideals and hope that in the near future Nazis from all cities will unite into one fascist party. There are thousands of us. The future belongs to us. Heil Hitler (Swastika.)

On behalf of the Kaluga fascists – Soloviov.

We believe that the Nazi movement is an outrage against the memory of

46,000,000 victims of fascism during the Second World War, 20,000,000 of our compatriots among them. Preaching fascism is calling for violence, new killings, new catastrophe. This is the regression of personality and of society too. This is an orgy of evil. Fascists must be disarmed and re-educated. We are for Peace and the Good of the land where the Hitlerites were beaten. We are for culture, moral health, joyful labour and the friendship of people.

'Peaceguard' Club, 315 signatures, Moscow.

Esteemed comrade Vitaliev! We are soldiers of a motorised unit. Your article 'Führers from Fontanka' was discussed at our political studies class. We are outraged by the fact that in our country, which lost so many lives in the struggle with fascism, there now live young mongrels with swastikas on their clothes and in their souls. We feel sorry for the people who, being well aware of these phenomena, tried to silence them and didn't take any measures against them. We are especially sorry for our Komsomol. We must all fight against fascism and the main weapon in this fight is glasnost'. We Soviet soldiers cannot allow these Nazi 'players' to walk upon the great land of our people. Respectfully,

Privates of the Guards (3 signatures), Gorky.

I know what fascism means from my own experience. I was ten years old and lived in Brest when it was occupied by the Germans. They shot people, sent them to concentration camps and gas chambers. It was not unusual for them to collect hostages and to shoot every tenth, fifth, second until somebody confessed he had contacts with partisans. Children, old people and the sick were burnt alive. Together with my parents, I went to the partisans to fight the fascist monsters. The fascist uniform was associated with death, tortures and violence. And suddenly, after forty-five years, some young scoundrels in our country are parading in this terrible attire. What a disgrace!

G–va, Magadan.

During the war, I didn't take part in military operations, but living in the occupied zone knew only too well what SS punitive actions meant. I was three years old and lived with my grandfather, a woodman. In our forest some Red Army soldiers were hiding and my granny used to cook food for them. Our local policeman, Timokha Burkhan, a Russian, came to know about this and had all three of us arrested. The grave – that was our only prospect. But suddenly we were set free by . . . an Italian commandant of our hamlet. (The Italians, not the Germans, were stationed in our district.) But our 'native' policemen didn't stop at that. They wanted to have us shot at any cost. The commandant had to appoint two Italian guards, Angelo and Nino, to protect us from the policemen. Wasn't that a paradox: occupiers protecting us from our own compatriots? . . . Though what kind of compatriots were they? Dirty traitors, much more cruel than the Germans themselves. The police beasts had no scruples about violating little girls, robbing old people . . . And before the war they used to be 'Stalin activists' . . . I think that our present-day fascists are similar to those traitors, the policemen. Their sole aim is to beat and torture people. They are worse than German fascists since they don't have any principles or convictions – just like the policemen during the war . . .

F–nko, Voronezh region.

Hello, editor! Vitaliev is finished. My friends and colleagues will avenge him for everything: for his job with the CPSU Publishing House and for his filthy writings denouncing us fascists. We beat Komsomols, Communists and ments, but we don't touch our soldiers whom you are sending to die in Afghanistan. We would even have beaten Oktyabriata [little children's organisation – for ages 7–10], but they are too small. There are many of us, we are united and we have no informers in our ranks. We have got uniforms and arms – both fire-arms and cold steel. We have motorcycles and we will ride them to Moscow soon to get you. We love Russia, but we hate Soviet power. We are eternal!

Günter, Organisation 'S-111', Stavropol. (Dozens of swastikas, skull and cross-bones etc.)

I am studying in the ninth form of a secondary school. This year we have a new history teacher, a young woman. Some of our boys started mocking her. During history lessons they drew swastikas on their hands. I reported them to the headmaster. That very evening the four of them came to my flat. They called me an informer and made me cry. One of them said: 'Do you think Communists and Pioneers are more numerous than us fascists?' 'Yes I do,' I said, 'and you are beasts.' 'The Soviet Union is just an empty space. Estonia is the best state and we will make it fascist,' one of them shouted and they left. And I just stood at the door crying. I think such brutes must be shot – that's all. They won't stop at anything . . .

H–va, Tallinn, Estonia.

The fascist bastards you write about and the Memory Society members are the same. Memory's anti-semitic leaflets are exactly like Hitler's. At their meetings they chant, 'Death to Yids'. They destroy graves at Jewish cemeteries. And their leader D. Vasiliev is a real paranoiac. Your article makes people think. But you should have mentioned Memory in it. Why do Russian nationalists defend this Society openly in *Nash Sovremennik* magazine? All this together with the recent events in Karabakh must make everyone think seriously about our country's future.

R–lin, an artist, Leningrad.

For the most part, V. Vitaliev is right. But I cannot agree with him on some points. I support the ideas of national-socialism and chauvinism. Hitler, as well as Stalin, was no fool. He knew what he was doing. One must be a great man to gain influence over thousands of people and to conquer almost the whole of Europe. I love my motherland and I am thinking of forming a new party in Russia. This party will be guided by Lenin's ideas but will be half military. A Happy New Year to all the staff of *Krokodil*! I hope you will be attracted by the principles of national-socialism in the coming year. Heil!

R–kov, Kuibishev region.

Fascists appeared in our country because of the lies which pervaded our society. You could easily blame Stalin and Brezhnev for everything. But where was the Party? When I served in the Army, our commander, a Communist, used the soldiers to renovate his house free of charge. What kind of Communist was he? It's no good when someone who has been stealing from the people for many years now cries: 'We are for perestroika!' Where was he before? And where were you?

S–ko, Amur region.

If only Stalin were alive, we would have had neither fascists nor strikes in Armenia and Karabakh. Under Stalin we had discipline. You could be imprisoned for being late for your work. Of course, he made some mistakes, but who didn't? To err is human. I feel sorry for Stalin when newspapers blame him for everything. The fascists were created not by him, but by our laziness and having too much to eat!

K–gin, Donetsk region.

I don't think we should burden ourselves with questions like, 'Where did the fascists come from?' They should just be shot on the spot, killed without a trial, destroyed mercilessly . . . A Happy New Year to you!

Sergei Ch., 22, Zlatoust.

Stalin is not to blame. He was strict but fair. I experienced this myself. In

1948 I was five minutes late for work. I wasn't allowed into the factory but sent directly to the district court, where I was quickly sentenced to four months' imprisonment. This was a good lesson for me, aged eighteen, and afterwards I was never late again . . .

P–va, Moscow.

In 1983 I too was a member of a fascist organisation. I was deceived by the girl I loved and joined the fascists from sheer disappointment in life. . . . Once we had several drinks and decided to hijack a Tu-154 plane to West Germany, to Bonn. We elaborated this plan for two months and it was a brilliant project! All details were allowed for. Somehow my mother found out about the plan. 'You are a blockhead,' she told me. 'What on earth are you going to do in West Germany?' 'The same things I am doing here,' I answered, 'and let's drop the subject, please.' We bought tickets for the Kuibishev–Moscow flight fifteen days in advance. It was a mistake, of course. We should have tried to hijack a plane from Brest, which is near the border. But anyway, nothing came of our plan. Ten days before the hijacking the same girl who had walked out on me came back and, kneeling, asked me to forgive her. I decided to quit the organisation on the spot. And without me the whole project was hopeless: my role was a major one. The organisation leader nicknamed Black Horse tried to stab me with his swastika-decorated knife, but I was a strong guy and broke his hand and jaw. Then I collected all the plane tickets and took them to the KGB. We had a lot of trouble but at least we were not tried. And my girlfriend committed suicide shortly afterwards. She cut her veins with a razor blade . . . Now I am twenty-five and I often think what makes young people call themselves Nazis. My opinion is that it happens simply because they have nothing else to occupy themselves with. And who is to blame? The adults! Respectfully,

Andy Black Snake, alias Gr–nko, Kuibishev.

I demand the immediate introduction of a law against fascist youngsters. But first of all, I demand protection for myself, since if I ever meet swastika-wearing thugs in the street, I will act as I did at the front – I will kill them. I will kill them for the millions who perished in the struggle against fascism, for those who were tortured to death or burnt alive. I will kill them for the future of my grandsons, of my Motherland. Death to Lavrov! Heil freedom!

O–lov, war and labour veteran, Chernigov.

We back the guys from Leningrad and fully agree with them. We don't believe you. For so many years you have been building Communism, but you haven't built it yet. Now you blame the stagnation time for this. You cannot prove the Nazis were butchers. Our partisans in 1941–2 were torturing German soldiers, but you keep silent about it. We won't forget these tortures. You are mistaken if you think we just play games. We will be heard soon! Heil Hitler!

(Swastika.) No signature, Pushkino, Moscow region.

I am proud we don't have all these Nazi scum in Kazan. Punks, rockeris, breakers and other informal youth groups are to blame for the existence of Nazis. They are all drug-fiends and are too feeble to resist fascists. On behalf of all my Kazan friends, I promise we will beat the hell out of all these bastards.

S–sky, 16, Kazan.

The press and the mass media are now full of anti-Stalin, that is anti-Soviet, propaganda. This breeds ideological havoc in the minds of young people and pushes them to fascism. Nothing but a preplanned campaign, initiated by capitalists and counter-revolutionaries, is taking place in the press now. I am enclosing a drawing published in *Horizont* magazine and depicting Stalin and Beria as inhuman mongrels. What is this but anti-Soviet propaganda?

L.P., Moscow.

I have just read your article and am crying from weakness and anger. Our boys are being killed in Afghanistan and meanwhile the fascist bastards are torturing our people. And we are helpless! They will spit in our faces and we will turn the other cheek . . . In Chernobyl the looters were shot on the spot. Are Nazis better than looters? Why are we so merciful to villains? To kill them is allegedly inhuman. But to tolerate them – is it human? Fire should be fought with fire.

Vika, 20, Nikolayev.

We are metallists from Novosibirsk. There are Nazis in our city. Not too many, but still . . . We are trying to destroy them, but the militia stands in our way. If we could only meet the bugger who has threatened Vitaliev, we would beat him to death. Our grandfathers shed their blood – and all in vain? No, not in vain! Let only one pig with a swastika appear here – we will cut his head off (literally). Fascists are blockheads! Hitler wanted to make us all his slaves. Happily, our grandfathers didn't let it happen. And now these pigs tattoo 'Adolf Hitler' on their chests . . . It's painful for us when some people say that metallists are fascists. Nothing of the kind. We are not like that! Long live Heavy Metal!

Twenty-five signatures, Novosibirsk.

My country is still far from being a model of democracy, but it is *my* motherland! I detest the Leningrad authorities and all the bureaucrats who turn a blind eye to the fascists. I feel like hitting the small führers on their stupid heads so that they understand what a great force is against them . . . My opinion is that our school system is not coping with its main task – to educate, not just to lecture. We lack real teachers, professional educators, able to implant our creed in children . . . The scoundrels who have swopped their consciences for swastika knick-knacks must know: we (and there are millions of us) will destroy them physically. Every force has a counter-force. A threat? Yes. Everybody must bear responsibility for his actions. Nail drives out nail.

L–sky, Dnepropetrovsk.

(*Telegram*) The paradox of our century is that yesterday's educators have pardoned themselves for all the mistakes which brought our country to stagnation, and socialism to degradation. In fact, they are now leading in perestroika. The Party of Lenin must not tolerate them in its ranks. Otherwise there will be no perestroika and 'Führers from Fontanka' will flourish.

S–va, Narva.

The main reason for the emergence of fascism is that our ruling bodies, supposed to lead society, were steeped in corruption and were beyond the law. The youth couldn't but see this special caste, the self-centred élite, who deemed themselves invulnerable. I think that anti-Communist views among some of our young people are rooted in just that. One can hardly believe in Communist ideals when those who are supposed to propagate them are wallowing in abuse and have monopolised the right to speak on behalf of the people. This creates protest which sometimes can take monstrous forms, as is the case with Nazis.

Ch–v, investigator, Dnepropetrovsk.

What have we done to our country! The shops have been empty since the Sixties. A lot of lip-service has been paid to people's well-being, but words remain words and things are going from bad to worse. Now you are speaking about stagnation under Brezhnev. But, comrades, where were the Communists? They were giving Brezhnev awards and praising him to the heavens. He was made a Hero of the Soviet Union five times. What for? For bringing the country to the brink of disaster? You must answer these questions first and then we will be able to understand where fascists come from.

R—na, a worker, Baltiysk.

I am strictly opposed to fascists. But I am no less against any totalitarian régimes and their leaders – Hitlers, Stalins, Brezhnevs, Pinochets, Maos, Khomeinis and the like. But because the head of Chile's junta or the leader of the Islamic revolution haven't done any harm to me personally, I detest our native dictators more than them. The terror of 1937, the forced hunger during collectivisation, crude dinosaurs of the Brezhnev time when the leaders lied shamelessly and everyone knew that they were lying, and they knew that everyone knew but went on lying, being sure that no one would dare to accuse them ... As you know, even the concentration camps were invented not by Nazis but by our 'experts' from OGPU [pre-war security police]. One of your readers recalls the execution of a sixteen-year-old girl by the Nazis. She was hanged only because her brother had gone over to the partisans. But, look: this was done by foreign soldiers on the enemy's territory. And what about children, brothers, sisters and parents of the 'enemies of the people'? They were mercilessly destroyed by Stalin mongrels in their own State. Isn't that much more terrible than the occupants' violence? What I mean is that if we insert a new law condemning fascism into the Criminal Code, it should be not just anti-fascist but anti-totalitarian, and should condemn totalitarianism in all its forms ... Children can only be morally healthy if their fathers are. Only when such seemingly outdated concepts as honour, conscience, dignity and justice return to our present-day life, when people feel shame in their son becoming a bureaucrat rather than a worker, when everybody's social status is determined by his abilities – not by his views or questionnaires – only then will all the social extremes, all the excesses, vanish by themselves.

P—nko, an engineer, Tiumen region.

Hello, Vitaliev! Haven't you hanged yourself yet? You have every reason to do so. We, Nazis from Nagatino [a district in Moscow], indulge in terror. And quite successfully! Go on writing and we will thank you in our own way. A Happy New Year – the year of the Black Snake! Heil!

(No signatures), Moscow.

Sieg Heil! We are Nazis from Zaporozhie. You won't frighten us with your lousy articles. You Communists strive to resemble Lenin and we want to be like the soldiers of the Great Reich! You will hear about us soon. Heil. (Six swastikas.)

Otto B., Adolf H., Zaporozhie.

Many people tend to draw parallels between fascism and Stalinism. They are right. These two régimes were similar in one way: people supported them. What about the millions who were imprisoned and shot, you would ask? But don't forget about many more millions who were neither shot nor imprisoned. When they shouted 'Heil Hitler!' or 'Long live Stalin!', they were profoundly happy! What do I have to shout now? You have killed all my faith. During the stagnation period I believed that our country was the best and that we lived better than anyone else. It was an illusion of course, but it helped me to survive. What do I have to believe now when you criticise everything? That we are a backward country? That we live like swine compared to Americans? That's what you say . . . When perestroika started and our best years were labelled as stagnation, you made millions of people miserable and they will never be happy again. No one can be happy without faith.

No signature, student, Komsomol member, Moscow.

Hello, editor! Hasn't Vitaliev been killed yet? We Nazis from Dzhezkazgan are laughing our pants off at your blasphemous articles. Your magazine is led on a leash by the KGB . . . And you, soldier from Afghanistan who praises Vitaliev's writings, you are a provocateur, an informer. What did you fight for? For peace? What do you need this peace for? They didn't touch you and you don't touch them. You fight for the pig who gives you orders – and you will kick the bucket thanks to him. And what did your fighting give you? A car? A dacha? A big country house with an attic? While you were rotting in Afghanistan, I bought myself the car and the dacha. And married a beaut. And got lots of clothes and a video from abroad. I would be completely happy if it were not for you, the Communists. I know that Communism is evil and it must be nipped in the bud. And we are struggling with you. We beat up Communists, Komsomols and Pioneers. We make Komsis eat up their cards and they do! We make Pioneers burn their red ties – and they do it too. We proudly bear our passports with swastikas. It is too late for you to stop us. We will pay you back for everything. Müller, the Gestapo chief, was right in saying: 'If after our defeat a single man cried Heil, it would mean that what we had done made sense.' Sieg Heil! Sieg Heil! Sieg Heil!

E–stov, Dzhezkazgan.

How do you do, comrade Vitaliev? I have read both your publications – 'Führers from Fontanka' and 'Passport with Swastika'. I will tell you on the spot: I am a member of the National-Democratic Union of Russian Fascists. Don't be afraid: we are not such imbeciles as your 'Führers' from Leningrad. We don't beat anyone, don't make uniforms. We are opposed to Hitlerism, the only thing we accept from it is Ordnung – the German order. Our organisation is strictly disciplined. Everyone has his code-name and grade, as in the old Russian Army. A lot of people are vocational schools' students, though there are no Komsomols, but here, excuse me, ideological disagreement... We concentrate on ideology. We study philosophy, literature, history, watch Fellini's, Tarkovsky's and Forman's films, read *Novy Mir* magazine and a lot of other publications. Why? To be ideologically fit, to know the enemy well. That's why we regularly study Marx and Lenin. To beat the enemy one must know his weapons. We don't believe in Communism, in the CPSU, in Komsomol, we doubt perestroika – we think it is just like Khrushchev's thaw. We think Russia must be solely for Russians. To hell with all national minorities – from Jews to Armenians and Azerbaijanis. Democracy, in our opinion, means a restriction on all non-Russian races, freedoms, and access to arms for the Russians, who should be able to protect themselves and their families. Frankly speaking, we rejoiced when we found out how many Armenians perished in the earthquake. We are not cannibals, as you may think. When we take power, we will kill just a few people – ten to twenty thousand, no more. Compared with Stalin's repressions, that is just a drop in the ocean. We will cleanse the Russian Federation (at least, its European part) of prostitutes (all, to penal servitude and hard labour), drug addicts (they will mostly be shot), homosexuals (to annihilation). As to liuberi, punks, hippies, metallists etc, we will re-educate them forcibly. These are only unwilling measures. In future, when our party gains real power and attracts masses of people, we will set about reorganising our society, its economy and agriculture, on the basis of private property. The army will be cut and made professional, that is more qualified. The Alaska peninsula, occupied by Yankees, will be returned to Russia. The dialogue with all other countries will be conducted only from a position of force. 'Banana republics' like Bulgaria, Poland, Czechoslovakia and others will be made part of Russia... Excuse my bad handwriting, but for obvious reasons I have been trying to change it (we learn to do this too)... By the way, can't you help us buy works by Nietzsche, Hegel, Kant and Kafka? They are very difficult to get and we are keen on philosophy... I hope, this letter is published, but...

On behalf of all the members

Colonel (signature) (two swastikas), Inta.
PS Excuse the swastika but this is our symbol for the time being: it attracts many people, you know. A Happy New Year! Happiness, good health and all the best! Excuse my terrible hand again. Heil, Russia! Death to Masons [Masons in the lexicon of the Memory Society are a euphemism for Jews].

The sudden emergence of fascism in our country has clear-cut socio-psychological roots. Let's consider them without emotion. The time of Stalinism, if we are not misled by the proclaimed lofty slogans and goals, had a lot in common with fascism. Totalitarianism is always totalitarianism – no matter how you decorate it ideologically. Stalinism was characterised by the physical destruction of dissenters, concentration camps, mass purges, hypocritical propaganda, terror, eradication of the intelligentsia, contempt for human culture, psychopathic searches for the 'enemies of the people', a barracks-style way of life, the cult of force and violence, amputated humanism, militarisation of life, personality cult ('leader' and 'führer' are synonyms), philistine psychology, rampant anti-semitism . . . Now we face the consequences of all these in the form of stagnation: sick economy and ideology and home-bred fascists . . . Our propaganda has never before dwelt upon a certain attractiveness of fascist ideas. But they were indeed able to attract and to lead the strong proletariat of Germany. Or were they only shopkeepers who went to war with us? No. These essentially inhuman but formally attractive ideas have something really rational and pragmatic about them – even if only for philistines . . . Their appeal lies in the prospect of reaching order, which is especially important in a period of crisis and moral degradation. And also the aesthetically primitive but enticing symbol: crosses, beautiful uniforms, swastikas etc . . . And also the possibility of promoting oneself to the detriment of others. Add a little demagogy – and everything can be justified. Humanism is the ideology of weaklings. The goal is primary. One's well-being is above all else. One's country too. Each to his own. Some violence and a war where the strongest will survive are also necessary. But ORDER will be the result. And even bad order is better than good disorder. This was the gist of it . . . And what did we contradict it with? Ideological fudging and propaganda detached from real life. As a result some of our philistines went crazy and were infected with inhuman ideas . . . Perestroika has exposed the boils and ulcers of society. When you open up a boil – no matter how thoroughly it is made up – pus comes out. Its stench upsets our sense of smell. We have got used to fragrances only. This has created panic in many people. But social medicine and

233

surgery must have strong nerves. Once the boil is opened up, let us cure it, let us wash away the pus and disinfect the gaping wound. Our organism is still strong enough. Extreme leftist tendencies are inevitable in every revolution. And we are having the revolution now . . . Fascism was born in the period of historical crisis of Capitalism – economic, political, ideological and moral crisis. We too have had crises recently, and to some extent are still having them. Any crisis presupposes a hidden longing for the broken order. Everyone is looking for a way out. Some people see it in perestroika. Others, perverted by the one-dimensional, stupid and hypocritical propaganda of our stagnation time, being ignorant and immoral, see it in fascism. This was the case with the Black Hundreds – a Russian fascist party of the pre-Revolutionary period . . . Terrible as it may seem, we must look the truth in the face: there were causes (if not roots) for the appearance of fascism in our country. And it did appear. Youth has always been keen on simple theories and quick solutions. If our ideals do not suit them or have been discredited in their eyes – then . . . We have proclaimed that we are all anti-fascists and have thought that was enough. It seemed so natural in a country which lost twenty million lives in the struggle with fascism, but natural processes are more characteristic of biology than of social life. There must be a sober, scientific, psychological approach to this terrible phenomenon. No more slogans, no more 'ideologically correct' and glib speeches! Meanwhile, we will have to limit ourselves to one-to-one struggle. I wish I had enough willpower and physical strength . . . I'm not sure my law-abiding and sober mind will prevent me from killing a Nazi. My grandfather perished in the Second World War during the forced crossing of the Dnieper. He gave his life to destroy fascism . . . Soberly or not – we won't tolerate Nazis. They are criminals.

Z–ga, psychologist, Rostov-na-Donu.

We strongly believe that everything will change for the better, that, by the will of the people and the Party, we will put an end to all the negative phenomena in our lives, to the 'sleep of reason'; and we will feel at last that we are living in the kind of socialist state that Lenin envisaged.

N. and S. P–chuk, livestock experts, Irkutsk region.

Prologue Instead of an Epilogue

I don't like epilogues for their finality and hopelessness. That's why I have decided to write a prologue instead.

There is still too much to say. Lots of changes occurred while I was writing this book. Soviet troops were withdrawn from Afghanistan and the Army's membership is being considerably reduced. Our country made public (for the first time ever) the full data about Soviet troops in Europe. The Declaration of Human Rights was published in our press. A number of previously banned books came to light. The names of Stalin's closest henchmen, together with those of Brezhnev, Chernenko and Suslov (Brezhnev's chief ideologist), were removed from our maps and city plans. The jamming of all foreign broadcasts – Radio Freedom and Free Europe included – was stopped. The crime figures were made public by the Ministry of the Interior. All those convicted for anti-Soviet propaganda and agitation were freed. Democratic elections with a choice of nominees to the Supreme Soviet were held.* It is noteworthy that most of the Leningrad Party functionaries were blackballed by the voters. Academician Sakharov was also nominated as a candidate to the Supreme Soviet and his election programme was issued. This programme included in particular: the scrapping of the administrative command system, to be replaced by a pluralistic one based on competition and the market; a free market for labour; social and national justice; freedom of political beliefs; freedom to choose one's country of residence, and place of residence inside the country; direct elections to the Supreme Soviet and of its president; the abolition of the internal passport system; the halving of the Army's size; and convergence of the socialist and capitalist systems (!).[1]

Could anyone have predicted just a couple of years ago that all these changes would be possible? Even the biggest optimists couldn't. Perest-

---

*A group of electors from Dnepropetrovsk expressed the desire to nominate me as a candidate but I refused: journalists should write, not sit in legislatures. Besides, I don't think of myself as a politician. The invitation itself was flattering though. It was something I couldn't possibly have anticipated even two months before.

roika sometimes proves much more promising than its most ardent supporters could have foreseen. And it's just the beginning.

Journalists are the watchdogs of democracy, so you say in the West. As for our country, I would rather say that journalists here are the caretakers of social renewal. The press is definitely the leading force in perestroika, but even it sometimes cannot keep abreast of the ever-changing life of our country. Several months ago I wrote an article for *Ogonyok* calling for the distribution of the Western press in the Soviet Union. The article never saw daylight but I bear no grudge: while it was being prepared for publication, some Western newspapers and magazines – the *Guardian* among them – appeared for sale in Moscow. This was the only time I was glad my article 'didn't go', as we journalists say.

It's fascinating to be a journalist in any country now, when reality is overtaking the boldest expectations. If formerly the press was way ahead of life, now it is often the other way around. This is the surest sign of social recovery.

I have tried to write a sincere book. If it helps you to understand our country better, I am satisfied. The very fact that I am sitting in my smallish Moscow flat and writing a book for Western readers is also a result of perestroika, though minor if compared to others.

I am full of plans. I am not going to stop. I am about to investigate the yet uncovered murder of Zinaida Reich (a prominent actress and the wife of the famous Soviet stage director Meyerhold), committed in 1938 on Stalin's orders. I am also nurturing the project of a book on Britain. On my desk now there is a file on one of the most terrible phenomena of the stagnation period – punitive psychiatry. There is no concealing the fact that under Brezhnev some of the country's best minds were put into special prison-type hospitals where they were spiritually and mentally destroyed for their dissenting views and words. This was the genial invention of the Brezhnev clique. 'Watch your tongue or you'll wind up in psikhushka [special psychiatric clinic]' – that was the popular saying in the Seventies. Even Stalin was not ruthless enough to invent this. He destroyed his opponents physically. It didn't occur to him that there existed the means to devastate someone's soul and brain without actually murdering him. No one has written about this in detail yet, though there have been some modest attempts by *Izvestia, Komsomolskaya Pravda* and *Moscow News*. They have dealt with separate cases rather than with the system. But the system did exist, and we must let everyone know.

'Memory, the warder of the brain,' Shakespeare said in *Macbeth*. I have been carrying this terrible story in my mind for thirteen years. In 1977 I was on a train to Kharkov returning from the Baltic sea coast where I had spent my first post-university leave. For some time I had been alone in my compartment, until at Chernyakhovsk station I was joined by a strange pair: a tall and burly red-headed man and a thin, sallow youngster. As soon as they entered the compartment they produced a tattered pack of cards and started playing. I pretended to read a newspaper but in fact was studying my fellow-travellers out of the corner of my eye.

They were playing lazily without a trace of interest or emotion. It was obvious they were on friendly terms but not related: the difference in their appearances was too evident. The man, with his rosy cheeks, and muscles bulging under his checked shirt, could have passed for a collective farmer if it were not for his hands – white and well cared for, which proved that he wasn't involved in any kind of manual labour. The young man's appearance was even more enigmatic: crew-cut hair, an elongated brownish face, and wretched clothes which could easily pass for rags. He would have resembled a new recruit (recruits have a habit of wearing their worst clothes when going into the Army) if it were not for his eyes – dark, slanting, and so sad that it became clear that he had suffered a lot, much more than an average recruit could imagine.

No matter how hard I tried, I couldn't tell who was who.

Then at one point the youngster threw down his cards and went out into the corridor for a smoke. His companion watched me with his radiant blue eyes. It was clear he was eager to have a chat.

'Do you know who this guy is?' he asked making a quick gesture towards the door. 'A dangerous criminal and murderer.'

For some moments he savoured the effect his words had made on me and then he went on:

'I am an orderly at the special hospital for mental prisoners.' He produced his red-backed identification card which stated that the bearer was an orderly at Institution OM-216-ST-2 (I will never forget these figures and letters). 'One of my duties is to accompany our patients home after the treatment is finished. That's what I'm doing now.' Only this guy will go to a local prison first – for a short while . . .

'Is he crazy or what?' I asked apprehensively.

'This one?' my interlocutor laughed. 'Nothing of the kind. It's simply that his uncle is a big shot at the Procurator's office. He helped to fake a psychiatrist's examination report and put his nephew into our prison hospital. So the lad was freed of any responsibility for his crimes. He has spent a month with us and is now on his way home.'

The orderly reached for his suitcase and produced a bulky file with copies of the man's record. I looked through the documents. They were terrifying: sadistic murders, sexual perversions, armed robberies. It was inconceivable that all this had been done by a single person.

'I am sure,' the orderly intervened as if reading my thoughts, 'he didn't commit all this on his own. Only knowing that lunatics are not subjected to criminal responsibility, he took the actions of the whole gang on himself.'

'Is your institution a prison or a hospital?' I enquired.

'It depends. When an inspection team comes from the Red Cross or somewhere, we, the staff, put on white robes to look like medical people, and warn our patients to keep their mouths shut. And so they do, in fact, because they know only too well that if they utter a complaint, we will beat the hell out of them afterwards.'

I was petrified and started stammering from excitement:

'D-d'you mean you beat the p-patients?'

'Yes. And what of it . . . They are maniacs. They don't understand words.'

A butcher was sitting in front of me, looking nonchalantly out of the window.

'Who else apart from the maniacs is kept in your prison?' I muttered.

'Politicians as we call them. The ones who are against our rulers and Comrade Brezhnev. Four loonies and one political in each ward. And no talking is allowed.'

I was struck dumb.

'Where on earth is the lad?' the orderly looked worried and rushed into the corridor. In a minute he returned in relief. 'Courting a girl. Why not? He's still young.'

'Aren't you afraid he'll escape?' I asked when the first shock subsided.

'Never,' the orderly answered gravely. 'He is not mad and understands that if he starts playing games this time, escape or no escape, he will have to return to us. And no one in his right mind would want to.'

I couldn't stand his talk any longer and went out of the compartment. My heart was pounding so loudly it seemed to muffle the rattling of the train wheels. Was the orderly serious? He must be. At least, the documents proved he was. But then it was terrible, terrible. Though I had heard rumours of people being put into psikhushka for telling a political anecdote, in my heart of hearts I never believed them. But here I had proof. The most striking thing was that the orderly wasn't afraid of boasting about his awful profession to an outsider, or of taking his victim home in an ordinary compartment of an ordinary train. Did he really feel that powerful?

I decided I must speak to the criminal. His first name was Sasha. (I won't mention his surname here for obvious reasons.) He was standing near the window smoking a cigarette. I came up to him, wondering how to start talking. But he forestalled me:

'You've spoken to the orderly, haven't you? So you know who I am. I've been to many prisons. But this one, it was like a nightmare. No fresh air, no nothing. And the stench of vomit and urine in the ward. When after a month there I went outside and had a whiff of fresh air, I nearly fainted. If it were not for the politicians, I wouldn't have survived. They supported me by secretly giving me cigarette butts and by speaking friendly words.' His speech was impeccable, even literary.

'But they could beat you for talking . . .'

'Yes, they could and they did. But a friendly word is sometimes worth a beating. Look what they did to me.'

He bared his left arm. His veins were covered in small marks left by syringes. There was not a healthy inch on them.

'They make you take a handful of unknown pills three times a day. And if you refuse, they beat you up and inject the same drugs intravenously. I kept refusing, so you see . . .'

'What are the medicines for?'

'Some of them paralyse your will, the others affect your liver, your heart, your brain and God knows what. You don't notice as you become crazy.'

'Who was there among the politicians?'

'A writer who wrote a kind of challenging book, a military colonel who refused to order his soldiers to disperse a demonstration, a guy who called the city mayor a fool. General Grigorenko was also there but he managed to get out.'

'Did he run away, or what?'

'No. He was just freed under pressure from the West. No one has ever escaped from that place. In fact it was an SS prison during the war.'

'Didn't they try to protest?'

'It's no use. Brezhnev said he didn't need them. They usually can't stand more than a year. After that they just go mad. They'd prefer to die but the beasts don't let them. And mind: this prison is not the only one of its kind. There's another in Dnepropetrovsk. But the most terrible, so people say, is in Sichevka, a village in the Smolensk region, where there was a Nazi concentration camp during the war.'

'But did you really commit all those crimes?'

'No. Look, I'm not a murderer, just a robber. But I don't care. My uncle won't let me be imprisoned because it would ruin his reputation.'

The train arrived in Minsk, the capital of Soviet Belorussia, and the orderly sent Sasha to buy some wine at the station. I watched his crew-cut disappear into the crowd. The orderly was nodding peacefully. He wasn't worried that Sasha would escape, and this was terrifying.

Sasha did return, with two big bottles of cheap red wine, and until late that night the butcher and his victim were drinking together in the compartment. I lay on the upper berth trying to catch some sleep, and couldn't.

When I arrived in Kharkov, I rushed to the militia to recount my terrible experience on the train. But then, in 1977, no one would listen to me. I was advised to keep silent if I didn't want to share the fate of my travel companion. No wonder: special prisons like that were under militia supervision.

But I knew the time would come. In 1988 I realised it *was* coming when a Decree of the Supreme Soviet transferred all special psychiatric clinics from the supervision of the Ministry of the Interior to the auspices of the Ministry of Health. The same Decree specified the conditions under which a person could be hospitalised in such a clinic: the permission of the patient's relatives or lawyer had to be granted.

On 23 March 1989, Leningrad TV in the '600 Seconds' programme announced that the similar militia clinic in Leningrad had been closed. Social sanity and humanism are returning to our society.

In 1977 I promised myself I would write about my awful train encounter. And I am going to keep my promise. It won't be just the story of Sasha, but of many innocent brave people destroyed by the infernal machinery of stagnation. Now I am collecting evidence from those who have been forcibly hospitalised at institutions similar to OM-216-ST-2. It will be a long sad story with old, yet unknown, facts. Truth can never grow out of date.

'Conscientious citizenship begins with the feeling of historical guilt. In saving the present by remembering the past, we save the future both for ourselves and for our children,' said my favourite Russian poet, Yevgeni Yevtushenko, at a session of the recently formed Anti-Stalinist Remembrance Society.[2] I have nothing to add to that.

There is still a lot to say and a lot to do. That is why I am not putting a full stop at the end of my book. A full stop is as hopeless as an epilogue. And I am hopeful.

So I am putting three dots instead. They imply continuation . . .

Notes

Chapter 1 'Clean Skies over the City of Kharkov'
1 *The Penguin Essays of George Orwell*, p. 6, Penguin Books, London, 1984.

Chapter 2 'Moscow Does Not Believe in Tears'
1 *Literaturnaya Gazeta*, 28 May 1980.
2 *Literaturnaya Gazeta*, 25 June 1980.
3 *Literaturnaya Gazeta*, 26 August 1981.
4 *Literaturnaya Gazeta*, 28 October 1981
5 *Literaturnaya Gazeta*, 25 November 1981.

Chapter 3 Just a Magazine Cutting
1 *Literaturnaya Gazeta*, 24 February 1982.
2 *Literaturnaya Rossiya*, 20 January 1984.
3 *Literaturnaya Gazeta*, 22 April 1982.
4 *Krokodil*, No 9, March 1982.
5 *Krokodil*, No 8, March 1983.
6 *Krokodil*, No 30, October 1982.
7 *Krokodil*, No 12, April 1983.
8 *Krokodil*, No 1, January 1983.
9 *Krokodil*, No 26, September 1985.
10 *Krokodil*, No 3, January 1986.
11 *Krokodil*, No 14, May 1985.
12 *Krokodil*, No 33, November 1983.
13 *Krokodil*, No 16, June 1986.
14 *Krokodil*, No 12, April 1987.
15 *Krokodil*, No 2, January 1986.
16 *Krokodil*, No 11, April 1986.

Chapter 4 'The Plague of Love'
1 *Krokodil*, No 3, January 1986.

2 *Krokodil*, No 9, March 1987.
3 *Sotsiologicheskiye Issledovaniya*, No 6, 1988.
4 *Moskovski Komsomolyets*, 19 November 1986.
5 *Argumenti i Fakti*, No 5, 1988.
6 ibid.
7 *Zhurnalist*, No 4, April 1988.

Chapter 5 Parabellum Jeans
1 *Krokodil*, No 36, December 1986.
2 *Krokodil*, No 3, 4, 5, 6, January–February 1987.
3 *Krokodil*, No 25, October 1987.

Chapter 6 Once Upon a Time in Amur
1 *Ogonyok*, No 48, December 1988.
2 *Sotsialisticheskaya Zakonnost*, No 9, September 1988.
3 *The Guinness Book of Records 1989*, p 204, Guinness Publishing Ltd, Enfield, 1988.
4 ibid.
5 *Sotsialisticheskaya Zakonnost*, No 10, October 1988.
6 *Ogonyok*, No 48, December 1988.
7 *Sovetski Entsiklopedicheski Slovar'*, p 1149, Sovetskaya Entsiklopediya, Moscow, 1983.
8 *Literaturnaya Gazeta*, 2 March 1988.
9 *Literaturnaya Gazeta*, 7 January 1987.
10 *Literaturnaya Gazeta*, 5 January 1989.
11 *Moscow News*, No 2, 1989.
12 *Ognoyok*, No 5, February 1989.

Chapter 7 Doublethink: Mechanism of Privilege
1 *Moscow News*, No 6, 1989.
2 Martin Walker, *The Waking Giant*, p. xiv, Abacus, London, 1986.
3 *Izvestia*, 3 March 1989.
4 *Ogonyok*, No 9, February 1989.
5 *Krokodil*, No 7, March 1988.
6 Martin Walker, *The Waking Giant*, pp xii–xiii.
7 ibid.
8 *Krokodil*, No 6, February 1988.
9 *Krokodil*, No 19, July 1987.
10 *Moscow News*, No 7, 1989; and *Izvestia*, 18 February 1989.
11 *Literaturnaya Gazeta*, 25 January 1989.

12 V. I. Polubinskiy, *Iz Istorii Sovetskoi Militsii* (From the History of the Soviet Militia), p 21, Znaniye, Moscow, 1987.
13 *Ogonyok*, No 40, October 1988.
14 *Ogonyok*, No 3, January 1989.
15 *Ogonyok*, No 47, November 1988.
16 *Moscow News*, No 39, 1988.
17 *Pravda*, 12 February 1986; and Martin Walker, *The Waking Giant*, p 202.
18 *Argumenti i Fakti*, No 11, 1989.
19 *Ogonyok*, No 4, January 1989.

Chapter 8 Passport with Swastika
 1 Andrew Wilson and Nina Bachkatov, *Living with Glasnost*, p 205, Penguin Books, London, 1988.
 2 *Moscow News*, No 1, 1988.
 3 *Demograficheski Entsiklopedicheski Slovar'*, p 564, Sovetskaya Entsiklopediya, Moscow, 1985.
 4 G. F. Petrov, *Pamyatnik Skorbi i Slavi* (Monument of Sorrow and Glory), pp 9–10, Lenizdat, Leningrad, 1986.
 5 Vyborg District Court of Leningrad, Case 1/1136, 1986.
 6 G. F. Petrov, *Pamyatnik Skorbi i Slavi*, pp 28–9.
 7 ibid., p 16.
 8 ibid., p 17.
 9 ibid., p 49.
10 ibid., p 9.
11 *Literaturnaya Gazeta*, 2 March 1988.
12 *Knizhnoye Obozreniye*, No 12, 1988.
13 *Moscow News*, No 13, 1988.
14 ibid.
15 *Knizhnoye Obozreniye*, No 12, 1988.
16 *Krokodil*, No 18, June 1988.
17 *Krokodil*, No 28, October 1988.
18 *Krokodil*, No 5, February 1989.
19 *The Penguin Essays of George Orwell*, p 133, Penguin Books, London, 1984.
20 *Literaturnaya Gazeta*, 1 February 1989.
21 *Krokodil*, No 34, December 1988.
22 *Ogonyok*, No 3, January 1989.
23 *Moscow News*, No 6, 1989
24 *Sovietskaya Kultura*, 4 February 1989.

25   *Pravda*, 4 October 1986.
26   G. F. Petrov, *Pamyatnik Skorbi i Slavi*, pp 61–2.

Prologue instead of an Epilogue
  1   *Moscow News*, No 6, 1989.
  2   *Literaturnaya Gazeta*, 1 February 1989.

Index